Beethoven

An Anthology of Selected Writings

BEETHOVEN
As depicted by the life mask taken by Franz Klein in 1812
(derived from a copy in the author's possession)

BEETHOVEN

AN
ANTHOLOGY
OF
SELECTED WRITINGS

Terence M. Russell

Jelly Bean Books

The right of Terence Russell to be identified as the
Author of the Work has been asserted by him in accordance
with the Copyright, Designs and Patents Act 1988.

Copyright © Terence M. Russell 2022

Published by
Jelly Bean Books
136 Newport Road
Cardiff
CF24 1DJ

ISBN:978-1-915439-07-9

www.candyjarbooks.co.uk

All rights reserved.
No part of this publication may be reproduced, stored in a
retrieval system, or transmitted at any time or by any means,
electronic, mechanical, photocopying, recording or otherwise
without the prior permission of the copyright holder. This book is
sold subject to the condition that it shall not by way of trade or
otherwise be circulated without the publisher's prior consent in any
form of binding or cover other than that in which it is published.

CONTENTS

AUTHOR'S NOTE — I
INTRODUCTION — IX
EDITORIAL PRINCIPLES — XI
BEETHOVEN'S FINANCIAL TRANSACTIONS — XIII

BEETHOVEN: AN ANTHOLOGY OF SELECTED WRITINGS
- Gerald Abraham — 1
- Theodor W. Adorno — 3
- Allgemeine musikalische Zeitung (AmZ) — 5
- Denis Arnold and Nigel Fortune — 8
- Matthew Arnold — 9
- Claudio Arrau — 10
- Boito Arrigo — 12
- Vladimir Ashkenazy — 13
- Mily Balakirev — 16
- Daniel Barenboim — 17
- Philip Barford — 19

Béla Bartók	22
Arnold Bax	23
Thomas Beecham	24
Paul Bekker	25
Alban Berg	27
Hector Berlioz	28
Leonard Bernstein	32
Georges Bizet	34
John Blacking	36
Arthur Bliss	36
Ernst Bloch	40
Pierre Boulez	43
Johannes Brahms	45
Alfred Brendel	46
Gerhard von Breuning	49
Benjamin Britten	52
Broadwood & Sons	55
Michael Broyles	60
Anton Bruckner	63
Hans von Bülow	65
Scott Burnham	66
Alan Bush	68
Ferruccio Busoni	70
John Cage	75
Neville Cardus	75
Elliott Carter	78
Barry Cooper	80
Martin Cooper	82
Aaron Copland	84
John Crabbe	86
Carl Dahlhaus	88
Collin Davis	90
Claude Debussy	91
Frederick Delius	96

David B. Dennis	97
Gaetano Donizetti	105
Paul Dukas	107
Antonín Dvorák	108
Sir George Dyson	108
Hanns Eisler	109
Ernst von Elterlein	110
Manuel de Falla	111
Amy Fay	112
Edwin Fischer	113
Nigel Fortune	114
Alain Frogley	114
Wilhelm Furtwängler	116
Hans Gal	118
Glen Gould	120
Percy Grainger	122
Cecil Gray	123
Franz Grillparzer	124
Donald J. Grout and Claude V. Palisca	126
Sir George Grove	130
Ivor Gurney	131
Sir William Henry Hadow	132
Sir Charles Hallé	133
The Harmonicon	137
Christopher Headington	138
Gustav Holst	139
Arthur Honegger	140
Victor Hugo	141
Vincent d'Indy	142
Charles Ives	143
Otto Jahn	144
Leoš Janáček	145
Joseph Joachim	146
Karl August Kahlert	149

Emanuel Kant	150
William Kinderman	151
Otto Klemperer	152
Zoltán Kodály	153
Nikolai Rimsky-Korsakov	155
Ernst Ludwig Kossak	156
Paul Henry Lang	157
Raymond Leppard	160
Franz Liszt	162
Heitor Villa-Lobos	175
Edward MacDowell	176
Sir John B. McEwan.	177
Gustav Mahler	179
François Martin Mai	183
Denis Matthews	183
Wilfrid Mellers	187
Felix Mendelssohn	190
Yehudi Menuhin	196
Olivier Messiaen	202
Darius Milhaud	203
Anton Neumayr	204
Ernest Newman	205
Carl Nielsen	209
Ludwig Nohl	210
Tia de Nora	212
Sir Hubert Parry	213
Giorgio Pestelli	215
Ildebrando Pizzetti	216
Andre Previn	217
Sergei Prokofiev	218
Philip Radcliffe	222
Maurice Ravel	224
Hans Richter	227
Ferdinand Ries	227

Romain Rolland	232
Eugène Ronteix (pseudonym for F. R. de Toreinx)	235
Charles Rosen	237
Gioachino Rossini	243
Anton Rubinstein	246
Arthur Rubinstein	248
Stephen Rumph	251
Camille Saint-Saëns	253
Anton Felix Schindler	255
Johann Aloys Schlosser	262
Artur Schnabel	265
Arnold Schoenberg (Schönberg)	274
Leo Schrade	277
Franz Schreker	279
Gunther Schuller	280
Marion Scott	282
Roger Sessions	283
Ignaz von Seyfried	286
George Bernard Shaw	288
Robert Shaw	292
Dmitri Shostakovich	293
Jean Sibelius	299
Bedrich Smetana	301
Maynard Solomon	303
Oscar George Sonneck	306
Louis Spohr	308
Glen Stanley	310
Erwin Stein	311
Karl Heinrich Stockhausen	313
Richard Strauss	314
Igor Stravinsky	315
John William Navin Sullivan	317
Karol Szymanowski	319
Samuel Coleridge-Taylor	321

Peter Tchaikovsky	322
Alexander Wheelock Thayer	328
Virgil Thomson	329
Michael Tippett	332
Ernst Toch	337
Prof. Sir Donald Francis Tovey	338
Edgard Varèse	341
Guiseppe Verdi	342
Cosima Wagner	343
Richard Wagner	346
Bruno Walter	358
Anton Webern	360
Kurt Weill	365
Felix Weingartner	366
Ralph Vaughan Williams	367
Hugo Wolf	368
BIBLIOGRAPHY	371
INDEX	407
ABOUT THE AUTHOR	410

AUTHOR'S NOTE

I have cherished the idea of making a study of the life and work of Beethoven for many years. This statement requires a few words of personal reflection. I first encountered Beethoven in my early piano lessons — Minuet in G major, WoO 10, No. 2. At the same time I became acquainted with his piano pupil Carl Czerny — *Book One, Piano Studies*. My heart sank when I discovered the rear cover advertised a further *99* books in the same series — scales, arpeggios studies for the left hand, studies for the right hand — all the way to his Op. 824! By coincidence, my *Czerny Book One* was edited by Alec Rowley — who had the same surname as my music teacher. In my childish innocence, I often wondered why *he himself* never appeared to give me a lesson!

In my teenage years I found myself drawn ever closer to Beethoven's music in the manner that ferromagnetic materials are ineluctably held captive in the sway of a magnetic field. The impulse to which I yielded is well described in words the conductor Bruno Walter gave in one of his rare public addresses: 'It is my belief that young people at that age are more easily impressed by what is heroic and grandiose; that they more easily understand works of art in which passionate feelings are violently uttered in raised accents, and that the lighter sounds of cheerfulness are less impressive to them.' I do indeed recall the stirring effect made on me on first hearing the Overture *Egmont*, the unfolding drama of the Fifth Symphony and the declamatory opening chords of the *Emperor* Piano Concerto.

I resolved to read everything I could about Beethoven, starting with Marion Scott's pioneering English-language study of the composer in the *Master Musicians series*. My father took out a subscription for me for *The Gramophone* magazine, enabling me to read reviews of the new 'LP' recordings — none of which though I could afford! The LP was then — 1950s — beginning to supplant the 78 rpm shellac records, stacks of which could be purchased for as little as six pence each in 'old' money. At this same time I had the privilege of hearing Beethoven's music performed by the *Hallé Orchestra* under the baton of Sir John Barbirolli, and experienced the *Carl Rosa Opera Company* perform the composer's only opera *Fidelio*; I borrowed the piano-reduction score from the City Library to become better acquainted with this moving work — only to find the score's fists full of notes were well beyond my capabilities. Nonetheless, since then *Fidelio's* every note has been woven into my DNA. I also recall the period when the *London Promenade Concerts* were designated 'Friday night is Beethoven night'.

Through these influences I resolved to visit Vienna to see where Beethoven had lived and worked. But how? The support for such travel was beyond the means of my family. Fortunately in my final year at school (1959) an opportunity presented itself. I saw a poster that stated *WUS — World University Service* — required volunteers to work in the Austrian town of Linz to help relocate refugees who were living there in improvised wooden shacks — displaced and dispossessed victims of the Second World War. To those participating all expenses would be paid together with free accommodation — in one of the crumbling wooden shacks! From Linz, I planned to make my way to Vienna.

I applied to *WUS* and, despite being a mere school-leaver, I was accepted. The *WUS* authorities doubtless reasoned the building-trade skills I had acquired during my secondary education in the building department of a technical school would be useful. This proved to be the case. At the refugee camp I dug trenches and was allowed to assist as a bricklayer. All about me were wide-eyed children eager to help but mostly getting in the way. I recall one afternoon when a reporter from *The Observer* newspaper paid a visit to our construction site to gather material for an article he was writing on European post-war recovery — he generously admired my trenches and brickwork!

Of lasting significance was another visit, this time from a Belgian priest. He took a group of us to the nearby *Mauthausen* Concentration Camp, recently opened as a silent and solemn memorial to those who had perished there. It was a deeply moving experience. Years later I learned of the views of the ardent Beethovenian Sir Michael Tippet. After the horrors of the *Holocaust*, he posed the question for mankind: 'What price Beethoven now?' He posited: 'Could we any longer find solace in Beethoven's setting of Schiller's *Ode to Joy* and its utopian vision — "Be embraced you Millions"?'

My refugee contribution duly came to end and Vienna beckoned. On arrival there I found scenes reminiscent of *The Third Man* and *Harry Lime*. I recall, for example, encountering cobblestones piled high in the streets waiting to be replaced after having been disturbed by the heavy armoured vehicles that had so recently passed over them. But Vienna was welcoming. I visited the houses where Beethoven had lived and worked and paused outside others associated with him that were identified by a commemorative plaque and the Austrian flag. A particularly memorable occasion was attending a recital in the great salon within the palace of Beethoven's noble patron Prince Lobkowitz — the very one where the *Eroica* Symphony had been premiered. Ultimately, my steps led me to the composer's first resting place in the *Währinger Ortsfriedhof.* I paid silent homage to the great man and, as I did so, discovered nearby the resting place of Franz Schubert to whom Beethoven was an endless source of admiration and inspiration.

I felt a youthful impulse to discover yet more about Beethoven and his music. But absorption in musicology would have to take second place. My chosen career beckoned in the guise of architecture — 'the mother of the arts' and 'the handmaid of society'. There was room though for Beethoven's music and from that time on it has been my constant companion through attendance at recitals, in concerts and music-making in the home. And at home a reproduction of Franz Kline's 1812 study of the composer has greeted me each day for more than half a century.

On my retirement from a career in architectural practice, research and university teaching, the opportunity finally presented itself for me to devote time to researching Beethoven musicology. Having attained my eightieth year also emboldened me to make progress with my good intentions!

With these autobiographical remarks outlined I will say a few remarks about my working method — see also the comments made in *Editorial Principles.*

As a member of staff of The University of Edinburgh, I had the good fortune to have access to the *Reid Music Library*, formed from a nucleus of books bequeathed by General John Reid and augmented over the years by such custodians as Sir Donald Francis Tovey, sometime *Reid Professor of Music* and renowned Beethoven scholar. Over a period of three years, I made a survey of the many works in the Reid collection. I consulted each item in turn making records on paper slips — many hundreds — that I deemed to be relevant for my researches. I confined my searches to book-publications, as reflected in my accompanying bibliography. All of this was quite some years ago, the cut-off date for my researches being 2007. Beyond this date I have not surveyed any further works. I am mindful though that Beethoven musicology and related publication continue to be a major field of endeavour in the manner of the proverbial 'ever rolling stream'.

In the intervening years since completing my archival researches, personal tribulations associated with family illness and bereavement slowed my progress in giving expression to my projected intentions. Latterly, however, with renewed energy, and more time at my disposal, I have been able to make progress. My studies take the form of a set of monographs. These trace the creation origins and reception history of each of Beethoven's piano sonatas and string quartets. The resulting texts also incorporate contextual accounts of Beethoven and his contemporaries. Also included in my musicological surveys are two related Beethoven anthologies. The set of monographs in question, identified by short title, are:

Beethoven: An anthology of selected writings.
Beethoven: The piano sonatas: An anthology of selected writings.

The Piano Sonatas:
Op. 2–Op. 28
Op. 31–Op. 81A
Op. 90–Op. 111

The String Quartets:
Op. 18, Nos. 1–6
Op. 59, Nos. 1–3 (Razumovsky); Op. 74 (The Harp);
  Op. 95 (Quartetto Serioso)
Op. 127, Op. 132 and Op. 130 (Galitzin)
Op. 131, Op. 135; Grosse Fuge, Op. 133 and Op. 134
  (Fugue transcription)

I provide further information about these studies in the introduction to each individual monograph. Suffice it for me to state here the basic premise upon which my work is founded. I believe it is rewarding, concerning the life of a great artist, to find connections between who he *was* and what he *did*; in Martin Cooper's words 'between his personality, as expressed on the one hand in human relationships, and on the other in artistic creation'. (*Beethoven, The Last Decade*) That is not to say I consider it essential to the enjoyment of Beethoven's music to know this or that fact about it. His music can be enjoyed, as millions do, with — in Robert Simpson's apt phrase —'an innocent ear', for what it is and how it reaches out to us in purely musical terms without any prejudging of its merits based upon extra-musicological facts.

I must make a further point. I am mindful that a scholar who ventures into a field of study that is not rightly his may be regarded with some suspicion. In this regard I can but ask the reader to place his or her trust in me in the following way. I have attempted to bring to my work the care which publishers and their desk editors have required of me in my book writings relating to architecture — listed elsewhere.

As inferred, it is now more than sixty years since I paid homage to Beethoven in Vienna's *Währinger Ortsfriedhof* and my warmth of feeling towards the composer and his music have grown with the passing of the years. My studies are not intended to be propaedeutic — that would be pretentious. However, if in sharing with others what I have to say contributes to their knowledge and understanding of the composer, and thereby increases their own feelings towards him and his works, my own pleasure in bringing my work to completion will be all the more enhanced.

It is perhaps fitting that my studies should appear in Beethoven's 250th Anniversary Year — I must confess more by chance than design!

When Beethoven arrived in Vienna, he was unknown. He was armed though with a note of encouragement from his youthful friend and benefactor Count Ferdinand Waldstein. It contained the often-quoted words: 'Receive Mozart's spirit from Haydn's hands.' Some forty years later Beethoven passed away in the House of the black-robed Spaniards at 200 *Alservorstädter*, the *Glacis* where he had lived since the autumn of 1825. Soldiers had to be called to secure the doors to the inner courtyard of the house from the pressure of onlookers. His body was blessed in the *Alservorsttädt Parish Church*, schools were closed and perhaps as many as 10,000 people formed a funeral procession — an honour ordinarily reserved for monarchs. The *Marcia Funebre* from the composer's Op. 26 Piano Sonata was performed at the funeral ceremony. Franz Grillparzer read the funeral oration. Franz Schubert, who, as remarked in life so admired Beethoven, was one of the pallbearers. The composer's mortal remains were lowered into a simple vault. Beethoven now belonged to history.

Dr Terence M. Russell
Edinburgh 2020

INTRODUCTION

As the title to this work implies, it consists of a compilation of texts that bring together views bearing on the life and work of Ludwig van Beethoven. As such, it provides a collective estimation of his achievements as expressed through the sayings and writings of fellow musicians, musicologists and performing artists. In selecting texts for inclusion, my primary intention has been to make available to the reader the opinions of recognised authorities bearing on such considerations as the composer's aesthetic and creative impulse; his philosophical and intellectual outlook; the expressive nature of his writing; the challenges with which he confronts the performer, relating to questions of interpretation and performance; and, above all, the continuing legacy of his musical inheritance.

Where applicable, prefatory remarks are incorporated with the selected texts to provide the reader with the original context from which the various writings have been derived. The bibliography at the close of the work will also be of value to the reader wishing to discover more about the original sources and others publications not cited in the text.

Following the death of Beethoven in 1827, the contemporary journal *Allgemeine Musikalische Zeitung* devoted a considerable part of its issue of 31 April 1829 to a reflection on the composer and his achievements. The reviewer's words have proved to be prophetic: 'The composer struck along new paths some thirty years ago.' He acknowledged his works had 'engendered hostility on the way' but concedes 'all that is now stilled for today, no other can touch this great spirit'.

TMR

EDITORIAL PRINCIPLES

By its very nature a study of this kind draws extensively on the work of others. Every effort has been made to acknowledge this in the text by indicating words quoted or adapted with single quotation marks. Wherever possible, for the sake of consistency, I have retained the orthography of quoted texts making only occasional silent changes of spelling and capitalization. Deleted words are identified by means of three ellipsis points ... and interpolations are encompassed within square brackets [ ]. Quoted words, phrases and longer cited passages of text remain the intellectual property of their copyright holders.

I address the reader in the second person notwithstanding that the work is my own – produced without the benefit of a desk editor. It follows that I must bear the responsibility for any errors of misunderstanding or misinterpretation for which I ask the reader's forbearance. A collaboration I must acknowledge is the help I received from the librarians of the Reid Music Library at the University of Edinburgh. Over the three-year period it took me to compile my reference sources, they served me with unfailing courtesy, often supplying me with twenty or more books at a time. In converting my manuscript into book format, I wish to thank my editorial coordinator, William Rees, for his support and painstaking care. I would also like to thank Shaun Russell for his work designing the cover for each of the twelve volumes.

My admiration for Beethoven provided the initial impulse to commence this undertaking and has sustained me over the several years it has taken to bring my enterprise to completion. That said, I am no Beethoven idolater. I am mindful of the danger that awaits one who ventures to chronicle the work of a great artist. I believe it was Sigmund Freud who suggested that biographers may become so disposed to their subject, and their emotional involvement with their hero, that their work becomes an exercise in idealisation. In response to such a charge let me say. First, I am no biographer. I do however make occasional reference to Beethoven's personal life and his relationships with his contemporaries. Second, I acknowledge Beethoven has his detractors. Accordingly, I have not shrunk from allowing dissentient voices, critical of Beethoven and his work, to be heard. These, however, are few and are silenced amidst the adulation that awaits the reader in support of the endeavours of one of humanity's great creators and one who courageously showed the way in overcoming personal adversity.

TMR

BEETHOVEN'S FINANCIAL TRANSACTIONS

Beethoven's negotiations with his music publishers make many references to his compositions. Today they are recognised for what they are — enduring works of art — but referred to in his business correspondence they appear almost as though they were mere everyday commodities — for which he required an appropriate remuneration. Beethoven resented the time he had to devote to the business-side of his affairs. He believed an agency should exist, for fellow artists such as himself, from which a reasonable sum could be paid for the work (composition) submitted, leaving more time for creative enterprises. In the event Beethoven, like Mozart before him, had to deal with publishers largely on his own. Beethoven, though, did benefit in his business dealings from the help he received from his younger brother Kasper Karl (Caspar Carl). From

1800, Carl worked as a clerk in Vienna's Department of Finance in which capacity he found time to correspond with publishers to offer his brother's works for sale and – importantly – to secure the best prices he could. In April 1802 Beethoven wrote to the Leipzig publishers Breitkopf & Härtel: '[You] can rely entirely on my brother who, in general, attends to my affairs.' Whilst Carl promoted Beethoven's interests with determination, he appears to have lacked tact and made enemies. For example, Beethoven's piano pupil Ferdinand Ries – who for a while also helped the composer with his business negotiations – is on record as describing Carl as being 'the biggest skinflint in the world'. The currencies most referred to in Beethoven's correspondence are as follows:

> silver gulden and florin: these were interchangeable and had a value of about two English/British shillings
>
> ducat: 4 1/2 gulden/florins: valued at about nine shillings
>
> louis d'or: This gold coin was adopted during the Napoleonic wars and the French occupation of Vienna and Austria more widely. It had a value of about two ducats or approximately twenty shillings or one-pound sterling.

Beethoven was never poor – in the romantic sense of 'an artist starving in a garret'. On arriving in Vienna in 1792, he was fortunate to receive financial support from his patron Prince Karl Lichnowsky who conferred on him an annuity of 600 florins that he maintained for several years. Between the months of February and July of 1796, Beethoven undertook a concert tour taking in Prague, Dresden, Leipzig and Berlin. He was well received and wrote to his other younger brother Nikolaus Johann: 'My art is winning me friends and what more do I want? ... I shall make a good deal of money.' Later on, in 1809, Napoleon Bonaparte's youngest brother Jérôme Bonaparte offered Beethoven an appointment at his Court with the promise of an income of 4,000 florins. Alarmed at the prospect of losing Beethoven — now the most celebrated composer in Europe — three of Vienna's most notable citizens, namely, the Archduke Rudolph (Beethoven's only composition pupil), Prince Kinsky and Prince Lobkowitz settled on the composer the same sum of 4,000 florins. Inflation, however, brought about by the Napoleonic wars, soon eroded its value; personal misfortune to Lobkowitz and Kinsky also took its toll.

Beethoven undoubtedly had to work hard to secure a reasonable standard of living. Notwithstanding, despite his occasional straitened circumstances, he contributed generously to the needs of others. For example, he allowed his works to be performed free of charge at charitable concerts; in 1815 his philanthropy earned for him the honour of Bürgerrecht — 'freedom of the City'.

Beethoven earned a great deal of money when his music was performed, to considerable acclaim, at several concerts held in association with the Congress of Vienna (1814-15). He did not though benefit from it personally; he invested it on behalf of his nephew Karl. It is one of the misfortunes of Beethoven's life that in money-matters he was culpably improvident. This is poignantly evident in a letter he wrote on 18 March 1827 to the Philharmonic Society of London just one week before his death; the Society had made him a gift of £100. He sent the Society 'his most heartfelt thanks for their particular sympathy and support'.

TMR

On 24 February 1824, a collection of musicians and devotees of music wrote to Beethoven to affirm their admiration of him. Their words have continuing relevance:

'Beethoven's name and his creations belong to all contemporaneous humanity and every country that opens a sensitive heart to art.'

SELECTED WRITINGS

GERALD ABRAHAM

The English-Jewish musicologist Gerald Abraham wrote extensively about music both in his capacity as Professor of Music at the University of Liverpool (1947–62) and as President of the Royal Musical Association (1970-74). He was General Editor to the multi-volume *New Oxford History of Music* (1982–85–88). Introducing Volume Eight in this series he writes:

> 'The title of no other volume of the *New Oxford History of Music* includes the name of a composer. But no other period of musical history is so completely dominated by one composer; in popular thought the years 1790–1830 are the *Age of Beethoven* ... In the first years of maturity he had opened a great symphony with an heroic

theme and rivaled Cherubini with a rescue opera which owes musical ideas as well as its subject to a French source and borrows its most dramatic stroke from Méhul's *Helèna*. A few years later he opened his greatest piano concerto with a quasi-military allegro ... But the spirit of the age is more comprehensively captured and preserved in Beethoven's first eight symphonies (1799–1812), his chamber music from the *Razumovsky* Quartets of 1806 to the *Archduke* works of 1811–12, the piano sonatas from the *Pathétique* (1799) to Op. 90 (1814).'

From the period following the Congress of Vienna (1814–15) Abraham observes:

'Post-war — or post-Congress — Beethoven is strikingly different: the piano sonatas, Opp. 101–111 (1816–22), the quartets that followed them, Opp. 127–135 (1824–6), and the two works fundamentally different from anything else he had written before, the Ninth Symphony and *Missa Solemnis* on which he worked side by side during 1818–23.'

Of Beethoven the putative romantic Abraham cautions:

'In Beethoven there are plenty of premonitions of romanticisms but not its full ripening. The romantic instrumental composers were more and more concerned with the expression of defined emotions, even pictorial or literary images: Beethoven during his last ten or twelve years was, except in the Mass and Ninth Symphony, almost exclusively concerned with the ineffable. He had become a more and more isolated figure, immensely respected but detached in spirit from the musical scene rather than at its centre ... [The] Age of Beethoven was above all an age of transition. Yet Beethoven, who had played the leading role in the process for so long, now stood apart, times had changed and he had changed, but not with them. He does not belong to German Romanticism.'

Gerald Abraham, *The Age of Beethoven, 1790–1830*, vol. eight: *The New Oxford History of Music*, Oxford, New York, Oxford University Press, 1988, pp. v–vi.

THEODOR W. ADORNO
The German philosopher, sociologist and composer Theodor W. Adorno spent many years compiling notes for a projected study of Beethoven. His work remained in this form at the time of his death but was edited and collated by the writer and philosopher Rolf Tiedemann, being published in English translation (Edmund Jephcott) as *Beethoven: The philosophy of music, Fragments and texts* (1998). Adorno worked on his projected Beethoven text through the years 1938–56. Despite this long period of gestation, his work did not progress beyond a great accumulation of diverse texts – 'fragments' – arbitrarily arranged in his files. In his reworking of this material, Tiedemann recast Adorno's texts into 370 numbered sub-texts to which he appended scholarly commentaries. Thereby, he sought 'to organize the material as Adorno himself might have done, had he written the projected book' (Preface). From the great body of material thus

co-ordinated by Tiedemann, we have selected the following citations:

> 'Beethoven's music is an image of that process which great philosophy understands the world to be. An image, therefore, not of the world but of an interpretation of the world.' p. 11.

> 'Beethoven's music does not merely contain "Romantic elements", as music historians maintain, but has the whole of Romanticism and its critique within itself.' p. 26.

> 'To understand Beethoven means to understand tonality. It is fundamental to his music not only as its "material" but as its principle, its essence: his music utters the secret of tonality; the limitations set by tonality are his own — and at the same time the driving force of his productivity.' p. 49.

> 'Among the most astonishing features of Beethoven's work is that nothing is ever type-cast, fixed, repeated, each work being a unique conception from a very early stage.' p. 66.

> 'If asked for the true reason for Beethoven's greatness I would probably answer first of all ... that he did not simply produce one good Beethoven piece after another, but incessantly — virtually infinitely — produced new characters, types, categories of music (compared to them, certain characteristics of the details, in which the spontaneity of other composers resides, are rather hackneyed). In Beethoven there is no reification of forms.' p. 159.

*

> 'Rage in Beethoven's music, is bound up with the priority of the whole over the part. As if rejecting the limited, the finite. The melody is growled in anger, because it is never the whole. Rage at the finitude of music itself. Each theme a lost penny.'

Adorno is making reference here to the composer's Rondo a capriccio, Op. 129: the so-called 'Rage over a lost penny'. p. 77.

> 'In what does the expression of the human manifest itself in Beethoven? I would say, in the fact that his music has the gift of sight. The human is its gaze. But this must be expressed in technical concepts.' p. 164.

ALLGEMEINE MUSIKALISCHE ZEITUNG (AmZ)

The Allgemeine musikalische Zeitung (General music newspaper) was a German language periodical that commenced publication in 1798 under the direction of its owner and founder Gottfried Christoph Härtel. Its publisher was Breitkopf & Härtel of Leipzig with whom Beethoven had many negotiations. The periodical reviewed musical events taking place in the German-speaking nations and in other countries. As such, it was amongst the first to bring to the attention of the musically minded public an awareness of Beethoven's compositions and of their originality — that the periodical's contributors frequently found to be disturbing. In 1800 the AmZ published a review ostensibly in celebration of Joseph Haydn to whom it accorded 'the first place' with regard to his symphonies and quartets, 'wherein no one has yet surpassed him'. Beethoven, a still relatively unknown composer, is not, however, overlooked; the reviewer comments how he may even usurp the venerable master 'if he calms his wild imaginings'. In due course the Allgemeine musikalische Zeitung received news of Beethoven's compositions with increasing respect. A music critic writing in issue XXVI of the AmZ of 1824 made a survey of Beethoven's pianos sonatas in what would be its longest contemporary review of his piano compositions. He enthused: 'The composer struck along new paths some thirty years ago.' He acknowledges his works 'engendered hostility on the way' but concedes 'all that is now stilled for today no other can touch this great spirit'.

Following the death of Beethoven in 1827, the AmZ devoted a considerable part of its issue 31 of April 1829 to a reflection on the composer and his achievements:

> 'Since the death of the great master, people have fought about his last works frequently and on occasions with bitterness. One side exhausts itself in praise and believes that the public is not yet ready for these works that are far beyond their times. They believe that only later on, after frequent listening, will people discover and enjoy their qualities of beauty. The others dismiss them as baroque, too lengthy, unclear products of an overheated fantasy.'

Beethoven's works were clearly held to be in advance of musical convention by the contributors to the AmZ:

> 'Beethoven's defenders admit that his last compositions have not yet been understood, but as proof that this will happen in the future they cite Mozart, for whom things didn't go any better.'

*

The AmZ editor then reflects more widely:

> 'The purpose of every work of art can be no other than to infuse our inner being with the highest possible degree of bliss in those moments when it engages us. This purpose is achieved when reason and feeling, equally occupied, are brought into harmonic play. In instrumental music, which we are concerned with first in regard to Beethoven's music, reason is satisfied through order, symmetry, and relationship to a major idea – theme and execution – in one word: through skilled thematic work. Feeling is satisfied through the beauty of the melody and through harmonious sound.'

Beethoven's deafness was acknowledged:

> 'Unfortunately, Beethoven lost that gem that for a musician is invaluable: hearing. Becoming melancholic and gloomy, he withdrew more and more from the external world and no longer heard music; he only saw it, and the longer this lasted the more the actual charm of the music faded in his memory and the more the consequences of this became evident in those of his works that now began to appear.'

The editor concludes his review with a misunderstanding of Beethoven's music — particularly that of his last period — that persisted for many years after his death:

> 'Gradually, Beethoven became an eye composer;

indeed, he had to become one because of the circumstances. More and more he enjoyed inventing odd motives and working out and interconnecting them in an artificial and strange way. He piled idea upon idea, and on paper they appeared very clear and delighted his eye, but in working them out they often become a chaotic image.'

Wayne M. Senner, Robin Wallace and William Meredith, editors, *The Critical Reception of Beethoven's Compositions by his German Contemporaries*, Lincoln: University of Nebraska Press, in association with the American Beethoven Society and the Ira F. Brilliant Center for Beethoven Studies, San José State University, 1999, Vol. 1 and Vol. 2. See also: H. C. Robbins Landon, *Haydn: The Years of the Creation*. London: Thames and Hudson, 1977. Many other reviews from the AmZ are cited in Anton Felix Schindler, *Beethoven as I knew Him*, edited by Donald W. MacArdle and translated by Constance S. Jolly from the German edition of 1860. London: Faber and Faber, 1966.

DENIS ARNOLD AND NIGEL FORTUNE

In their Preface to *The Beethoven Companion*, Denis Arnold and Nigel Fortune attest to the continuing influence Beethoven exerts on contemporary musicology:

'Modern statistical methods could no doubt calculate whether more words have been written about Beethoven than any other composer (although Mozart must be a close competitor). The list only begins with the musicologist and music critic; novelists and politicians, philosophers and poets have all added to the riot of words, using a sometimes mythical figure for their own ends. In spite of a literature which already presents a formidable challenge to the bibliographer, it is safe to say that there will be no halt to its growth.'

Denis Arnold and Nigel Fortune, *The Beethoven Companion*, London, Faber and Faber, 1973, p. 15.

MATTHEW ARNOLD

The English poet and critic Matthew Arnold was a contributor to *Macmillan's Magazine* that was highly regarded in the late nineteenth century in cultural circles. Edited by Sir George Grove, its other contributors included such luminaries as George Elliot, Thomas Huxley, William Morris and the poet Tennyson. Writing to Grove on 29 May 1878, Arnold revealed some knowledge of Beethoven's many illnesses:

> 'My Dear Grove ... Look out the Beethoven passage for me [unspecified], when you have time. All that sort of thing interests me much. I see he died at fifty-six; I shall be fifty-six next Christmas, and am not loath to depart, but hope I shall not have dropsy first, and be punctured, and the punctures turn to sores. But "an enduring heart have the Destinies given to the sons of men," as Homer says.'

Charles L. Graves, *The Life & Letters of Sir George Grove*, Hon. D.C.L. (Durham), Hon. LL.D. (Glasgow), formerly director of the Royal college of music, London: Macmillan and Co., Ltd.; New York: The Macmillan Co., 1903, pp. 157–8.

*

CLAUDIO ARRAU

The Chilean pianist Claudio Arrau was celebrated for his interpretations of a large repertoire including the works of Beethoven, Schubert, Chopin, Schumann, Liszt and Brahms. In 1938 Arrau gave the first rendering of the complete Beethoven piano sonatas and piano concertos in Mexico City. He repeated this feat several times in his lifetime, including in New York and London. He is remembered for being one of the leading Beethoven keyboard authorities of the 20th century. As a tribute to his accomplishments, New York City conferred on him its Beethoven Medal.

When in conversation with the American cultural historian Joseph Horowitz, Arrau expressed his high regard for Beethoven, to the interpretation of whose works he had dedicated so much of his life:

> 'For me, Beethoven has always stood for the spirit of man victorious. His message of endless struggle concluding in the victory of renewal and spiritual rebirth speaks to us and to young people today with a force that is particularly relevant to our times. In the sense that his life was an existential fight for survival, Beethoven is our contemporary. In the sense that he mastered both his life and his art to reach the ultimate heights of creation and transfiguration, he will last as long as man's spirit to prevail lasts on earth.'

Turning to the piano sonatas, Horowitz discussed the question of metronome indications as a guide to performance. In particular he cited the case of *the Hammerklavier* Sonata for which the composer's suggested metronome settings are today considered to demand too fast a tempo.

Arrau responded:

> 'If you play the first movement of *the Hammerklavier* at the metronome tempo, it loses all its majesty.' He revealed he had tried to perform it at Beethoven's metronome tempo but, although he considered it 'feasible', he personally found it to be 'very difficult technically ... Almost impossible'. He thought Carl Czerny's metronome markings for the sonata deserved respect for being 'the only markings from somebody who actually studied with Beethoven and performed under his influence'. Of these though he accepted – 'they're not too reliable either'. In response to Horowitz's generalization: 'Do you think there is such a thing as a proper tempo for a given piece?' Arrau averred, somewhat laconically: 'There is a proper range, I think. A rather narrow range.'

Horowitz also asked Arrau what his position was concerning the redistribution of notes between the hands in performance to facilitate evenness or accuracy. Arrau acknowledged that an audience may not notice such things but he maintained 'one should play for the ideal listener'. He believed the ideal listener will notice the difference, and cited passages in the first movement of Op 106:

> 'People play it with two hands because they don't want to risk dirty octaves. Well, first of all, it sounds different played with one hand, as written. And then technical difficulty has itself an expressive value.'

On another occasion, in the 1970s, the pianist Philip Lorenz assisted Arrau to conduct a series of master classes; these were in connection with the Beethoven Bicentennial. It was a first-time experience for Arrau. Students attended from Europe, Japan and America. One student elected to perform the Op. 111 Piano Sonata. Lorenz recalls how, in guiding the pupil, Arrau did not play a single note. Instead he encouraged her with his views about the composition, remarking on 'the emotional world the music occupies' and how to realise the work's technical challenges. At the close of the student's performance there was thunderous applause. Lorenz remembers:

> 'I think a lot of people were moved to tears ... it wasn't so much for her playing, although she played very well. It was for [Arrau].'

Joseph Horowitz, *Conversations with Arrau*, London: Collins, 1982, p. 21, p. 170 and pp. 214–5.

BOITO ARRIGO

The Italian Boito Arrigo is remembered today for his collaboration with Giuseppe Verdi, notably for supplying the libretti to his operas *Otello* and *Falstaff*. In his day, however, Arrigo enjoyed a reputation for being a poet and writer on music. Arrigo's musical articles adopt vivid word-imagery to convey his thoughts about the character of a composer. Thus:

> 'Haydn proceeds from Bach as the flowering laburnum from the terrible rock' and Schumann is 'the sail of a ship before the wind'. In this scheme of things: 'Beethoven [is] a solar intelli-

gence, a nature almost divine, amphibian of sky and earth'. Arrigo pronounced Beethoven to be 'the greatest of all' in stature: 'Bach comes up to his chest, Mendelssohn to his heart, Schumann to his elbow, Haydn to his knee, Wagner to the clavicle of his foot.'

Frank Walker, *The Man Verdi*, London: Dent, 1962, p. 454.

In an essay on what constitutes beautiful, Arrigo wrote:

'The Beautiful can come to life in many kinds of forms, the most bizarre, the most varied, the most different; regarding the Sublime, one can only point to its great form, the divine form, universal and eternal: the form of the sphere. The horizon is sublime; the sea is sublime; the sun is sublime. Shakespeare is spherical, Dante is spherical, Beethoven is spherical.'

Mary Jane Phillips-Matz, *Verdi: A biography*, Oxford: Oxford University Press, 1993, p. 474.

VLADIMIR ASHKENAZY

In an interview with the American pianist and author David Dubal, and the Russian-born pianist and conductor Vladimir Ashkenazy, Beethoven became the subject of conversation, prompting the following exchange:

Dubal: 'Which brings to mind Beethoven and his hard-fought creative developments. Do you know the little book called *Beethoven: His Spiritual Development*, by J. W. N. Sullivan?'

Ashkenazy: 'It is my favourite book on Beethoven and perhaps on music itself. It's such a marvelous little volume'.

Dubal: 'Sullivan felt that music on the level of Beethoven's communicates great depths of consciousness that contain invaluable lessons for humanity'.

Ashkenazy: 'How much he understood of Beethoven, one of the great geniuses? That we have a Beethoven in our midst is a great solace and a never-ending experience.'

David Dubal, The World of the Concert Pianist, London: Victor Gollancz, 1985, p. 42.

On another occasion Ashkenazy compared Beethoven with Mozart:

'I have always been puzzled by the fact that Beethoven composed with great difficulty while Mozart did so effortlessly and very, very fast. And most of his music is so incredible, so transcendental, that there are no words to describe it. Beethoven's case seems more understandable because the greatness of the music was the result of so much effort. He certainly had the feeling, the musical idea and the image corresponding to his feeling. But it took a lot of time, anguish and torment before his ideas crystallized into something that could be written on paper, in notes. He did hundreds of sketches. But we know what finally came out. And when it is imperfect or clumsy from the formal point of view, as it very occasionally is, it is still perfect from the point of view of communicating ultimate reality — or, in other words, true to life.'

'When I say that I can understand Beethoven's case more easily, I am not saying that he is closer to me, but merely that he reflects life in all its states. Mozart, on the other hand, is so elevated, so perfect that he almost seems removed from life — because life is not perfect. But Mozart is. Maybe he represents some essence of life, a transcendental essence, the ultimate meaning of life. But I can't explain it. I don't know and can't reconcile the apparently easy process of composition with the unfathomable depth and complete, integral, organic vision contained in his music. Some critics and musical people say that the music was already made up, stamped in his mind all the time. I don't believe this, but cannot provide any answers of my own, either. Perhaps the only conductor who came close to explaining this mystery was the late Josef Krips who stopped an orchestra during a rehearsal of a Mozart symphony, tapped his baton and said, "Gentlemen, please! Remember: Beethoven goes to heaven: Mozart comes from heaven!" '

Helena Matheopoulos, *Maestro: Encounters with conductors of today*, London: Hutchinson, 1982, pp. 478–9. See also the entry for J. N. W. Sullivan.

*

MILY BALAKIREV

Rimsky-Korsakov recalled his Saturday evening visits to see the Russian pianist and nationalist composer Mily Balakirev — founder of the famous 'Five' who included, together with Rimsky-Korsakov himself, Borodin and Mussorgsky. His recollections shed light on the state of musical appreciation at the period of these visits — the 1860s:

> 'As far as I recall, Balakirev was then composing a piano concerto, excerpts from which he would play for us. Often he explained to me instrumentation and forms of composition. From him I heard opinions that were entirely new to me. The tastes of the circle learned towards Glinka, Schumann, and Beethoven's last quartets. Eight symphonies of Beethoven found comparatively little favour with the circle.'

Reflecting more widely on the musical tastes of his distinguished circle of friends, Rimsky-Korsakov adds:

> '[Under] the influence of Schumann's compositions, melodic gifts were then looked upon with disfavour. The majority of melodies and themes were regarded as the weaker part of music ... Nearly all the fundamental ideas of Beethoven's symphonies were thought weak; Chopin's melodies were considered sweet and womanish; Mendelssohn's, sour and bourgeois.'

Carl van Vechten, editor, *Nikolay Rimsky-Korsakov: My Musical life*, London: Martin Secker & Warburg Ltd., 1942, p. 20 and p. 28.

DANIEL BARENBOIM

In his autobiography *A Life in Music*, the Argentine-Israeli born pianist and conductor Daniel Barenboim outlined his views on the nature of Western European music, as we typically know it in recital and concert. He remarks:

> 'The paintings we know date back two thousand years, the literature we read goes back three or four thousand years, but the music we live with only dates primarily from the end of the seventeenth century. Three hundred years is a very short time.'

He adds:

> 'The majority of today's audiences who attend concerts regularly, and with great interest, still think of the music of Stravinsky and Bartók as modern or contemporary.'

He further observes that many of their works were written between 1910 and 1920.

Turning to present-day interest in music Barenboim comments:

> 'There has never been as much interest in music as there is today. There have never before been so many people able to listen to music. But I am not sure about the quality of the audiences. Beethoven's works must have been just as difficult to listen to in the 1820s as some of the work of Boulez, Messiaen, or Lutoslavski is today. But Beethoven's audiences had something that came from an active musical education: many of the

listeners at those first performances had a knowledge of music that today's audiences lack.'

Daniel Barenboim, *A Life in Music*, London: Weidenfeld & Nicolson, 1991, pp. 93—4.

Turning to Beethoven, Barenboim outlined his views on the manner in which the composer brought order to his creations though the apparent disorder of his preliminary thoughts:

> 'Complexity - until methodically analysed - is chaos. After analysis, it is revealed as an accumulation of orderly details. Beethoven's sketchbooks show that his method of composing went from the complex to the simple. The final version, as we know it, is often considerably simpler than his first version. A composer's initial inspiration, like the initial reaction of an interpreter, is often disorderly and therefore unnecessarily complex. If one wanted to oversimplify it, one could say that the distinction between a great composition and a lesser one is that the great compositions have all been worked out from the complex to the simple - not in a primitive sense, but from the point of view of greater clarity.'

Barenboim makes the following remarks concerning interpretation in music:

> 'Every masterpiece is open to any number of interpretations, as long as they do not falsify it. However, it is not possible to combine all interpretations in any one performance, just as it is impossible to live more than one life. The

interpreter or the performer can never perceive all the many details of the many possible interpretations in any one performance, he can only glimpse them. We often become obsessed with one particular viewpoint or idea, and thus become blind to its opposite. But to me, dualism, the paradoxical nature of things, is the very essence of music. It is no coincidence that the sonata form, which is based on this dualism, is one of the most perfect forms of expression. The structure of a classical sonata or symphony by Beethoven is based on this principal of dualism.'

Daniel Barenboim, *A Life in Music,* London: Weidenfeld & Nicolson, 1991, p. 170 and pp. 215–216.

PHILIP BARFORD

In his portrait of *Beethoven as Man and Artist* the musicologist Philip Barford expresses candid and uncompromising views:

'Totally opposed to the romantic image of "Beethoven the Creator and Conqueror" is the psychological, psychiatric, even clinical view. Beethoven was a genius with the characteristic marks of genius – neurotic without a doubt, unstable, oscillating between moody introspection and depression on the one hand and back-slapping exaltation and enthusiasm on the other, with his own view of himself enlarged by solid convictions of his own worth and tainted by excursions into self-pity. He was aggressive, over-sensitive, restless, undisciplined in his life, gross and crude with an "unbuttoned" sense of humour, devious, intolerant and sometimes hypocritical. He suffered a great deal of ill-health.'

Notwithstanding these many personal shortcomings, Barford gives the following affirmation of Beethoven's continuing relevance to humankind — almost as an antidote to his previous raw candor:

'Beethoven's enduring monument is his music. There, in the notes, are his intellectual functions revealed. Beethoven *is* the music. The symphonies, quartets, sonatas — these are the very structure of his consciousness, the framework of his being enshrined in symbols, which reveal the truth to us in the only language that matters ... And yet the traditional romantic images must be given their due. A bust, an engraving or a painting that is a true work of art brings something through which is true to its subject, something discerned intuitively by the artist who has made it, however fleetingly, living contact with the inner life behind the appearances. From this point of view, images projected in idealized busts and portraits by artists who never even saw Beethoven could be allowed their measure of truth.'

Barford considers Beethoven in the context of Freedom:

'Beethoven believed in Freedom and in God, and like many others in his day and ours saw no reason to waste time saying what he meant by these terms. Like many he had felt the impact of the French Revolution. Unlike most his notion of freedom rose quite above political considerations and the local circumstances of his life, although he was interested in politics and freely criticized politicians and the police during a period of Viennese history when it was unwise to do so. His cavalier treatment of sonata conventions reveals a mind which, of its own creative momentum, had broken through previously accepted limitations.'

Barford identifies Beethoven's personal credo by which he sought to live:

'Freedom from theological restraints is clearly indicated in Beethoven's credo, which he adopted from an inscription on a temple in Jean-François Champollion's *Pictures of Egypt*. "I am that which is. I am everything that is, that was, and that will be. No mortal man has raised my veil. He is of himself alone, and it to this aloneness that all things owe their being." '

Beethoven copied out these words, framed them, and kept them on his desk.

Of Beethoven's continuing legacy Barford states:

'Beethoven is still very much before us, not only as a musical genius but as a challenge to the further growth of humanity, the symbol of man's eternal rejection of negative attitudes to life, and all narrow cleaving to petty ambitions of the finite self. The forces of his personality, which overflowed into unrefined excesses and offensive behaviour, were reflections of forces transmuted

> at a higher level of his being — the level of his
> better self, his individuality — into music.'

Phillip Barford, *Beethoven as Man and Artist*, In: Denis Arnold and Nigel Fortune: editors, *The Beethoven Companion*, London: Faber and Faber, 1973, p. 22, p. 31 and p. 37.

BÉLA BARTÓK

In 1911 the Hungarian composer, pianist and ethnomusicologist Béla Bartók wrote an essay on the subject of Liszt's music that he had first encountered when he was a student. Reflecting on this period, he concedes he 'did not understand Beethoven's last sonatas' but adds, aphoristically:

> 'It is not given to every composer to be able, like
> Beethoven, to break down every difficulty himself, and to create perfection in every single work.'

Janos Demény, editor, *Béla Bartók: Letters*, London: Faber and Faber, 1971, p. 453.

On another occasion Bartók compared Beethoven with Debussy and Bach:

> 'Debussy's great service to music was to reawaken
> among all musicians an awareness of harmony
> and its possibilities. In that, he was just as important as Beethoven, who revealed to us the
> meaning of progressive form, and as Bach, who
> showed us the transcendent significance of counterpoint.'

Serge Moreux, *Béla Bartók*, London: Harvill Press, 1953, p. 92.

Whilst teaching at Harvard University in 1940, Bartók arranged to give piano lessons to his private pupil Dorothy Parrish. She must have been a pianist of considerable talent, given the nature of Bartók's response to her requests for study material:

> 'As for works to study, you may choose whatever you like from all the works of Beethoven (except the last sonata, and the *Hammerklavier*), by Mozart, Bach Schubert, Chopin, Schumann, Debussy and — Bartók.'

Janos Demény, editor, *Béla Bartók: Letters*, London: Faber and Faber, 1971, pp. 279–80.

ARNOLD BAX

The English composer, poet, and author Sir Arnold Bax confided his views about music in a letter to the pianist Harriet Cohen, written sometime in 1930. These have been described as 'intuitive ... ecstatic' and 'unhampered by the artificialities of civilized accretions'. Their essence is expressed in the extract from the following letter in which Bax positions Beethoven amongst other composers:

> 'I can't help being (fundamentally) a very primitive being. I believe in conditions of ecstasy — physical or spiritual — and I get nothing from anything else. I think all the composers who appeal to me — Beethoven, Wagner, Delius,

Sibelius — were primitive in that they believed that the secret of the universe was to be solved by ecstatic intuition rather than by thought.'

Colin Scott-Sutherland, *Arnold Bax*, London: J. M. Dent, 1973, pp. 67–68.

THOMAS BEECHAM

The English writer and critic Sir Neville Cardus was widely read for his contributions to *The Manchester Guardian* on both cricket and music. He counted several distinguished musicians amongst his personal friends, including Sir Thomas Beecham. In conversation with Beecham, Cardus ventured to say he believed most geniuses to be ahead of their time. Beecham responded:

> 'As far as I have been able to study the doings of the most far-seeing of geniuses, I am led to believe that they have invariably expressed themselves in terms more-or-less understood by average educated listeners of their own period.'

Cardus raised the proposition that Beethoven was once considered 'fit for the madhouse' – a recollection, doubtless, of Weber's remark, 'Our Beethoven is now fit for the madhouse' in response to passages written for the double basses at the close of the first movement of the Seventh Symphony. Beecham responded:

> 'Perhaps at one time, perhaps at many times, Beethoven *was* fit for the madhouse. We must remember, too, that performances in those distant years were often incapable of doing justice

> to a new work. And few means existed then whereby a new work could become familiar to the public. Scores were not easily acquired. And there was no radio, no gramophone.'

Sir Neville Cardus, *Sir Thomas Beecham, A Memoir*, Collins, 1961, p. 77.

PAUL BEKKER

One of the most articulate and influential of German music critics of the 20th century comments on the origins of Beethoven's creativity:

> 'Beethoven's work is based on the pianoforte: therein lie its roots and therefore it first bore perfect fruit.'

Considering the aspect of faith in Beethoven's art, Bekker writes:

> 'It makes no real difference to us whether Beethoven did or did not, as a performer, answer to his own ideal; or whether, in later years, his performance deteriorated on account of his deafness, or his neglect of the technical side of his art. What matters is the certainty that in the pianoforte works we possess an absolutely subjective confession of faith from a practising artist. They give us a glimpse into his workshop. Through them we get authentic tidings of his wishes and purposes; they form a diary of the deepest, most individual and intimate description.'

Paul Bekker, *Beethoven*, London: J. M. Dent & Sons, 1925, p. 80 and p. 145.

Placing Beethoven in the context of other composers, Bekker states:

> 'Compared with the works of other musicians of the first rank, Beethoven's compositions are few in number and restricted in kind; a glance at the collected works of Bach, Handel, Haydn and of the short-lived Mozart and Schubert confirms this. But to deduce that Beethoven was therefore less creatively fertile would be wrong. The explanation lies in the peculiar nature of his genius as an artist. He was first a thinker and poet, and secondarily a musician. He never subordinated his ideas to the limitations of tone or of his craft. His whole work is ever a struggle of idea with tone-material, which he made for ever more adaptable, more expressive as a vehicle of thought, It is this process, with its many difficulties, which accounts for Beethoven's slow development and the comparative fewness of his works. The thought-infused nature of his art and the types of problem which he chose for artistic treatment demanded evolution and continuous refinement of style.'

Elaborating on the foregoing, Bekker adds:

> '[Beethoven] expressed the thought of Kant, Schiller and their compeers, and struggles of the revolutionary epoch, in terms of music. His philosophic attitude conditioned his position as

the greatest of all instrumental composers in musical history. The world of abstract thought, which clamoured in him for expression, demanded a correspondingly pure and absolute form of musical revelation. The great epoch of idealism and classicism in Germany found its most perfect artistic expression in the idealistic instrumental music, not depending on any connection with the sung or spoken word ... Regarded from this aspect, Beethoven's art might appear to be a product and expression of the cultural ides of his period, but it is, of course, rooted in the remoter past. The impulse towards abstraction, which is the driving force behind his work, is ever discoverable as the motive force in the history of musical development ... It seems as if Nature herself were bent on proving the inexhaustible possibilities of that aspect of creative activity which we call art, when she chose for the apparently limitless genius of Beethoven his date in the history of musical art.'

Paul Bekker, *Beethoven*, London, J. M. Dent & Sons, 1925, pp. 337–9.

ALBAN BERG

The Austrian composer Alban Berg had occasion to write to his wife Helene on 2 June 1907. In his affection for her he enthused:

'We must believe in the miracle of love, just as we believe in the miracle of death, since "the secret of love is bigger than the secret of death".' (Oscar Wilde, *Salomé*).

Turning first to Wagner and then to Beethoven, he added:

> 'Someone who could write *Tristan* must surely have believed in love with the utmost conviction. Would all those who are transported into ecstasy by it, explain their state of mind as the effect on their nervous system of the altered diminished seventh? No, my beautiful one, you must surely believe that this music, written in love, will touch strings in you to produce a purer, truer tone — unaffected by the intellect and (in your phrase) "keeping the eyes wide open". For, as Beethoven tells us, "Music is truly a higher form of revelation than all philosophy".'

Bernard Grun, *Alban Berg: Letters to his Wife*, edited and translated by Bernard Grun, London: Faber and Faber, 1971, pp. 24—5.

HECTOR BERLIOZ

Hector Berlioz's enthusiasm for the music of Beethoven is well documented. He himself gave expression to it in his *A travers chants, etudes musicales, adorations, boutades et crtiques,* an English edition of which was translated and edited by Edwin Evans and was published in 1911 under the title *A critical study of Beethoven's nine symphonies, with a few words on his trios and sonatas, a criticism of Fidelio and an introductory essay on music,* London, W. Reeves, 1911. More than thirty years after Beethoven's death his works were little known in France. Those that were performed, in particular the orchestral works, were usually premiered in severely edited and truncated form and were typically received with hostility. The symphonies were condemned for being 'bizarre, incoherent, diffuse, bristling with harsh modulations and wild harmonies, bereft of melody, over the top, too noisy, and horribly difficult to play'.

Amidst such clamour, the views of Hector Berlioz were an oasis of calm and reason, albeit with more than a touch Gallic passion. In 1828 Berlioz heard Beethoven's Third and Fifth Symphonies for the first time when they were performed at the Paris Conservatoire — an experience he found overwhelming. In the same year he submitted an entry in a bid to secure the coveted *Prix de Rome*. His composition, a cantata *Herminie,* was one of four attempts; it was not until 1830 that he was eventually successful. In his *Memoires*, Berlioz writes of the passion for Shakespeare that Beethoven's music had stirred within him:

'I was haunted by my Shakespearean passion, which had been painfully intensified by the effect produced on me by Beethoven; and [I] was at that time a dreamy, savage creature, silent to the verge of dumbness, disorderly in my attire, as great a burden to my friends as to myself, and my only occupation the occasional production of a small and shapeless article on music.'

On 10 December 1831, Berlioz wrote enthusiastically to his fellow countryman Victor Hugo; Berlioz was by then becoming more fully aware of Beethoven's music:

'Oh! You are a genius, a man of power, a colossus who is both tender, pitiless, elegant, monstrous, raucous, melodious, volcanic, affectionate and *scornful.* This last constituent of genius is certainly the rarest, neither Shakespeare nor Molière had

> it. Beethoven alone among the *great* gauged correctly the size of the human insects that surrounded him and on his level I see none but you.'

Hugh Macdonald, editor: *Berlioz: Selected Letters*, London: Faber and Faber, 1995. p. 95.

An entry from Berlioz's *Memoires* from 1837 bears testimony to the slow progress Beethoven's music was taking in France to infiltrate into even the more musically enlightened circles. This derives from remarks made by the then Director of the Fine Arts. Berlioz discretely withholds his name but describes him as being the 'arbiter of the destinies of art and artists' who, apparently, did not condescend to recognise the worth in any music except that of Rossini. One day, in conversation with Berlioz, the individual in question endeavoured to recall the names of past and present musicians whom he considered to be of standing. He appeared to falter, stopped and remarked:

> 'But surely there must be another – what is his name? A German, whose symphonies they play at the Conservatoire. You must know *him*, M. Berlioz. Beethoven? Ah, Beethoven. Well, *he* was not devoid of talent.'

Berlioz later recalled, scarcely able to contain his disdain:

> 'I myself heard the Director of the Fine Arts express himself thus, and admit that Beethoven *was not devoid of talent!*'

In 1854 Berlioz was asked to supply biographical details for his *Memoires* and to explain the grounds why he himself had encountered such opposition in Paris as a composer. It is worth recalling what a modernist Berlioz was. His *Symphonie Fantastique* was composed only seven years after the death of Beethoven and occupies an entirely new and different musical landscape. Depicting 'An episode in the life of an artist', Leonard Bernstein described the symphony as 'the first musical expedition into psychedelia' because of its hallucinatory and dream-like nature. Berlioz's response to the request he had received for details for his *Memoires* provides further evidence, albeit indirectly, of the challenges Beethoven's music was proving to be almost thirty years after his death. Berlioz first states:

> 'The principal reason for the long war raged against me lies in the antagonism existing between my musical feeling and that of the great mass of the Parisian public. Many of them looked upon me as a madman.'

Berlioz concludes:

> 'All music deviating from the beaten track of the manufacturers of *opéras-comiques* necessarily seemed to these people the music of madmen, just as Beethoven's Ninth Symphony and colossal pianoforte sonatas are to them the compositions of a lunatic.'

Ten years later in 1864, Berlioz was reunited with his son who had been away in Mexico. He relates:

> 'Towards evening, as we walked along the banks of the Seine and talked of Shakespeare and Beethoven, I remember we got into a state of

immense excitement, in which my son only shared as far as Shakespeare was concerned, he being still unacquainted with Beethoven. We ... agreed finally, however, that it was good to be alive, to worship the beautiful, and that, if we could not destroy its opposite, we must rest satisfied with despising and forgetting it as far as possible.'

Ernest Newman, annotated and translated: *Memoirs of Hector Berlioz from 1803 to 1865, Comprising his Travels in Germany, Italy, Russia, and England*, New York: Knopf, 1932, p. 81, p. 95, pp. 180–1, pp. 483–4 and p. 510.

LEONARD BERNSTEIN

The American composer, conductor, pianist, educator and humanitarian Leonard Bernstein was described by the music critic Donal Henaham as 'one of the most prodigiously talented and successful musicians in American history'. His admiration for Beethoven approached reverence. This is evident in the many recordings he made of the composer's music alongside his equally numerous performances of the five piano concertos. Moreover, he expressed his thoughts about Beethoven's music in lectures, not least when he held the tenure of the Charles Eliot Norton Professorship of Poetry at Harvard University (1973–74). His lectures on Beethoven's symphonies, originally destined for television, are today available on *You Tube*.

The following is a characteristic Beethovenian Bernstein utterance:

'When you get the feeling that whatever note succeeds the last is the only possible note that can rightly happen at that instant, in that context, then

> the chances are you're listening to Beethoven ... Our boy has the real goods, the stuff from Heaven, the power to make you feel at the finish: Something is right in the world. There is something that checks throughout, that follows its own law consistently: something we can trust that will never let us down — But that is almost a definition of God — I meant it to be.'

Leonard Bernstein, *The Joy of Music*, New York: Simon and Schuster, 1959.

In one of his YouTube recordings, Bernstein states:

> 'I have studied [Beethoven's music] and re-studied it, rehearsed and performed it over and over again and I may report that I have never tired of it for a single moment. The music remains endlessly satisfying, interesting and moving and has remained so for almost two centuries and to all kinds of people. In other words, this music is not only infinitely durable but perhaps the closest music has ever come to universality and that dubious cliché about music being the universal language almost comes true with Beethoven. No composer has ever lived who speaks so directly to so many people, to young and old, educated and ignorant, amateur and professional, sophisticated and naive, and to all these people of all classes, nationalities and racial backgrounds, this music speaks a universality of thought of human brotherhood, freedom and love.'

Bernstein about Beethoven's music, YouTube.

Georges Bizet

When studying at the Paris Conservatoire under the guidance of Charles Gounod, Georges Bizet completed his Symphony in C — only a month after his seventeenth birthday — 'revealing an extraordinarily accomplished talent' (Grove's Dictionary). Notwithstanding this precocious achievement, Bizet felt a sense of insecurity as a composer — and his symphony languished in obscurity in the library of the Paris Conservatoire until its discovery in 1933. Bizet shared his doubts in a series of letters that he wrote to close friends. In these Bizet reveals his thoughts about music and musicians. In one, sent to an artist friend in December 1858, he writes:

> 'At the Conservatoire I was a good pupil; here I am beginning to think of myself as an artist, I go forward alone ... I know what is good and what is beautiful ... Happy the men like Raphael, Mozart, Correggio and Rossini who have received from Heaven the artistic gift in all its purity and perfection; happy also those who like Michelangelo and Beethoven, have by the power of their *reason* and their genius come to discover the last word in greatness and beauty.'

At the end of the same month Bizet wrote his friend, the opera singer Hector Gruyer, outlining his views on genius in music:

> 'There are two sorts of genius: natural genius and rational genius. While immensely admiring the second, I shall not conceal from you that the first has all my sympathies. Yes, I dare to prefer Raphael to Michelangelo, Mozart to Beethoven,

and Rossini to Meyerbeer ... It is solely a matter of taste, one type of ideas has a greater attraction for me that the other.'

In another passage Bizet attempts to find an underlying correspondence between the arts:

'All the arts touch, or rather there is only one art. Whether one expresses one's ideas on canvas, in marble or in the theatre, is of little importance: the idea is always the same. I am more that ever convinced that Mozart and Rossini are the two greatest musicians. While admiring Beethoven and Meyerbeer with all my faculties, I feel my nature brings me to love art that is pure and fluent rather than dramatic passion.'

A few years later Bizet gave further expression to his worries and unsatisfied longings in another letter, this time written to his fellow musician-friend Ernest Guiraud — like Bizet a winner of the coveted *Prix de Rome*. His concerns had clearly disturbed his sleep:

'I dreamed last night that we were all at Naples, installed in a charming villa; we were living under a purely artistic government. The Senate consisted of Beethoven, Michelangelo, Shakespeare, Giorgione and people like that.'

Winton Dean, *Georges Bizet: His life and work*, London: J.M. Dent, 1965, p. 86 and pp. 238–9.

*

JOHN BLACKING

The British ethnomusicologist and social anthropologist John Blacking likened Beethoven's working method to that of an architect and carver — bearing upon his wider belief in music's social and cultural virtues:

> 'Composing is essentially a problem of capturing force within form. Although a composer ostensibly "puts together" patterns of sound, like an architect who builds up the design of a cathedral, he is also like a carver who chips away at an existing mass in order to give it new, culturally significant form. Beethoven is one of many musicians for whom we have evidence of a composing process in which precise, but amorphous, ideas and lumps of sound are eventually crystallized into patterns of melody. The process by which a musician puts together or chips away, as well as the materials which he assembles or "carves", are influenced by the patterns of both his culture and the behavioral processes which he has learned as an individual member of it.'

Reginald Byron, *Music, Culture, & Experience: Selected papers of John Blacking*, Chicago: University of Chicago Press, 1995, p. 81.

ARTHUR BLISS

The English composer Arthur Bliss writes of his early musical experiences whilst at preparatory school:

> 'I shall always be grateful to the self-effacing and dedicated music master there who introduced me

> to the Beethoven Sonatas ... My introduction to Beethoven through practising his *Andante con Variazioni*, Op. 26, and then through hearing in London his *Coriolan* Overture and Fifth Symphony fired me with a longing to find out all there was to know about his personality and life.'

Later Bliss wrote about the capacity of Beethoven's music to heal:

> '*All* Beethoven's music is a continual protest against the cruelty, misery and evil in this world, but he *does*, after a lifetime's struggle, supply and answer in the music of his last period, envisaging a world of compassion and serenity. I believe that through whatever changes and transformations music is passing it must unswervingly keep its idealistic aim; otherwise, it may cease to retain its mysterious power of healing and of giving joy, and just dwindle into an excitant aural sensation, and nothing more.'

In the spring of 1934, Bliss was invited to deliver a series of lectures at the Royal Institution. H. G. Wells was in the audience of one of these and later invited Bliss to compose the music to Alexander Korda's film-adaptation of his *Things to Come*. In discussing unity and form in music, Bliss made a passing, but significant, reference to Beethoven:

> '[Unity] in diversity [is] the employment not of one idea that spreads, but of two or more antagonistic ideas that are gradually compelled to harmonize and form one complete whole. This implies drama and struggle, and is the formal idea

lying behind the first movement of a Beethoven sonata, for instance. The first develops from a single thematic idea, the second is based on the interaction of several contrasted ones.'

Arthur Bliss, *As I Remember*, London: Thames Publishing, 1989, pp. 18–19, p. 102 and p. 247.

In the first of his Royal Institution Lectures, published as *Aspects of Contemporary Music*, Bliss summed up his personal creed:

> 'I believe that the foundation of all music is emotion, and that without the capacity for deep and subtle emotion a composer only employs a half the resources of his medium. I believe that this emotion should be called into being by the sudden awareness of actual beauty seen, or by the vision of beauty vividly apprehended. I believe that the emotion resulting from apprehended beauty should be solidified and fixed by presenting it in a form absolutely fitting to it, and to it alone.'

Bliss's view of contemporary music was bleak:

> 'There is not great music today in the sense that Bach or Beethoven are great'. Bliss conceded though: 'There is most certainly music that is good, good that is in the aesthetic sense, good art.'

In a BBC radio broadcast delivered on the Overseas Service on 3 October 1941 – published under the title *Music in Wartime* – Bliss conveyed his impressions of musical appreciation in England — his audience being American. In this he remarked:

> 'In serious music there is one composer whom the people need and demand above all others, and he is Beethoven. In the recent Promenade Concerts in the Albert Hall the top galleries were filled on a Beethoven night — this generally happens only on boxing nights, or when there are great spectacular shows. Before the Queen's Hall was destroyed by bombing, Basil Cameron gave a series of five Beethoven concerts there. It was impossible to get a seat. Beethoven has supplanted Bach in general favour.'

In a speech Bliss gave at a Royal Academy Dinner on 10 June 1971, Bliss reflected on the musical profession — and of its members' need to earn a decent living. He first called to mind a conversation with the English composer Sir Edward Elgar who told him of the struggles he had in his early years due to lack of means and, moreover, how, at the start of the century,

> 'any young man or young woman who aspired to be a composer without private income was regarded as [being] either mad or suicidal'.

This prompted Bliss to reflect: 'In spite of a Beethoven and a Schubert, a squalid garret is no place for inspiration — except in novels.' Bliss is here exaggerating somewhat; Schubert benefited, albeit in his all too short life, from the support of close friends and admirers and Beethoven received a regular annuity conferred on him by three of Vienna's most high-born citizens.

At a Royal College of Music prize giving held on 18 July 1974, an address was read on behalf of Bliss to the students by the Director of the College David Willcocks – Bliss was unwell at the time. His address touched upon what Bliss referred to as 'the mysterious, magical world of sound' and of the pleasure to be derived from making music with others and of the privilege of being a composer endeavouring 'to extend the boundaries of our art'. Calling Beethoven to mind, he quoted the composer's then acknowledged authority:

> 'I think it was Donald Tovey who said of Beethoven that when we are listening to him there come rare moments when we seem for an instant to be standing at the same high inspirational summit. The sad difference between Beethoven and us is simply that while he can remain there, we cannot.'

Gregory Roscow, editor, *Bliss on Music: Selected writings of Arthur Bliss, 1920–1975*, Oxford: Oxford University Press, 1991, p. 73, p. 179 and pp. 278–279.

ERNST BLOCH

The philosopher Ernst Bloch is known for his Marxist views and outlook for a humanistic world free from oppression and exploitation. Alongside his major intellectual interests, he also had close friendships with musicians, including Bertold Brecht and Kurt Weill, and writers on music including Theodor Adorno. Concerning the latter, he once remarked:

> 'I have from Beethoven that whenever something seems to me false, absurd or unreal (in his music),

I should defer entirely to him and seek fault in myself.'

Theodor W. Adorno, *Beethoven: The philosophy of music; fragments and texts*, Cambridge: Polity Press, 1998.

In his colourful, spirited and deeply thoughtful essay, relating to the structures and moods to be found in aspects of Beethoven's music, Bloch's text is interpolated with such expressions and imagery as '*Luciferan* music', 'flashes of lightning', 'notes [that] spiral upwards', 'architectonic', 'growing intensity', and the 'the struggle or soul of the emergent relationship'. With the foregoing in mind, he offers the following generalization about the music of Beethoven:

'Hence in Beethoven's music the detail is nothing and vitality in the broad context is everything — energy, directness, conflict-torn departure and resolution which is not re-possession but entirely gain. Thus in his developments, so thoroughly torn apart, Beethoven never acknowledges the theme's opportunity for delicate, calm, solitary self-enrichment. He recognises only the emotive quality of its exploration as the boldness, the *élan* of an adventure stated in the intrinsic harmonic-rhythmic substance. With Beethoven we enter the room and breathe the relationship. We have the most vivid feeling that here, everything is compressing itself by turns, and thus through the changing atmospheric pressure, so to speak, we ascertain the height and depth of the terrain — more than that, we acquire a true sailor's instinct and even genetic instinct for the atmosphere and its laws.'

Bloch also considers the rhythm and energy to be found in Beethoven's music:

> 'Above all, rhythm in Beethoven's music has taken possession of harmony, contributed a dynamism with strong drive and capped it with this dynamism's *rhythmic cultivation of the tonic.* The respiration of the rhythm no longer allows the parts to give themselves out simply as chords, vertically, or even to relax homophonically, any more than it permits all the parts to state uniform conviction, by which we mean the frictionless fugal self-differentiating of a single idea. Instead the rhythmicising energy constructs in depth. It annexes a polyphonic action by encompassing the vertical segments and, notwithstanding its tendency towards filigrane [sic] polyphony, by showing a preference for climaxes which settle in a single layer, passages where the notes fit together to form sonic columns supporting the achieved splendour and are thereby capable of subordinating highly daring, self-intensifying, self-deciding dynamic-rhythmic harmony to a new form, *sequential counterpoint.*'

Later Block adds:

> 'Another element arises continuously and with growing intensity: the struggle or soul of the emergent relationship. Hence, in Beethoven's music, the detail is nothing and vitality in the broad context is everything — energy, directness, conflict-torn departure and resolution which is not re-possession but entirely gain.'

Discussing the spirit in Beethoven's piano sonatas he writes:

> 'Passion, pain, cheerfulness and liberation are, and always will be, the components of the sonata as the authentic and encompassing Beethovenian form. The headings *Allegro*, *Adagio*, *Scherzo* and *Finale* generally correspond to these, although, on occasion to be sure, there is marked change in meaning. The first movement itself is frequently anything but an allegro, while the last occasionally incorporates rondo and even variation form. Normally the latter is diametrically opposed to strict, antithetical development. But when located in the final movement, it nonetheless constitutes the most significant part of the sonata besides the opening movement, precisely because it expands at will, loosely, more feely.'

Ernst Bloch, *Essays on the Philosophy of Music*, Cambridge: Cambridge University Press, 1985, p. 32, p. 70 and pp. 109–110.

PIERRE BOULEZ

In an interview with Pierre Boulez, the American musicologist and lecturer on music James R. Briscoe invited Boulez to remark on the response of an audience to music. Boulez answered:

> 'I find there are always works that communicate with a large group and those that communicate with fewer. For instance, I might take Beethoven,

the epitome of a musician known everywhere. If you play the Ninth Symphony, everyone would flock to the performance. If the Mass [D minor Op. 123], then many fewer. And if you play the last quartets, then you reduce to a few. I find that I am not at all shocked by that. One day Beethoven must express himself in a quite expansive way but on another much more for himself. Shakespeare wrote dramas that are played constantly, but he also wrote the sonnets, known by very few people. I do not find that unrealistic to expect a different appreciation from audiences.'

James R. Briscoe, editor, brief description: *Debussy in Performance*. New Haven: Yale University Press, 1999, pp. 89—90.

On another occasion Boulez compared the audience that might attend a popular sporting event to that which might be attracted to a Beethoven concert:

'Even the greatest conductor with the most standard repertoire does not have the popularity of, for instance, a boxing match. You have, for a football match, let's say two hundred thousand people and, even for a Beethoven symphony, you have only five thousand.'

Michael Oliver, editor, *Settling the Score: A journey through the music of the twentieth century*, London: Faber and Faber, 1999, p. 299.

*

JOHANNES BRAHMS

It is well reported that Brahms, as a young composer, found it difficult to escape from Beethoven's shadow, remarking 'You do not know what it's like to be followed by Him' — or words to that effect depending on the translation. In conversation with the Austrian music critic and teacher Richard Heuberger he shared some thoughts about his predecessor:

> 'I understand very well that the new personality of Beethoven, the new outlook, which people found in his works, made him greater, more important in their view [than Mozart's later works]. But 50 years later this judgment has been altered. The attraction of novelty must be differentiated from inner value. I admit that the [Third Piano] Concerto of Beethoven is more modern, but not so important! I am able to understand, too, that Beethoven's First Symphony did impress people colossally. In fact, it was the new outlook! But the last three symphonies by Mozart are much more important! Some people are beginning to feel that now.'

Originally published in Richard Heuberger, *Erinnerungen an Johannes Brahms: Tagebuchnotizen aus den Jahren 1875-1897*, editor K. Hofman, Tutzing, 1970. The quotation is derived from: John L. Holmes, *Composers on Composers*, New York: Greenwood Press, 1990, p. 14.

Brahms shared many views about music with Clara Schuman. The following extract, from a letter he wrote to her on 14 August 1855, is typical of what he had to say:

> 'Incidentally I ought to tell you that Shakespeare made a close study of Plutarch. In *Coriolanus*, *Julius Caesar* etc., whole speeches are taken bodily out of Plutarch, and in *Coriolanus* particularly the action is based entirely upon him (the sequence of scenes). Beethoven also loved to read Plutarch, and when listening to his music one often imagines that one can see the outline of one of Plutarch's heroes.'

Berthold Litzmann, editor, *Letters of Clara Schumann and Johannes Brahms, 1853–96*, New York, Vienna House. 2 Vols., 1971, Vol. 1, p. 44.

ALFRED BRENDEL

Alfred Brendel is universally acknowledged for being among the greatest interpreters of Beethoven and has the distinction of being the first performer to record his complete solo works for piano. In conversation with Brendel, the Swiss writer Martin Meyer invited him to place his gift for music alongside his other interests. Brendel replied:

> 'When I was very young, about sixteen, I went through a phase of playing a game with friends in which you had to pair composers with painters ... We used to agree about the following pairings: Mozart-Watteau, Beethoven-Michelangelo. And then I read in an essay by a very earnest and famous colleague that Beethoven was like Michelangelo, only greater! If I needed something to put an end to such a game, that was it.'

When asked about the particular challenges posed by

Beethoven's piano music, Brendel remarked:

> 'These are for me, as a performer, the most important points: to understand the concentration, then to convey the processional manner of the composition, the inevitability, the logic, in other words the erection of a building structure, block upon block, in order to achieve something especially stable. Finally, the quality of feeling, the genuineness, yes, the poetry of feeling, if such a phrase can be used today, without making people laugh.'

In explaining to Meyer why Brendel finds Beethoven's music so compelling in nature he remarked:

> 'There is something inevitable, continually self-justifying in this music, that commands respect through the logic and psychology of its compositions. There is, in addition, a development from Op. 1 to Op. 135, which is enormously far-reaching; from the beginning to the end, this music provides something new, formulates it with mastery, formulates the mastery anew, if you will. If masterpieces differ from one another, by creating something new each time, through something that was not previously there, then Beethoven is the master par excellence. The more I get to know him, the more I admire him, love him, respect him. I've realized this again and again in recent years, above all when I played all the sonatas.'

Alfred. Brendel, *The Veil of Order*, Alfred Brendel in conversation with Martin Meyer, London: Faber and Faber, 2002, p. 74, p.106 and p. 112.

In conversation with the pianist and musicologist David Dubal, Alfred Brendel remarked:

> 'For me, Beethoven, a master of the Classical style, always shows the listener where the music goes, and always justifies why it goes there. He also gives the reasons for why it happens as it does. I do not mean that Beethoven is in any way predictable, but that it is his plan to explain himself throughout. In other words, Beethoven is in control.'

Alfred Brendel in conversation with David Dubal in: Dubal, David, *The World of the Concert Pianist*, London: Victor Gollancz, 1985, p. 95.

In his essays on music, Brendel offers the following generalisation regarding the virtues of various composers:

> 'We readily extol composers for their "greatest" and "most personal" or exemplary achievements. Bach is granted primacy in organ music, sacred choral music and in fugue; Mozart primacy in opera, the piano concerto and the string quintet; Beethoven highest rank with the symphony and sonata, and — according to our preferences and perspective — either Haydn or Beethoven supremacy with the string quartet.'

Alfred Brendel, *Alfred Brendel on Music: Collected Essays*, Chicago, Ilinois: A Cappella Books, 2001, p. 9.

GERHARD VON BREUNING

Gerhard von Breuning was the son of Beethoven's lifelong friend, Stephan von Breuning. Beethoven held a particular affection for Gerhard, whom he knew as a child, referring to him as Hosenknopf — 'trouser button' — because he attached himself like a button to the composer's trousers. In the last two years of his life, Beethoven had rooms in the so-called *Schwarzspanierhause*. Unlike many of Beethoven's other residences it has not survived being demolished in 1903–4. Von Breuning is remembered in musicology today for his reflections on Beethoven in the title of which he adopted the name of *Schwarzspanierhause*. These were originally published in Vienna in 1874 under the title Aus dem *Schwarzspanierhause: Erinnerungen an L. van Beethoven aus meiner Jugendzeit*, known today in English translation as *Memories of Beethoven: From the house of the black-robed Spaniards*. This work has the authority of being one of only three book-length writings written by authors who knew Beethoven personally, the other two being the *Biographische Notizen über Ludwig van Beethoven* — *Remembering Beethoven: the biographical notes of Franz Wegeler and Ferdinand Ries* — and Anton Schindler's *Biographie von Ludwig van Beethoven* — *Beethoven as I new him*. In his editorial commentary to the modern-day edition of von Breuning's study (1992) Maynard Solomon describes it as 'a minor classic of the Beethoven literature, [and] an important source for our knowledge of the composer's later years'. From this text we have derived the following extracts:

> '[Beethoven] was powerful-looking, of medium height [in fact, Beethoven was of short stature being no more than 168 cms. — 5 feet 2 inches tall], vigorous in his gait and lively in movements,

> his clothing far from elegant or conventional [when von Breuning knew the composer, he had become negligent in his dress but as a young man he took greater care of his appearance]; and there was something about him overall that did not fit into any classification.' p. 19

Von Breuning inherited a piano that Beethoven had owned early in his career as a virtuoso pianist. This disposed him to exclaim:

> 'When one looks at the [Josef] Brodmann grand piano ... considered one of the best makes at that time, with its tiny tone and its mere five and a half octaves, one finds it hard to conceive how it could have been adequate for Beethoven's tempestuous improvisations, while realizing that it was as a consequence of Beethoven's sonatas that the piano was altered and strengthened into its present state, indeed it had to be almost made afresh.' footnote to p. 38

Later in life Beethoven owned a full six-octave Brodmann grand that today forms part of the Berlin Collection of Musical Instruments. See: Tilman Skowroneck, *Beethoven the Pianist*, Cambridge University Press, 2010, p. 128.

It is from von Breuning that we learn how completely deaf Beethoven was in his final years. He recalls a visit to see the composer at the period when he was at work on the so-called Galitzin string quartets. He tells us how he entered unnoticed by Beethoven who was preoccupied at his desk.

He continues:

> 'I was quiet for a while and then went over to the Graf piano [Conrad Graf loaned one of his 6 1/2 octave grand pianos to the composer around 1825–6] ... and began to strum lightly on the keys ... I kept looking in his direction to see whether he might be bothered. When I saw that he was completely unaware of it, I played louder ... I had no more doubts. He heard nothing and kept on writing.' p. 72

In the months just before his death, Beethoven derived great pleasure in leafing through a forty-volume edition of Handel's collected works that he had received as a gift in December 1826 from the London harp manufacturer Johann Stumpff. The young von Breuning assisted the now ailing composer to enjoy these works:

> 'I began to bring one volume after another over to his bed. He leafed through them one volume after another ... sometimes stopping at particular passages ... [He] started to sing the praises of the great Handel and to call him the most classic and most accomplished of all composers.' p. 96

Gerhard von Breuning was in Beethoven's presence until half an hour before he passed away. At the ensuing internment, the poet and dramatist Franz Grillparzer wrote the funeral oration. Later in life, von Breuning's father presented him with a copy of Grillparzer's text. See under Franz Grillparzer.

Gerhard von Breuning, edited and part-translated by Maynard Solomon: *Memories of Beethoven: From the house of the black-robed Spaniards*, Cambridge: Cambridge University Press, 1992.

BENJAMIN BRITTEN

By the age of twelve Benjamin Britten had already passed the Associated Board Grade VIII examination in piano. Nevertheless, as he recorded in a youthful letter — styled with youthful spelling — he did not esteem his playing very highly:

> 'After nearly eight years of study, I had a very flimsy *technick*; he [his teacher Greatorex] as good as said I had none at all. His words were, when I finished playing, "And who taught you that?" Afterwards he made out that it was hopeless for a boy of my age to play later Beethoven, and that my love of Beethoven will soon die, as it does with everyone!'

Donald Mitchell, editor, *Letters from a Life: The selected letters and diaries of Benjamin Britten 1913–1976.* London: Faber and Faber, 1991, Vol. 1 p. 30.

In 1962, the University of Hull conferred an honorary degree on Britten that prompted him to reflect on his formative years:

> 'When I was very young, my music was inclined to be hectic, to reply on exciting crescendos and diminuendos, on great climaxes — in one word, to reply on "gestures". At this time I was absorbed in the music of Beethoven. But for myself I felt the danger of this technique, so I turned away from that great pillar of music, turned to another — to Mozart, the most controlled of composers, who can express the most turbulent feelings in the most unruffled way.'

*

In a speech Britten gave on the occasion of being conferred the Freedom of Lowestoft, he expressed his general views on music:

> 'Before Beethoven music served things greater than itself – the glory of God or the glory of the State, for example. After Beethoven the composer was the centre of his own universe. The romantics became so intensely personal that it looked as though we were going to reach a point at which the composer would be the only man capable of understanding his own music. Then came Picasso and Stravinsky. They loosened up painting and music, freed them from the tyranny of the purely personal. They passed from manner to manner as a bee passed from flower to flower.'

Paul Kildea, editor, *Britten on Music*, Oxford: Oxford University Press, 2003, pp. 110–111 and p. 214.

Despite his youthful reservations concerning his abilities as a pianist, as remarked above, Britten matured into a performer of considerable accomplishments, especially as an accompanist. During his temporary wartime exile in the USA he gave a number of recitals together with his companion Peter Pears. At one of these, in December 1941, he played a Beethoven piano sonata and a Chopin scherzo prompting the reviewer to comment:

> 'His performance of these works was truly electrifying and one could sense that here was a master pianist. Some technical flaws marred an

> otherwise magnificent reading of the Chopin opus, but we understand that Mr Britten approaches music as a composer-conductor, rather than as a keyboard virtuoso. On the whole, however, we left feeling that we should like to attend some further concerts by these two.'

Donald Mitchell, editor, *Letters from a Life: The selected letters and diaries of Benjamin Britten 1913–1976*, London: Faber and Faber, 1991, Vol. 2, pp. 999–1000.

In 1963 musicologist Murray Schafer asked Britten as to his sympathies towards Beethoven and Brahms. Britten responded:

> 'I'm not blind to them. Once I adored them. Between the ages of thirteen and fourteen, I knew every note of Beethoven and Brahms. I remember receiving the full score of *Fidelio* for my fourteenth birthday. It was a red letter day.'

Of his present-day feelings toward Beethoven, Britten added:

> 'I certainly don't dislike all Beethoven but sometimes I feel I have lost the point of what he's up to. I heard recently [1963] the Piano Sonata Op. 111. The sound of the variations was so grotesque I just couldn't see what they were about.'

Original source: Murray Schafer, *British Composer's Interview*, London, Faber and Faber, 1963, pp. 113–24. The quotation is derived from: Paul Kildea, editor, *Britten on Music*. Oxford: Oxford University Press, 2003, p. 228.

BROADWOOD & SONS

When on his tour of the continent in 1817, Thomas Broadwood, then manager of the celebrated firm of John Broadwood & Sons of London, made the acquaintance of Beethoven. Doubtless aware of the prestige it would confer on his business he put in hand arrangements for one of his latest pianos to be sent as a gift to the composer. Given the importance of this instrument to Beethoven musicology — and to cultural history — we provide the following details.

The firm had been founded by John Broadwood in the eighteenth century and included amongst its patrons the painters Reynolds and Gainsborough and the composer Joseph Haydn. It is on record that in 1785 Thomas Jefferson, later to be third President of the United States, visited Broadwood's premises in Great Pulteney Street, London, to discuss musical instruments. The instruments of this period are most aptly described as being 'fortepianos'. However, by the time of Broadwood's meeting with Beethoven, his firm had made significant improvements to the mechanism of the instrument in consultation, no less, with members of the Royal Society of London. Furthermore, the range of the keyboard had been progressively expanded from 5, to 5 1/2, to 6 octaves. The term 'piano' becomes more appropriate for the description of these later instruments that were the precursors of the modern-day grand piano. Beethoven himself, ever eager to promote improvements to his chosen instrument, endeavored to adopt the term *hammerklavier*, by way of indicating the newer-type of instrument with its greater sonority and improved action. His Piano Sonata Op. 106 is his most enduring — and formidable — testament to this desire.

Thomas Broadwood was not the first to appreciate the entrepreneurial advantages of having his business associated with the name of the most celebrated composer of the day.

In 1803, the French instrument maker Sébastien Érard presented Beethoven with a splendid, state-of-the-art fortepiano that incorporated several innovations such as foot pedals that replaced the cumbersome knee-action lever-arrangement typical of the older instruments. Érard's pianos were sturdily constructed and offered greater sonority than most other fortepianos of the day.

On 27 December 1817, Broadwood selected from his warehouse a six-octave grand piano, No. 7362, that was carefully packed in a deal case with a waterproof lining of tin foil; this was then delivered to a Mr. Farlowe of London ready for shipment to Trieste. The choice of particular instrument was, in part, made by a small group of distinguished musicians of the day. As a measure of their respect and esteem for the recipient, they test-played and signed the piano before it was sent away. The musicians involved in the enterprise were John Baptiste Cramer, Jaques Godfroi, Friedrich Kalkbrenner, Charles Knyvett and Beethoven's former pupil Ferdinand Ries. They each inscribed the piano with their signatures alongside the inscription: *Hoc Instrumentum est Thomae Broadwood (Londrini) donum propter ingenium illustrissime Beethoven* – 'This instrument is a proper gift from Thomas Broadwood to the great Beethoven.' Broadwood's own, more prosaic, inscription reads: 'John Broadwood & Sons, Makers of Instruments to His Majesty and the Princesses. Great Pulteney Street, Golden Square, London.'

Dieter Hildebrandt, *Pianoforte: A social history of the piano.* London: Hutchinson, 1988, p.27. See also: Derek Melville, *Beethoven's Pianos* in: Denis Arnold and Nigel Fortune, editors *The Beethoven Companion*, 1973, p. 47 and pp. 50–1. Melville describes a Broadwood piano, No. 8074, exactly similar to Beethoven's in the Colt Collection, Bethersden, Kent, England.

Typical of Broadwood's solicitude towards Beethoven is that he arranged for his own piano tuner, Johann Andreas Stumpff, to travel to Vienna to tune and regulate the piano; significantly, Broadwood refers to his instrument as a *piano*, rather than *pianoforte* of *fortepiano*. When Beethoven received news of Broadwood's intended gift, he responded fulsomely in a letter of 3 February 1818. He expressed his pleasure at the prospect of receiving the piano that he intended to regard 'as an altar on which to place the beautiful gifts of his spirit before the divine Apollo'. In addition, he promised to send Broadwood 'the first fruits of his inspiration on playing it' — an undertaking that, however, he does not appear to have fulfilled.

Emily Anderson, 1961, Vol. 2, Letter No. 891, pp. 755–6. See also: Dieter Hiderbrandt, *Pianoforte: A social history of the piano*, 1988, pp. 87–8 and Edwin Marshall Good, *Giraffes, Black Dragons and other Pianos: A technological history from Cristofori to the modern concert grand*, 1982, pp. 83–8.

Beethoven received the Broadwood piano in late spring 1818. It had been delayed in Trieste so that the required customs formalities could be completed; Broadwood had born the cost of the freightage but customs dues still had to paid. Beethoven turned to his friend and patron Count Moritz Lichnowsky to assist him to obtain the necessary exemption, as Beethoven insisted, from payment of the customs duty. Given Beethoven's standing in Vienna these circumstances appear to have been regarded as having something of national significance since the arrival in the Imperial City of Broadwood's instrument — then the only one of its kind in Europe — was subsequently reported in the *Wiener Zeitung* of 8 June 1818 and the *Vienna Gazette of the Arts*:

> '[The] Broadwood Piano is a true masterpiece, in its interior structure as well as in its outward form, which is chiefly distinguished by its unadorned simplicity, solidity and portability to any place whatsoever.'

Emily Anderson, 1961, Vol. 2, Letter, No. 890, pp. 754–5. For a facsimile reproduction of this letter see: Beethoven House, Digital Archives, Library Documents, NE 196. See also: Dieter Hildebrandt, 1988, p. 27.

Beethoven's new Broadwood had a range of six octaves, from the third C below middle C to the third C above. This was in fact a half octave less than the contemporary Viennese piano made by Johann and Nanette Streicher, personal friends of Beethoven's and his preferred Viennese makers of keyboard instruments. The Broadwood's case was constructed from Spanish mahogany inlaid with marquetry. It was triple strung and equipped with a una-chord pedal enabling the action to move the keys to the right so that the hammers would strike one string only. The soundboard was thicker than that of equivalent Viennese instruments and the hammers were heavier. These gave the piano a more sonorous tone than its Viennese rivals but at the expense of a heavier action, making the performance of passages requiring additional velocity more challenging.

See: David Wainright, *Broadwood by Appointment*, The Book Service, 1982 and Reginald Gerig, *Famous Pianists and their Technique*, Washington: R. B. Luce, 1974, p. 44. See also: Derek Melville, *Beethoven's Pianos* (Plate 4a) in: Denis Arnold and Nigel Fortune, editors, *The Beethoven Companion,* 1973.

When the Broadwood piano arrived, it was unpacked by men from Streichers' piano-manufacturing establishment in Vienna and from there it was sent on to the composer, then residing in Mödling. Doubtless Johann and Nanette Streicher were eager to see for themselves the latest product of a rival instrument maker, albeit a foreign one. Ignaz Moscheles and Cipriani Potter were allowed to try out the piano. They confirmed its beautiful tone but Moscheles found the action to be too heavy; not surprising, the piano was out of tune. On a later visit to see Beethoven, Potter remarked on this to the composer whose response was tart: 'That's what they all say; they would like to tune it and spoil it, but they shall not touch it.'

Emily Anderson, 1961, Vol. 2, Letter, No. 890, pp. 754–5. For a facsimile reproduction of this letter see: Beethoven House, Digital Archives, Library Documents, NE 196. See also: Dieter Hildebrandt, 1988, p. 27.

In the following years, in his desperate attempts to hear his new instrument, Beethoven appears to have tormented it severely. Visitors to see him have left poignant accounts of how many of its strings were snapped and lay coiled about 'like a wind-spent thorn bush'. It was also left to gather dust when, a few years later, the Austrian-German piano maker Conrad Graf loaned Beethoven one of his latest instruments. This had a range of 6½-octaves – a larger span therefore than the Broadwood. Like the Broadwood it was triple strung to make it more audible to the composer. Today it can be seen in the Beethoven House in Bonn.

Following Beethoven's death in 1827, the Broadwood became a prized possession of Franz Liszt, who kept it in his salon alongside a fortepiano previously owned by Mozart. On the death of Liszt, in accordance with his will, the Broadwood was preserved for the nation; it now resides in the Hungarian National Museum. In 1991, the Los Angeles piano maker and restorer David Winston undertook an extensive programme of work, with great integrity, to restore the Broadwood to something like its former glory.

The guiding principle in its restoration was, as Winston remarks:

> '[To] stand back and let the instrument itself give the clue, rather than try to impose one's own ideas. I hope that this approach will bring the piano closer to the way Beethoven found it, and will guarantee its conservation for future generations.'

Today we are able to enjoy the benefits of Broadwood's original manufacturing skills, allied to the restoration efforts of David Winston, through the medium of Melvin Tan's recording on EMI Classic: *The Beethoven Broadwood Fortepiano*.

MICHAEL BROYLES

The American musicologist Michael Broyles outlines Beethoven's contribution to the transformation of the classical world in music:

> 'The ten-years in Beethoven's life, from approximately 1800 to 1809, comprise one of the crucial decades in the history of Western music. During that time Beethoven not only wrote an astonishing number of major compositions which still form the core of the concert repertory — the first six symphonies, the Third, Fourth and Fifth Piano Concertos, the Triple Concerto, the *Razumovsky* Quartets, as well as fourteen piano sonatas that include the *Moonlight*, the *Tempest*, the *Waldstein*, and the *Appassionata*, in addition to *Fidelio* and other large vocal pieces — but created a body of works of such individuality that their shadows

haunted composers throughout the nineteenth century. In 1800 Beethoven's compositions still resided in the Classical world of Haydn, Mozart and Clementi. By 1809 Beethoven had fundamentally reordered that world.'

Broyles gives an estimation of the standing of Beethoven's late music:

'For years Beethoven's late compositions, because of their profundity, complexity and individuality, have held a special fascination for analysts. And because Beethoven's late works stand in such splendid isolation both biographically — due to Beethoven's deafness and his own personal inclinations — and chronologically — due to Beethoven's compositional hiatus in the early teens — they have appeared as a corpus in themselves, naturally suited to stylistic considerations on their own. As a consequence the principal stylistic characteristics of Beethoven's late works have been carefully and minutely described. And scholars have shown a remarkable consistency in their results. Penetrating the formidable intellectual difficulties posed by Beethoven's late music has presented a real challenge, but once done, there has been little disagreement over its principal features.'

Broyles outlines its singular individuality:

'The uniqueness and relative isolation of Beethoven's late compositions, which has made them so appealing to so many of the best musical minds, has at the same time obscured their evolutionary nature. Thus far we have detailed a conflux of factors that are found in Beethoven's music in the early nineteenth century: tonal relations at the structural level became more distant; motivic gestures within the phrase toward the cadence; flowing lyrical lines began to dominate allegro movements; and a rhetorical, even declamatory type of motion began to appear.'

Broyles next considers the expansive nature of Beethoven's music:

'All of these developments occurred upon an greatly expanded overall time scale. Movements not only became longer, but Beethoven made many attempts to break beyond the boundaries of the individual movement, either by linking movements directly to each other or by extending organicism to encompass entire pieces.'

Broyles concludes his opening remarks to his essay *Towards the Late Music*, with reference to its poetic qualities:

'At the same time expressive qualities took on a new power. The poetic element became a central aspect of post-1800 compositions. Scholars may disagree today about the substance, the meaning and the extent of a poetic connection in specific middle Beethoven compositions, but few would deny the existence of such as a common characteristic of many works of this time. Whether described as individuality, personal subjectivity, an ethical quality, or out and out tone painting, its presence is acknowledged by even the severest formalists. And it is accorded a prominence that its Classical antecedents seldom receive.'

Michael Broyles, *Beethoven: The Emergence and Evolution of Beethoven's Heroic Style*, New York: Excelsior Music Publishing Co., 1987, p. 1 and p. 222.

ANTON BRUCKNER

The Austrian composer and organist Anton Bruckner is known for his monumental symphonies — once pejoratively described by Brahms as 'symphonic boa constrictors' — and religious music including several masses and motets. Notwithstanding his musical originality he was deferential to other composers, notably Wagner, to whom he showed humility often bordering on subservience. He was in awe of Beethoven as is illustrated by the following anecdote. After a triumphant performance of his *Te Deum* in Berlin, in 1891, he learned that a music critic had favoured him by likening him to 'a second Beethoven'. This was a novel experience for Bruckner who normally had to endure criticism of his music, in particular from the Viennese critic Eduard Hanslick. On this occasion, however, being compared with Beethoven was too much for the modestly inclined Bruckner who is reported to have exclaimed: 'Good Lord, how could anyone say such a thing?' Being profoundly religious he promptly crossed himself to expunge the possibility of sin.

Originally published in: Max Graf, *Legend of a Musical City*, New York, 1945 and quoted in: *The Book of Musical Anecdotes*, editor, Norman Lebrecht, London: Andre Deutsch, 1985, p. 187.

The Dresden composer and conductor Jean Louis Nicodé visited Bruckner in March 1891. Bruckner was then age 67 and was enjoying his hard-earned celebrity. Nicodé was greeted by Bruckner at the door to his apartment whilst still wearing his nightshirt and holding a candle before him. As they entered the composer's music room Nicodé noticed Bruckner's eyes began to gleam with tear drops shining in them. His recollection continues:

> 'Finally he led us next door into his bedroom, which was just as big as his study. He pointed to the portraits of Beethoven and Wagner above his bed and said: "They are my dear Masters".'

As further testimony to his modesty, Nicodé describes Bruckner making a deferential gesture to the portraits.

Carl Hruby studied with Bruckner and published reminiscences of the composer in his *Meine Erinnerungen an Anton Bruckner* – 'My recollections of Anton Bruckner'. He describes the morning when he arrived for a lesson and found Bruckner seated at the piano lost in thought, not initially acknowledging his pupil's entry. Collecting himself he then remonstrated against the injustice he felt towards the critics who found fault in his music, disposing him to exclaim: 'Beethoven! Beethoven! Recalling this years later, Hruby writes:

> 'For Bruckner [Beethoven] was the incarnation of everything lofty and sublime in music. He connected that hallowed name with all the twists of fortune in his own life, and at crucial moments he often asked how Beethoven would have behaved in the same situation.'

In 1863 Beethoven's remains were exhumed, together with those of Franz Schubert. Bruckner was invited to take part in the official ceremony that took place in Vienna's old

Währinger cemetery. After some discussion it was decided to open Beethoven's coffin as part of the proceedings. This provided Bruckner with the opportunity to press forward and stare at Beethoven's mortal remains. According to Hruby, Bruckner was 'deeply moved' and 'shaken to the core'. On the way home it was only after some reflection that Bruckner realized, in his eagerness to stand close by the remains of the composer he so revered, his eyeglasses had fallen into the coffin. The thought they would be reinterred with Beethoven's remains according to Hruby gave Bruckner 'great delight'.

Stephen Johnson, *Bruckner Remembered*, London: Faber and Faber, 1998, p. 158 and pp. 168—169.

HANS VON BÜLOW

Although today remembered as one of the most famous conductors of the 19th century, and for his aphorism 'Bach is the Old Testament and Beethoven the New Testament of music', recollections from his early days remind us of his formidable powers as a virtuoso pianist. He pioneered the innovation of performing the complete series of Beethoven piano sonatas and was known for the challenging nature of some of his recitals — challenging both to himself and his audience. On one occasion von Bülow played the last five Beethoven piano sonatas in a single evening and on another occasion he opened his recital with a performance of the *Hammerklavier* Piano Sonata and concluded the evening with the *Diabelli* Variations.

As recalled in: Peter Yates, *Twentieth Century Music: Its evolution from the end of the harmonic era into the present era of sound*, London: Allen & Unwin Ltd., 1968.

The Czech composer and music critic Joseph Foerster has left recollections of Hamburg's musical scene in the late nineteenth century. In particular, he recalls the exacting demands von Bülow imposed upon himself. Foerster writes:

'His effervescent spirit could bear no easy-going manner approach, his pure artistry no half measures.' He remembers the occasion when von Bülow was performing the F-sharp major Piano Sonata in Hamburg's Konviksaal. Although he was well into his performance he stopped because one string of the piano was out of tune, only resuming when the problem was rectified. In his role as orchestral conductor, von Bülow could be no less demanding of his audience. There was the occasion, for example, when, following a performance of Beethoven's Ninth symphony, he thanked the audience for their applause, apologised that Beethoven, who should receive it, could not attend but as a mark of respect proceeded to have the whole of the Finale repeated.

As recalled in: Kurt Blaukopf and Herta Blaukopf, *Mahler: His life, work and world*, London: Thames and Hudson, 1991, p. 92.

SCOTT BURNHAM

The American musicologist Scott Burnham considers Beethoven as hero:

> 'Beethoven. When asked to name the single most influential composer of the Western world, few would hesitate. And the specific style that has come to define the nature of Beethoven's accomplishment is his heroic style, a style to which only a handful of his works can lay unequivocal claim: two symphonies, two piano sonatas, several overtures, a piano concerto. For nearly two

centuries, a single composer has epitomized musical vitality, becoming the paradigm of Western compositional logic and of all the positive virtues that music can embody for humanity. This conviction has proved so strong that it no longer acts as an overt part of our musical consciousness; it is now simply a condition of the way we tend to engage the musical experience. The values of Beethoven's heroic style have become the values of music.'

Burnham asks: 'And what is the nature of the heroic experience represented in this music?'

He responds:

> 'The short answer usually invokes the necessity of struggle and eventual triumph as an index of man's greatness, his heroic potential.'

By way of substantiating this contention, Burnham cites a letter Beethoven wrote in 1815 to countess Anna Maria von Erdődy, a Hungarian noblewoman and among the composer's closest confidantes. Beethoven made the following declaration:

> 'We mortals with immortal spirits are born only to suffering and joy, and one could almost say that the most distinguished among us obtain joy through suffering.'

Burnham concludes:

> 'It would be hard to imagine a more direct transcription of the popular view of the meaning of Beethoven's heroic style.'

*

Scott Burnham *Beethoven Hero*, Princeton, Princeton University Press, 1995, pp. Xiii–xiv.

ALAN BUSH

The British composer, pianist and political activist places Beethoven in the context of humankind:

> 'The greatness of Beethoven has never been in question. In 1792, when Beethoven was 21 years old, he left his birthplace, Bonn, on a second visit to Vienna. His friends inscribed their farewells in an album. Count Waldstein, a young aristocrat and amateur of music, to whom Beethoven subsequently dedicated one of his most famous piano sonatas, wrote as follows: "Dear Beethoven, you are travelling to Vienna in fulfilment of your long cherished wish. The genius of Mozart is still weeping and bewailing the death of her favourite. With the inexhaustible Haydn she found a refuge, but no occupation, and is now waiting to leave him and join herself to someone else. Labour assiduously and receive Mozart's spirit from the hands of Haydn".'

A measure of Beethoven's standing in Vienna is evident by the scenes that attended his funeral cortege as it made its way through the streets of Vienna to his resting place in the Währinger cemetery:

> 'Beethoven's funeral in Vienna on 29 March 1827 was attended by a vast number of people; the coffin was borne by eight leading musicians

of the city and surrounded by thirty-six torchbearers, including the composer, Schubert, and the famous piano virtuoso and teacher, Carl Czerny, familiar to, though perhaps not exactly beloved by, millions of children on account of his innumerable piano studies. The crowd surrounding the funeral procession was so enormous that soldiers were called in to clear a way through the streets; even so it took an hour and a half to cover the short distance between Beethoven's house and the church.'

Bush comments on Beethoven's only opera *Fidelio*:

'In *Fidelio* Beethoven chose a subject of the very greatest significance in the fight for freedom ... During the opera occurs the "Prisoners' Chorus". This is the longest single musical number in the opera. From a dramatic point of view it does not advance the action at all. Leonora, or "Fidelio", as she is known to the gaoler, persuades him to allow the prisoners out of their cells into the open air of the prison courtyard. With much trepidation he does so. The prisoners issue from their cells, scarcely able to believe that they are breathing the air of heaven again. Nervously they emerge and fearfully retreat, with scarcely time to raise their voices in a chorus of joy at seeing once again the blue sky and greenery of nature. In this chorus, one of the most beautiful pieces of music ever written, Beethoven has expressed the piteous plight of the unjustly imprisoned.'

Bush concludes:

'The greatness of Beethoven does not lie solely in his flow of melodic invention and his command of technical resources, but in the fact that he used his great musical gift and painfully acquired technical capacity to express in every way open to him the problems of his time, so as to bring to the men and women around him the clarity of mind and courage of heart which would enable them to take a step farther along the radiant path of human progress.'

Alan Dudley Bush, *In my eighth Decade and other Essays*, London: Kahn & Averill, 1980. p. 61.

FERRUCCIO BUSONI

The Italian composer and virtuoso pianist Ferruccio Busoni revealed his remarkable aptitude for piano at an early age, being elected to the Academia Filharmonica of Bologna at just fifteen — the youngest person to receive the honour since Mozart. Busoni's views about Beethoven and his music are scattered throughout his many letters and diary entries. The following is a selection.

On 12 October 1910 Busoni wrote to the Swiss composer Hans Huber. Busoni had recently performed his taxing Piano Concerto in C major — one of the largest works ever written in this genre with a performing time of around seventy minutes. Busoni was vexed by its reception by the Berlin music critic Karl Nef who had written:

'One may not look for German profundity in the Concerto but it is true Italian sensuous music' — which may be taken as recognition, if somewhat backhanded, of Busoni's nationality and artistic temperament. Busoni wrote to Huber:

'The critic of the *Basler Nachrichten* thinks that
one should not look for German profundity in
my Italian work. If only I knew what was meant
by German profundity in music. I am quite at a
loss! In Beethoven I hear great humanity,
freedom and originality, in Mozart *joie de vivre*
and beauty of form, in Bach feeling of devotion,
grandeur and skill.'

Antony Beaumont, editor, *Ferruccio Busoni: Selected letters*, London: Faber and Faber, 1987, p. 114.

Whilst on tour in America, Busoni wrote to his wife Gerda from Los Angeles on 15 March 1911; she had earlier requested advice on how best to practice the piano. In his reply, Busoni added some additional remarks about his views on music in general:

'It can be said — contradict it who may — that
Wagner was the first to recognize melody as the
supreme law, and not only theoretically. On the
whole, the older art of composition suffers from
neglect of melody. Unconsciously we feel another
standard in the classical works, and we do not
measure them so strictly.'

Directing his attention to Beethoven he then writes:

'With Beethoven, this strikes one most forcibly
in his second period, which is the weakest, and is
exemplified in its principal compositions, the
Fifth Symphony, the *Waldstein* and the *Appassionata*, and the three *Quartets*, Op. 59. I should

> like to repeat — and let them contradict me again
> — that in Beethoven's first period, feeling conquers helplessness; in the third, feeling is overshadowed by symphonic breadth and symphonic brilliance. Beethoven, in his second period, exploits the forceful ideas contained in the first.'

Busoni, perhaps prompted by Gerda's requests for guidance with her piano playing, turned his attention to Beethoven's piano sonatas:

> 'The heroically passionate defiance of the *Pathétique* continues to be the basis for all pieces similar in feeling (only more extended) in the following period, headed by the *Fifth Symphony*. But the melodic element does not keep with step with this extension and gets lost in ... a kind of table-land of modulatory and figurative eloquence. I am thinking of, for example, of the working out in the first movement of the *Appassionata*, where the persistent rush and intensity of temperament take the place of content. In this case it is more as if the thrilling eloquence and infectious conviction of an orator were making the effect, rather than his theme or the wealth of his ideas. It makes an effect, accordingly, on larger masses of people and with more direct impact.'

John L. Holmes, *Composers on Composers*, New York: Greenwood Press, 1990, pp. 352–3.

A diary entry of Busoni's for 27 September 1914 reveals his anguish at learning that Belgium had been stormed, Riems attacked and that the French composer Albéric Magnard had been shot — or possibly burned alive — whilst defending his property. Busoni reacted:

> 'The Germans have ascribed to Beethoven German attributes which he does not possess. Therefore, I believe that the Germans are now at the furthest remove from a just assessment of Beethoven.'

Antony Beaumont, editor, *Ferruccio Busoni: Selected letters*, London: Faber and Faber, 1987, p. 186.

In 1916 Busoni wrote to his former pupil, the Dutch-born German pianist Egon Petri — he assisted Busoni in editing Bach's keyboard works. He writes:

> 'The Latin attitude to art, with its cool serenity and its insistence on outward form, is what refreshes me. It was only through Beethoven that music acquired that growling and frowning expression which was natural enough to him, but which perhaps ought to have remained his lonely path alone. Why are you in such a bad temper, one would often like to ask, especially in the second period?'

From a letter to Egon Petri originally published in E. J. Dent, *Ferruccio Busoni*, London: Oxford University Press, 1933, p. 230 and quoted in John L. Holmes, *Composers on Composers*. New York: Greenwood Press, 1990, p. 15.

The following year Busoni appears to have felt more warmly disposed to Beethoven as he enthused in a letter of 20 June 1917 to his friend and confident the pianist, composer and conductor Philipp Jarnach:

> 'To live for and to love humanity, which was Beethoven's chosen goal, fulfils the ethical requirement of the notes: "Trance" as contrast to "Existential norm".'

Two years later an encounter with Mozart's music appears to have displaced Beethoven in Busoni's favour as he explained in a letter to Hans Huber, written late January or early February 1919. Busoni had been studying the score of Mozart's opera *Idomeneo*. Composed at the age of just twenty-four, Busoni marvelled at its 'virility' and 'maturity' and the abundance of original ideas in its orchestration that includes parts for no fewer than three trombones — Beethoven would not use the trombone (in his Fifth Symphony) until almost thirty years later. Busoni pronounced *Idomeneo* to be 'phenomenal for its time' and 'today [is] still amazing'. As remarked, this experience seems to have disposed him to favour Mozart over Beethoven:

> 'Those of us born in the middle of the nineteenth century have been incorrectly educated: it would have been shameful not to know a work of Beethoven's but no discredit to ignore a masterpiece of Mozart's. Now I am turning progressively away from the former's sulky seriousness and perceiving more and more the great seriousness of the latter, which is actually superior, behind its serenity. At a time when much is changing, the symbolic and legally enforced cult of Beethoven should be restrained within its fair limits.'

Antony Beaumont, editor, *Ferruccio Busoni: Selected letters*, London: Faber and Faber, 1987, p. 262 and pp. 282–3.

JOHN CAGE

In 1975 the German composer Walter Zimmermann interviewed the American composer and music theorist John Cage. He proposed if Cage could speak to anyone from the past, with whom would he like to talk? Caged responded:

'James Joyce, Gertrude Stein, Erik Satie. If we went back further, I wouldn't mind meeting Mozart.'

Zimmerman asked 'Why Mozart?' to which Cage replied:

> 'I think he was a great musician. It's his tendency toward complexity and away from unity. Now I would let Bach stay on his side of the street. And I wouldn't bother with Beethoven or Haydn.'

He elaborated his views citing the reaction of the composer Eric Satie to the music of Beethoven:

> 'The reason is that Beethoven's music is based on a marriage of form and content, involving beginnings, ends and middles, and all kinds of ideas and expressions of individual feeling that have nothing whatsoever to do with sounds, whereas Satie's music is essentially based upon an empty space of time, in which one thing or another could happen.'

Richard Kostelanetz, *Conversing with Cage*, New York: London: Routledge, 2003, p. 37 and p. 50.

NEVILLE CARDUS

The English writer and critic Sir Neville Cardus was widely read for his contributions to *The Manchester Guardian* on both cricket and music. He counted several distinguished musicians amongst his personal friends. In 1962 he contributed an article to an issue of *The Manchester Guardian* in which he outlined his feelings towards Beethoven and his music:

> 'Today, more than one hundred and thirty five years after his death, Beethoven's music remains close to the consciousness and feeling of ordinary humanity. Time hasn't diminished its significance or its power. On the contrary, it comes home to us more urgently that ever before. The clash of man's ideas, ambitions, and vanities, the struggle between the individual will and the irresistible massed stupidity of instinct, the littleness of the ego in the fact of the tidal waves of the changing years — Beethoven has told us of the mysterious immensities and fluctuations which since the revolution in his own period created the nineteenth-century, setting into motion forces that have caused the greatest upheaval in civilization of all.'

Turning to the present day — we recall Cardus was writing in the 1960s — he continues:

> 'At the present time Beethoven is neither to be claimed by the "new" or the "old". He is neither of the "right" nor of the "left". He himself was a rebel, but one who didn't run away from the past. "I have never believed in the *Vox populi*" he once said, yet in the finale of the Ninth Symphony he strove to embrace the "millions". He was, in fact, aristocratic in intellect and a democrat in sympathies. He was perhaps not the most truly and

wholly musical of all composers, the most *suffused* by music. This distinction is Mozart's. But Beethoven was the greatest man ever to live and find a way of life in music.'

Cardus believed, like every other genius, Beethoven had become a legend and, thereby, his life and work had become distorted through the prism of history. As he put it:

'He is often thought of as a grim perpetually heroic, fate-driven Prometheus, setting himself against the order and propriety of the ordained gods of music.'

Cardus acknowledged he had 'shattered the immaculate palace of the eighteenth-century symphony', remarking how a mere eighteen years separated the G minor Symphony of Mozart and Beethoven's *Eroica* Symphony and argued that in no other art had such an advance been taken in a single step. Cardus was of the view that in the genre of the symphony Beethoven had dramatized its classical patterns and procedures and, for the first time, had made it 'an organic, single-minded, single-purpose whole'. More widely, Cardus considered Beethoven 'changed the face of music'. Quoting his friend Sir Thomas Beecham, who was not a Beethovenian without reservations:

'Beethoven was the cause of all wrath later to come in music – the subsequent discordance.'

That said, Cardus acknowledged Beethoven thought of music as language and that to compose music was akin to writing poetry and sprang from the same creative and imaginative process.

Cardus concluded his article for *The Manchester Guardian*:

> 'The mind of Beethoven, the entire mental make-up of him was forward-reaching, forward looking. He was a "Modern" in his day. He is still a "Modern" in ours. Where was he leading music in the variations of the Opus 111 piano sonata, with its mysterious trills and transitions moving upward and onward, in an upper ether and light? Here the scientific music-maker and the prophetic poet work hand in hand. It is pretty certain that if Beethoven were alive today he would be investigating and making use of all the latest "atonal" and "serial" discoveries. But he wouldn't have employed these discoveries for any "abstract" purposes or ends. He would have drawn them into his own creative forge, endowing them with a living identity, unmistakably Beethoven, embracingly human and humane.'

Neville Cardus, *Talking of Music*, London: Collins, 1957, pp. 47–50.

ELLIOTT CARTER

The American composer Elliott Carter must be a candidate for holding the record for being the oldest amongst composers, living to the remarkable age of 104. More significantly, he won the coveted Pulitzer Prize twice, composed forty works between the ages of 90 – 100 and twenty more after he had turned 100, in 2008. In 1940 he wrote an article for the journal *Modern Music* titled *American Music in the*

New York Scene. In this, as his title implies, he sought to evaluate the then present state of American music. He believed literature, for example, had a good head start over music that had not yet produced a composer of comparable standing to that of Walt Whitman. In attempting to explain this Carter argued:

'The plain facts ... are that now, as in the past, composers have less importance than painters or writers.'

Carter, however, acknowledged the virtues of composers from other countries such as Mussorgsky, Purcell, Couperin, Berlioz, and Debussy where, as he puts it, 'music is generally overshadowed by the other arts'. Carter summed up the situation as he saw it:

> 'Nor do parallels between the cultures of other nations and of America come to much either, for it grows steadily clearer that America cannot and will not follow in Europe's footsteps. We won't have an American Beethoven or an American Mussorgsky, even though we may have composers who work toward the same high musical standards Europe has raised.'

Carter added a note of defiance:

'Nevertheless, important composers are already with us in America.'

Originally published as *American Music in the New York Scene*, 1940, and reproduced in: *Modern Music, 17,* 2 Jan.–Feb. 1940. Derived here from: *The Writings of Elliott Carter: An American composer looks at modern music*, Else Stone and Kurt Stone, editors, Bloomington: Indiana University Press, 1977, pp. 68–9.

In a BBC broadcast in the summer of 1972, Elliott Carter discussed the problem in musical appreciation of attaching words and meaning to sounds. He made a wry reference to Beethoven:

> 'Beethoven's answer to someone who asked questions about some music he had just played was to play it over again. This is, of course, the composer's true response about his own work.'

Else Stone and Kurt Stone, editors, *The Writings of Elliott Carter: An American composer looks at modern music*, Bloomington: Indiana University Press, 1977, p. 310.

BARRY COOPER

The British musicologist Barry Cooper is internationally recognised for his scholarly studies of the life and work of Beethoven. In addition, Beethovenians have him to thank for his reconstruction of a performing edition of the composer's 10th Symphony — from the many surviving sketches that were left incomplete at the time of his death. Pianists are no less in debt to Cooper for his recently released edition of the Piano Sonatas for The Associated Board of the Royal Schools of Music (ABRSM). This incorporates Beethoven's three youthful *Kurfürstensonaten* (WoO 47) — dedicated to the Elector (Kurfürst) Maximillian Fredrick — that Cooper is known to believe are unjustly neglected.

At the conclusion of his *Beethoven*, Cooper writes:

> 'It was the end of an era — the "Age of Beethoven" as it is sometimes known. Never since, and probably never before, has one composer been so dominant for such a long period; and his successors, though often using his ideas, had to find new paths, since he had traced his to

its limits. Beethoven is still in many ways the central figure in western music, the culmination of the Classical period and an archetype for the Romantic concept of a genius — heroic, individualistic, eccentric, single-minded, and visionary. His art ranged over the whole gamut of human emotion, from the ecstatic joy of the Ninth Symphony to the profound suffering of the *Pathétique* Sonata, and from the deep mysticism of the *Missa Solemnis* to the playful humour of his many scherzos. And his compositional technique far surpasses that of most composers, manipulating themes, pitches, intervals, registers keys, instruments, rhythms, phrases, and structural patterns in ways previously unimagined — halving note values in a triple-time fugue, for example, or creating a form that is simultaneously both a single movement and a multi-movement structure, or exploring the utmost extremes of the piano, or using timpani as a melody instrument. Yet a nobility and seriousness of purpose invariably underlie his music — a desire to "raise men to the level of gods" through his art.'

Barry Cooper, *Beethoven: The Master Musicians Series*, Oxford: Oxford University Press, 2000, pp. 349–50. See also: Barry Cooper, *Beethoven and the Creative Process*, Oxford: Clarendon Press, 1990 and Barry Cooper, in collaboration with Anne-Louise Coldicott, Nicholas Marston and William Drabin, *The Beethoven Compendium: A guide to Beethoven's life and music*, London: Thames and Hudson, 1991.

*

MARTIN COOPER

In his study *Beethoven: The Last Decade, 1817–1827*, the music critic and author Martin Cooper considers what Beethoven means to the typical music lover:

> 'Beethoven's case is unique in the history of music: there is no other instance of a composer whose works, one hundred and fifty years after his death still form the staple basis of the repertory in the concert hall, in chamber music, and amongst pianists of all degrees, from the beginner to the greatest virtuoso, satisfying in different ways the simplest, most ignorant listener and the most intellectual, most exclusively "musical" professionals. The extraordinary position that he occupied in the imagination of his contemporaries — "one God in heaven and one Beethoven on earth", as a young English admirer put it — he has really never lost ... No reputable musician has seriously questioned the quality of Beethoven's music, though they may, like Stravinsky, have delighted in finding flaws in a popular idol, may have resented the domination of the repertory by often unintelligent, routine performances of his music and felt that the concept of the "Beethoven symphony" weighed like a dead hand on the further development of the art and must therefore be violently rejected. The ordinary music lover, on the other hand, has been unswervingly loyal to the great works by which he has known Beethoven — the symphonies and the concertos in the first place, perhaps a dozen of the thirty-two piano sonatas, half a dozen of the chamber works, *Fidelio* and its overtures ... These works of

> Beethoven "speak" to quite uncultivated human sensibilities and command their attention in a way that is literally unique.'

Martin Cooper, *Beethoven: The Last Decade, 1817–1827*, London, Oxford University Press, 1970, pp. 4–5.

In his study *Ideas and Music*, Cooper, considers Beethoven in 'Human Terms' and as 'Revolutionary'. With regard to Beethoven in human terms he observes:

> 'No hero has been more fantastically misrepresented, more assiduously idealised than Beethoven; and it is easy to understand why. The extreme disparity between an artist's work and his personal life is still a mystery to psychologists and a stumbling-block, even an offence, to simple people; and in no case is the disparity more extreme than in Beethoven's.'

With regard to Beethoven as revolutionary Cooper remarks:

> 'Towards the three points of the trident which the French Revolution aimed at the heart of the old régime, Beethoven's attitude throughout his life was always unambiguous — though that is not to say that it was always the same, or that his understanding of Liberty, Equality and Fraternity was that of the politicians. For Beethoven was a rebel, but not a revolutionary. He judged the laws and conventions of the society of his day by a wholly subjective standard, that of his own nature. His exuberant and powerful character would have found any system likely to win general acceptance

with the rest of mankind and irksome and full of illogical anomalies. His passionate belief in Liberty never faltered, though it changed in character; but it was in the first instance a wholly natural, instinctive egoism, the emotional reaction of a high-spirited, hugely talented youth increasingly aware of his exceptional gifts and irritated by the difficulties and frustrations which lay in the way of their development.'

Martin Cooper, *Ideas and Music*, London: Barrie and Rockliff, 1965, p. 45 and p. 51.

AARON COPLAND

The American composer and all-round musician Aaron Copland has been described by his peers and critics as 'the Dean of American Composers' and for many his harmonies epitomize the very sound of American music, evoking its vast landscape and the American pioneer spirit. He considered Beethoven to be a composer of 'the first rank', alongside Palestrina and Bach, singling out for mention the psychological depth of his music, its dramatic instincts, his dynamic forms and their 'sense of inevitability'. In response to the proposition 'What made Beethoven so compelling?' he responded:

'How can one not be compelled and not be moved by the moral fervour and conviction of such a man. His finest works are the enactment of a triumph — a triumph of affirmation in the face of the human condition. Beethoven is one of the great yea-sayers among creative artists; it is exhilarating to share his clear-eyed contemplation of the tragic sum of life. His music summons forth our better nature; in purely musical terms Beethoven seems to be exhorting us to be noble, be strong, be great in heart, yes, and be compassionate.'

Howard Pollack, *Aaron Copland: The life and work of an uncommon man*, New York: Henry Holt, 1999, p. 60.

Copland set out his views about music in an essay titled 'What to listen for in music' (1939). In this he remarks:

'Don't get the idea that the value of music is commensurate with its sensuous appeal or that the loveliest sounding music is made by the greatest composer. If that were so, Ravel would be a greater creator than Beethoven. The point is that the sound element varies with each composer, that his usage of sound forms an integral part of his style and must be taken into account when listening.'

Copland addressed the challenge of attempting to pin down the 'meaning' that might be ascribed to a particular musical work:

'In the first place it is easier to pin a meaning-word on a Tchaikovsky piece than on a Beethoven one. Much easier. Moreover, with the Russian composer, every time you come back to a piece of his it almost always says the same things to you, whereas with Beethoven it is often quite difficult to put your finger right on what he is saying. And any musician will tell you that that is why Beethoven is the greater composer.'

Richard Kostelanetz, editor, *Aaron Copland: A reader; selected writings 1923–1972*, New York: London: Routledge, 2003, pp. 4–5.

JOHN CRABBE

The British writer compares Beethoven's influence on Western culture with that of Shakespeare's:

> 'Apart from Shakespeare I can think of no other figure in Western culture who commands such supremacy and veneration in his own art, yet is known to a universal public. What is it that still confers on Beethoven, more than 150 years after his death, the universal public? [Crabbe was writing in 1982]. What is it that still confers on Beethoven, more than 150 years after his death, the mantle of a prophet with a perennially vital message for each new generation? Why does his music radiate such energy that it shines right across the romantic age to probe even today, beyond the boundary of ordinary musical feelings?'

Of the Fifth Symphony he asks:

> 'Why, when elated by the Fifth Symphony's exaltation or absorbed in the questing mysteries of the late quartets or piano sonatas, do we feel the urge to wonder what Beethoven is saying or to ask what he means?'

More generally, he continues:

'Similar questions are sometimes asked of new composers whose musical aims and idioms seem obscure, but Beethoven has been dead for two whole lifetimes and ordinary music-lovers have been familiar with his idiom for almost as long. Yet still we sense an extra-musical "something" behind the notes, an intense individual person striving with all his might to direct our attention to things of great human concern, then — his last utterances — towards the transcendental. The very least that can be said is that he brought to music a passionate and visionary element, a sense of drama and struggle that was absolutely new. It has been emulated since, but never repeated on the same scale by ay one man.'

Crabbe extends his views:

'Paradoxically, I believe that Beethoven's very individuality contributes to his universal appeal: his craggy turbulence; his love of nature; his contempt for authority and etiquette; an assertive will contrasted with humility before his God; a careless disregard of physical surroundings; a passionate desire to beg, borrow or steal fire from the gods in order to benefit mankind with his art; and above all, strong feelings that we should direct our attention to higher things, beyond the hurly-burly and chaos of the world ... He believed that his music could in some fashion provide men with new liberties. He was a dreamer who ultimately might conquer the world, and if the poet Arthur O'Shaughnessy had

> lived and written at an earlier time, the words of his, which Elgar set as *The Music Makers*, would surely have been clothed with the music of Beethoven:
>
> "We are the music makers/And we are the dreamers of dreams." Such sentiments are of Beethoven's very essence, an epitome of that spiritual empire in which his own dreams had an all-conquering power.'

John Crabbe, *Beethoven's Empire of the Mind*, Newbury: Lovell Baines, 1982. Crabbe's book title is derived from one of Beethoven's most cherished sayings: 'I much prefer the empire of the mind. I regard it as the highest of all spiritual and worldly monarchies.'

CARL DAHLHAUS

The German musicologist Carl Dahlhaus outlined his views on the music of Beethoven in his *Ludwig van Beethoven: Approaches to His Music*. Translated by Mary Whittall, Oxford: Clarendon Press; New York: Oxford University Press, 1991. In considering the composer's legacy he makes the following generalizations:

> 'Beethoven overwhelmed the limits of Classical form in his sonata movements by blurring the demarcations between sections and theme-groups and in creating such gigantic structures as the first movements of the *Hammerklavier* Sonata and the Ninth Symphony ... No composer of the nineteenth century could wholly escape Beethoven's influence, for his musical activity was so universal that he must be regarded as the trunk

of the tree of nineteenth-century music from which so many branches sprang ... Beethoven gave the strongest impetus, at least for music, to the idea that art was a substitute for, or at least as noble as, religion.'

Later on Dahlhaus discussed what he described as 'Beethoven: Myth and Legend' in the following terms:

'The Beethoven myth ... is separated from empirical biography by a chasm that represents something more than a simple opposition of truth and falsehood. Still, it would be a gross oversimplification to claim that the myth of Beethoven is a direct imprint of his music. The mythical figure in the "romantic image of Beethoven", whether, sorcerer, or saint, cannot be conveniently equated with the persona behind his works, however close the connection between them. Just as the aesthetic subject that we sense in Beethoven's music bears little relation to the man we know from his biography, it s no less foolish to try to identify this subject with the Beethoven of myth and legend. First of all, the works on which the Beethoven myth thrives represents a narrow selection from his complete output: *Fidelio* and the music of *Egmont*; the Third, Fifth and Ninth Symphonies; and the *Pathétique* and *Appassionata* Sonatas. It is not a fact in support of the Beethoven myth that these works are "representative", but rather are one of the claims that make up the myth. To the same extent that the myth was abstracted from the music, the reception of the music was tempered by the myth. And if the myth, once it impinges on biography, transforms anecdotes into allegorical cyphers, it also creates an order that separates symbolic works from non-symbolic ones.'

Dahlhaus closes his discussion of 'the Beethoven myth' with an expression of regret:

'We seldom think how much we lost as the Beethoven myth tradition took root. His characteristic first-period works, which drew on the divertimento tradition, especially that of chamber music with wind instruments, vanished virtually without trace from the late nineteenth-century repertoire and sank into oblivion ... Once the "grand concert" had crystallized into the "symphony concert" around the middle of the century, there was no longer any room for works of a divertimento character; and these works likewise slipped through the gaps of chamber music culture, which came to be dominated by string instruments and the piano. Moreover, being places with a social function, they did not fit the "romantic image of Beethoven", which increasingly determined the choice of repertoire.'

Carl Dahlhaus, *Nineteenth-century Music*, Translated by J. Bradford Robinson, Berkeley; London: University of California Press, 1989, p. 29, p. 32 and pp. 75–6.

COLLIN DAVIS
The English conductor Sir Colin Davis was interviewed by the American cultural historian Joseph Horowitz. Their subject was primarily the Chilean pianist Claudio Arrau —

an acknowledged interpreter of Beethoven. In passing Davis made some characteristically modest remarks:

> 'I'm reading this biography of Beethoven, by Maynard Solomon [*Beethoven*, New York: Schirmer, 1977]. I'm learning an awful lot of things from it, about Beethoven and about myself. Not that I think I'm in any way comparable; I'm unworthy to untie his shoes, I wasn't born into a professionally musical family, as Beethoven was. I wasn't a child prodigy, as he was; I didn't start studying an instrument until I was twelve. I don't have that kind of musical background. I am therefore full of reverence for those who do.'

Of Arrau he added:

> 'So when I meet a man of Arrau's background, and a man of his integrity, *and* a man after my own heart ... [who] accepts me as a musician ... I feel devoted to him.'

Joseph Horowitz, *Conversations with Arrau*, London: Collins, 1982, p. 236.

CLAUDE DEBUSSY

Claude Debussy's views about Beethoven oscillate between respect, on the one hand, and disdain on the other. The essence of this is captured in the recollections of some of those who met him. We offer the following selection:

The English composer and poet Cyril Scott met Debussy early on in his long life — he lived to be ninety-one — and left several recollections of the composer. He considered

Debussy to be one of those Frenchmen who sacrificed politeness to sincerity:

'He was charming to those whom he liked but was the opposite to those he disliked.'

Scott recalls Debussy's dislike of Beethoven whom he was given to describing as *le vieux sourd* – 'the old deaf [one]'.

The English writer and collector Simon Harcourt-Smith met Debussy at the period when his father was head of the British School at Athens. Harcourt-Smith was then still only a child but recalls the composer seizing him by the arm and saying:

> 'If you have any affection, my boy, for me, *never* play or even talk of Wagner or Beethoven to me, because it is like somebody dancing on my grave.'

The French writer on music Georges Jean-Aubrey was a staunch supporter of contemporary composer's and met Debussy when he was in his forties. He remarks how the composer was then disposed to speak very little and when he did it was in brusque phrases that seemed to contain ill-restrained wrath and irony for those who did not understand him or who endeavoured to falsify his beliefs. Of composers he ridiculed Grieg, whose music he described as 'a pink bon-bon stuffed with snow' and of Saint-Saëns he exclaimed: "I have a horror of sentimentality and I cannot forget that its name is Saint-Saëns!" Jean-Aubrey recalls Debussy expressed his liking for Mozart but Beethoven did not escape his critical censure:

> 'He believed Beethoven had terrifically profound things to say, but that he did not know how to say them, because he was imprisoned in

> a web of incessant restatement and of German
> aggressiveness.'

Roger Nichols, *Debussy Remembered*, London: Faber and Faber, 1992, p. 105, p. 120 and p.166.

In New York's 1908 music season, Claude Debussy's *Pélleas et Mélisande* made the composer the subject of keen interest in America. As a consequence, the columnist Emily Bauer secured what is thought to be the first interview with the somewhat unapproachable composer. This was published in *Harper's Weekly* on 29 August 1908. Bauer interviewed Debussy in his Paris apartment that she describes as,

> 'his interesting workshop, a large room lined with
> books and hung with pictures, a close scrutiny of
> which further accentuates the personal tastes of
> a man of genius'.

When pressed about his way of life, Debussy retorted:

> 'I live in a world of imagination ... I find an
> exquisite joy when I reach deeply in the recesses
> of myself and if anything original is to come from
> me, it can only come that way.'

Bauer, somewhat provocatively, questioned Debussy about his early studies and asked him if he had then been as antagonistic to the classics as she believed him to be in his own compositions. Debussy responded with a question of his own:

'What do you call classics?' He eventually replied, confirming his known alleged antipathy towards Beethoven:

> 'I acknowledge one great master, but I do not know why he should be called a classic, because he lives, breathes, and pulsates today. This is Bach; but I will not say the same of Beethoven, as I consider him a man of his epoch, and with a few exceptions his works should have been allowed to rest. I can never understand why all people who study music, all countries that work to establish original schools, should be built upon a German foundation.'

The French writer and academician Georges Delaquys interviewed Debussy, the text of their conversation being subsequently published as an article in *Excellsior* on 18 January 1911. In this, Debussy affirmed his love of music and what it meant to him:

> 'I love music passionately, and through my love I have forced myself to break from certain sterile traditions with which it is encumbered. It is a free art, a wellspring, an art of the open air, an art comparable to the elements — wind, the sea, and the sky!'

Debussy then attempted to put the record straight with opinions that were being attributed to him:

> 'All kinds of attitudes toward the great masters have been attributed to me, and I have been quoted as saying things about Wagner and Beethoven that I never said. I admire Beethoven and Wagner, but I refuse to admire them uncritically just because people have told me that they are masters! Never! In our day, it seems to me

that we adopt poses in regard to the masters more becoming to bitter old cleaning women; I wish to have the freedom to say that a boring page of music is annoying no matter who its author.'

In 1913 Debussy contributed an article on taste in the February issue of *SIM* – Société Internationale de Musicology. He considered the true meaning of the word 'taste' was in decline merely signifying a difference of opinion – usually settled, in Debussy's words 'with knuckle dusters'. Turning to taste in music he remarks – with a dig at Beethoven:

'Geniuses can evidently do without taste: take the case of Beethoven, for example. But on the other hand there was Mozart, to whose genius was added a measure of the most delicate "good taste." And if we look at the works of J.S. Bach – a benevolent God to whom all musicians should offer a prayer before commencing work, to defend themselves from mediocrity – on each new page of his innumerable works, we discover things we thought were born only yesterday.'

In 1903 Prince Ludwig-Ferdinand of Bavaria consented to be the President of a committee conveyed to erect a monument in honour of Richard Wagner. Debussy was incensed when he learned that such a statue was 'to the glory of the first and the greatest composer of Germany'. He railed:

'I will not dwell on the historical impossibility of Wagner being the first real German composer. What about Bach? Just a man who had a lot of children? Or Beethoven? A man who was so ill-bred that he decided to become deaf so that

> he could better annoy his contemporaries with
> his last quartets.'

Richard Langham Smith, editor, *Debussy on Music: The critical writings of the great French composer Claude Debussy*, London: Secker & Warburg, 1977, p. 96, pp. 232–3, pp. 244–5 and p. 277.

FREDERICK DELIUS

The English composer Frederick Delius outlined his views on composers in a letter to Peter Heseltine, better known as Peter Warlock:

> 'When I first heard Chopin as a little boy of six or seven, I thought heaven had been opened before me. When also as a little boy I first heard the *Humoresken* of Grieg a new world was opened to me again. When at the age of 23 I heard *Tristan* – I was perfectly overcome – also when I heard *Lohengrin* as a schoolboy. Beethoven always left me cold and reserved – Bach I always loved more – it seemed to me more spontaneous – Brahms I never liked much and never shall – it is philistine music – although some of the chamber music is good – But to have to get accustomed to music is a fearfully bad sign – The sort of people who get accustomed to music are the unmusical and when once accustomed to it they will hear no other.'

Lionel Carley, *Delius: A life in letters*, London: Scolar Press in association with the Delius Trust, 1988, pp. 91–2.

*

On another occasion Delius remarked:

> 'Beethoven's music has never given me a great thrill, though he was, of course, an intellectual giant. I like the symphonies and some of the chamber music, but his choral work I find tedious.'

Christopher Redwood, editor: *A Delius Companion*, London: John Calder, 1976, p. 59.

DAVID B. DENNIS

David B. Dennis is an American professor of history with particular interests in the Western humanities, and modern European cultural and intellectual history. His *Beethoven in German Politics, 1870-1989* (Yale University Press, 1996) examines evocations and uses of Beethoven's biography and music by all of the major parties of 19th- and 20th-century German political culture. Dennis reworks many of his views, concerning the place of Beethoven in Western culture, in his essay *Beethoven at large: reception in literature, the arts, philosophy, and politics* as outlined in the *Cambridge Companion to Music*, editor Glen Stanley, 2000, pp. 292–304. We cite the following from this text:

Dennis first considers what Beethoven means to the typical music lover:

> 'Amid the enormous collection of Beethoven inspired lyric in the Beethoven-Haus archives of Bonn stands a thick folder overflowing with poems "on single sheets", in other words never published. Hand-written or carefully typed, these verses were submitted by their authors themselves, often after visits to the Geburtshausmuseum. Such

amateur but heartfelt words remind us that the majority of artistic responses to Beethoven come from men and women whose names remain unfamiliar to the world of high letters; they might reveal more about how his music and life-story for general listeners than all "expert" disputations. Above all, the collection symbolizes a compulsion widely felt by persons who encounter this composer, his music, or simply memorabilia and places associated with him: Beethoven lovers tend to react to his art in active, often creative fashion, not passively. Such is the intense, ongoing influence that he and his works have on Western and even world cultures, both inside and outside musical life.'

Dennis adds:

'His triumphs over deafness and loneliness fixed his reputation as a paradigm of the "artist". Inspired by this heroic image and the élan of his most popular works, musicians, writers, visual artists, politicians, and a host of others have attempted to imitate aspects of his personality, and convince others to do likewise.'

Dennis acknowledges:

'That Beethoven was a complex character, partly explains the diversity of ways listeners set him into their cultural and ideological horizons. Combing through records of his inconsistent, even volatile nature, interpreters have found evidence to support associating the composer and his music with almost every modern current thought and behaviour.'

In the context of Beethoven's own time Dennis states:

> 'Scholars generally agree that common perceptions of Beethoven were strikingly — and permanently — coloured by his young contemporaries; the Romantics E.T.A. Hoffmann and Bettina Brentano urged listeners to interact emotionally with music, Beethoven's in particular, seeking and expressing soulful responses instead of merely being entertained.'

Dennis quotes the following passage from a letter of Brentano to Goethe:

> 'I believe in a divine magic that is an element of spiritual nature; and this magic, Beethoven exercises in his art.'

In this context, Dennis continues:

> 'Romantics underscored Beethoven's self-description as a *Tondichter* or "poet of tones" [consider for example the *Pastoral Symphony*] in order to associate him with their own goal of synthesizing the arts. This epithet functioned as a beacon summoning interpreters to mine his music for poetical ideas.'

Franz Grillparzer had the honour of eulogizing Beethoven at his Vienna funeral. In Dennis's estimation:

> '[He] portrayed the composer as outcast and ignored, doomed to suffer alone, but — like a fairy-tail wizard — in possession of magnificent powers.'

Dennis quotes the following lines from Grillparzer's oration:

> 'An enchanter, tired of the world and life/Sealed his magic in an impregnable chest/Threw the key into the sea, and died.'

In his all-embracing survey of the manner in which Beethoven has been absorbed into Western culture, Dennis quotes the following: Charles Baudelaire and his *La Musique* (1857), dedicated to Beethoven; Walt Whitman's lines:

> 'Hastings, urging, restless — no flagging, not even in the "thoughts" or meditations — to be perceived with the same perceptions that enjoys music — free and luxuriant — as in Beethoven's; and E. M. Forster's *A Room with a View* (1908) and *Howard's End* (1910). We remind the reader that both of these provide instances when Lucy Honeychurch 'disturbs her friends by playing the Piano Sonata Op. 11 on a rainy day in Florence and when Helen Schlegel listens to "the most sublime noise that ever penetrated the ear of man".'

These are illustrations, Dennis suggests, of the 'register [and] the ongoing influence of Romanticism on literary allusion to Beethoven'.

Continuing his survey of Beethoven, as instanced in Romantic literature, Dennis contributes the following further illustrations:

Of Victor Hugo, he notes that whilst he never made specific reference to the composer in his own novels, he considers he sketched the main lines of Beethoven's representation in such allusions to: ' "crippled body, flying soul", producing music like a "deep mirror in a cloud" that reflects everything his listeners desire: in it "the dreamer will recognize his dream, the sailor his storm ... and the wolf his forests".'

For Dennis, Romain Rolland presented the composer as 'a holy martyr who sublimated pain through creative acts'. He quotes Rolland's words: "Blessed is the misfortune that has come upon thee! Blessed the sealing of thine ears!" He interprets this as Rolland's recognition of the manner in which Beethoven overcame 'the terror of deafness' and was shown 'a path to self-redemption: "poor, sick, alone — and yet a victor!" ' He places Rolland as a central figure in the popularization of Beethoven in France 'in spite of ... his hero's Germanic origins'. High in Dennis's estimation of Rolland's prose works is what he considers to be his masterwork *Jean Christophe* (1904–12), an epic concerning an artist whose youth was mirrored on Beethoven's especially in the sense of obstacles to be overcome. To this work of Rolland's we may add his: *Life of Beethoven* (1903); *Beethoven and Handel* (1917); *Beethoven the Creator* (1929); and *Goethe and Beethoven* (1930).

In the representational arts, Dennis's survey encompasses the manner in which Beethoven has been portrayed in sculpture, portraiture, illustration and indeed a wide variety of other media relating to the Western music tradition. Concerning these he notes:

> '[The] commercialisation of Beethoven's physiognomy ... overshadows a long tradition of fashioning his likeness for reasons other than marketing. Through every phase of modern

> history, painters and sculptors have conveyed
> their regard for this musician as a source of
> inspiration across artistic boundaries ... Portraits
> done during Beethoven's life, often in a Romantic
> vein, established a number of constants in the
> visual representation of this genius. Unruly hair,
> tensed brow, frowning mouth, gaze directed
> elsewhere'.

Dennis laments the later trivialisation of Beethoven's visual imagery as is often depicted in the least accomplished of Biedermeier, the term used to identify the sentiment that permeates much early to mid-nineteenth century illustrative work — watercolour, line drawing and the like. A typical example, from literally hundreds, is Johann Peter Lyser's depiction of Beethoven seated by the bank of a stream composing his *Pastoral* Symphony. The reader for whom such Beethoven iconography holds particular fascination is encouraged to consult the Beethoven Haus 'Digital Archives'.

Franz Klein's life mask of Beethoven, taken in 1812, provided the basis for numerous later depictions of the composer in sculptural form. More than any other work this study identified Beethoven with the characteristic expression of defiance we have come to associate with him. Alessandra Comini has devoted an extended essay on this very subject in her *The Visual Beethoven: Whence, why, and whither the scowl?* See Scott G. Burnham and Michael P. Steinberg, editors, *Beethoven and his World*, Princeton, New Jersey; Oxford: Princeton University Press, 2000, pp. 287–312.

By the mid-nineteenth century, attempts began in earnest to capture Beethoven the titan in stone and bronze, and locations associated with the composer began to erect monuments in his honour. Dennis comments:

'Taken together, these monuments embody the conflicting motives of depicting the composer "as he really appeared" while simultaneously idealizing him.'

He considers: 'One of the most successful placements of Beethoven on a pedestal to be Kaspar Clemens Zumbusch's Vienna monument (1880): 'Scowling downward, the composer is as imposing as Michelangelo's Moses.' Alongside this work, we may cite that of the German artist Max Klinger. He depicted Beethoven partly robed — Roman fashion — seated in a chariot and worked in an array of marble, alabaster, ivory, bronze, amber and semi-precious stones (now located in the Museum der bilden Künst, Leipzig).

Dennis makes reference to the French sculptor Antoine Bourdelle who created over forty-five versions of Beethoven in various media between 1887 and 1889. Bourdelle left many of his busts with rough and ragged surfaces suggesting to Dennis 'primal forces in the composer's character: like Michelangelo's bound slaves, Bourdelle's Beethovens emerge from earth's stony veins.'

Dennis cites examples of artists seeking to liberate 'the earthbound and monumentalised image of Beethoven to a more spiritual level'. He comments:

'This is nowhere more true than in the friezes Gustav Klimt designed to compliment Klinger's sculpture [see above] at the 1902 Vienna Secession exhibition. Fashioned in Klimt's suggestive style intimating psycho-sexual drives then being postulated by Sigmund Freud, each of the three panels proposes psychological correlates for portions of Beethoven's *Ninth Symphony*.'

*

Among philosophers who discuss Beethoven and his music, Dennis cites Friedrich Nietzsche, Theodor Adorno, and Ernst Bloch. In his estimation, these writers and thinkers stand out:

> 'They genuinely incorporated ideas about the composer into their thought.' In particular, Dennis remarks how, as a young man, 'Nietzsche set forth in poetry the awe he felt before this sublime creator: "I look upon you mutely/Wishing to ask your eyes/Why, you miraculous man/Does my pulse beat stormily/When you pass through the forest of my soul?" ' Nietzsche clearly felt a strong affinity with Beethoven, recognizing that, like himself, he both suffered and gained from solitude: 'It was only with Beethoven, in Nietzsche's view, that music 'began to discover the language of pathos, of passionate desire, of the dramatic events which take place in the depths of man ... Beethoven was the first to let music speak a new language, the hitherto forbidden language of passion'.

Of Adorno, Dennis remarks:

> 'Adorno advanced a musical sociology in which the "inner syntax" of musical language correlates with social conditions and cultural patterns.' (see our following entry) Of Bloch, Dennis quotes: "How elated we feel when at the thought of you, infinite one! ... Our soul bubbles up to the stars in the initial rough, tempestuous, eloquent sea of

this music. Beethoven is Lucifer's benign offspring, the eloquent, the demon that leads to the ultimate things." Dennis also quotes Bloch's admiration of Beethoven's opera: "Every future storming of the Bastille is implicitly expressed in *Fidelio* ... Here and nowhere else ... music becomes a rosy dawn, militant-religious, the dawning of a new day so audible that it seems more than simply a hope."

Dennis cites the universal popularity of the Ninth Symphony:

'Since Second World War it has become [the] tradition to perform [the Ninth Symphony] every December throughout the country.'

He cites performances with a chorus of ten thousand given in Japan. Beethoven's Ninth Symphony has also been adopted as a symbol of peace by the United Nations.

Dennis concludes his majestic survey of Beethoven's influence:

'This Western composer's life and music have clearly become touchstones in world culture.'

David B. Dennis, *Beethoven in German Politics, 1870-1989*, Yale University Press, 1996. Passim.

GAETANO DONIZETTI

In 1842 Gaetano Donizetti was nominated to be a Corresponding Member of the French Academy. On the occasion of his acceptance of this considerable honour he expressed his views on music. He opened his address with the general remarks:

> 'Music is only a declamation accentuated by sounds, and therefore every composer must instinctively apprehend and give rise to vocal melody based on the accent of the declamation of the words. Whoever does not succeed in this, or does not do it felicitously, will only compose music devoid of feeling.'

Donizetti urged the would-be composer to follow the example of Rossini and 'imitate the good where you find it'. He acknowledged the importance of melody in music but did not place it before everything, believing that Italian music had sinned too much in the past in this regard, to the neglect of orchestration. He then turned to Beethoven:

> 'Many preach: imitate Beethoven; and may God will it so. Imitate him then, but imitate something beyond the instrumental effects and the rhythm. Have musical science before everything; afterwards take all the liberties that are taken in the symphonies and the last writings; but write me a *Septet*, a *Mount of Olives*, a *Fidelio*, etc., and everything will be pardoned you.'

In a throwaway line he added:

> 'German composers should sing a little more; Italians a little less.'

William Ashbrook, *Donizetti*, London: Cassell, 1965, pp. 273–4.

PAUL DUKAS

The name of Paul Dukas is firmly established in popular culture with his Symphonic Poem *L'apprenti socier* – 'The Sorcerer's Apprentice' – a musical setting of Goethe's ballad *Der Zauberlehrling* made famous by Walt Disney's filmic adaption *Fantasia* (1940). In his lifetime, however, Dukas was widely known as a writer and scholar-musicologist. During the course of his literary career he contributed many articles to the Journal *Revue hebdomadaire*. In the issue for September 1894, he considers the question of 'the comic' in music – by which he means *wit* and *humour*. Turning his attention to Beethoven, whose sense of humour was irrepressible – and often found expression in his correspondence in the form of contrived puns – he writes:

> 'Schuman, one of the first to take into account the comic power of music, points out, in several places in his writings, a number of passages from the symphonies of Beethoven which seem to suggest to him what he calls *grotesque* relations. The word is unfortunate and conveys the meaning badly. Yet, on examination of the passages in question, one gets a clearer picture of Schuman's idea. Beyond doubt these melodic or harmonic caprices of Beethoven, which sometimes occur in the midst of the most serious passages, must have had in his mind a certain humorous significance.'

Sam Morgenstern, editor, *Composers on Music: An anthology of composers' writings*, London: Faber & Faber, 1956, pp. 344–5.

*

ANTONÍN DVORÁK

Otakar Dvorák, writing about her composer-father relates:

> 'Some critics have not taken my father seriously as a composer because he did not have much of an education ... But father's self-education and, of course, his talent gave him more than any music conservatory could have. He said to me, "How much time I spent learning the rich forms of Beethoven's sonatas!" ' Recalling a later occasion she adds: 'Father adored Mozart and Beethoven. A very small bust of Mozart's head stood on Father's desk, and next to that a small picture of the gloomy face of Beethoven. Once, after a concert, Father received a wreath inscribed with the words, "To the greatest genius ever." Father took this wreath home and draped the ribbon over the picture of Beethoven.'

Otakar Dvorák, *Antonín Dvorák, My father*, Spillville, Iowa: Czech Historical Research Center, 1993. p. 91 and p. 109.

GEORGE DYSON

The English musician and composer Sir George Dyson was invited to contribute to Beethoven's Death Centenary (1927) in a special edition of *The Musical Times*. The following is an extract from his essay concerning questions of expression and interpretation — couched in suitably laudatory terms:

> 'The outstanding pianist will always demand problems of interpretation on which to feed the zeal of his evangel. For him Beethoven is food indeed. And there has been no player of high

rank who has not counted it a triumph to present to the world, at whatever expense of labour and thought, the truth of a message so exacting. In the pursuit of expression Beethoven was merciless. Pianoforte, quartet, orchestra and chorus, all alike he stretched to the utmost. He forgets that there are limits to the powers of an instrument, limits to the capacity of a human interpreter. Above all, he forgets himself. He would crouch under the desk to suggest a pianissimo. He would gesticulate wildly and ludicrously to emphasize a fortissimo. He would caress the piano into quiet ecstasies which his friends never forgot. He would thrash it into turmoil that made them almost afraid. Moods so intense are not for every man, though there can be no supreme artists without them. When the heat of his passion demands the impossible, it is because his vision is of things beyond man's power to describe. In pursuit of that transcendence Beethoven spent himself. And if his fire sometimes scorches us it consumed his own ardent soul no less.'

George Dyson, in: *Music & Letters: Beethoven: Special Number*, London: Music & Letters, 1927. p. 210.

HANNS EISLER

The Spanish Catalan composer and musical scholar Roberto Gerhard studied for a period with Arnold Schoenberg where he became acquainted with fellow composition student Hans Eisler. The latter was, by all accounts, difficult to get along with 'like a dog to a cat' and the day came when

Gerhard and Eisler almost had a duel. Like true musicians they made up, in their case by playing through four-hand versions of three or four Beethoven symphonies on an old boarding house piano — disturbing the whole establishment in so doing. Although Eisler was an extreme Marxist, and an enemy of what he condemned as 'Bourgeois' music, he affirmed his deeply held conviction to Gerhard on the value of 'true' music and the role Beethoven had in placing it central to society:

> 'Without a society there is not music and without collective ideals society does not exist. Great musicians have only existed during periods of great social ideals. The Beethoven who was a protégé of the Archduke Rudolf and the great lords of the Austrian aristocracy, was the singer of the Revolution, of universal fraternity, of human rights.'

Meiron Bowen, editor, *Gerhard on Music: Selected writings*, Brookfield, Vermont: Ashgate, 2000, pp. 59–60.

ERNST VON ELTERLEIN

The nineteenth-century pianist and musicologist Ernst von Elterlein, published one of the earliest comprehensive treaties on the subject of Beethoven's piano sonatas. In this he makes the following remarks:

> 'The gradual growth and ripening of [Beethoven's] mind — surely one of the most interesting psychological periods in the course of a great artist's evolution — is more clearly illustrated in his sonatas than in his other works. Nowhere else are those fine gradual changes, that

> progress towards an ever increasing independence, so noticeable and so traceable. In Beethoven, imagination, feeling, intellect and character are developed with equal potency and import, and in perfect harmony with each other. It is to these fundamentals that the finest works are unmistakably to be traced, indeed, they seem to me to be their inevitable outcome. Nor can this close connection of fancy, feeling, intellect and character be realized except by a strong subjectiveness, not one-sided or wrapt up in itself, but in unison with objective qualities equally potently'.

Ernst von Elterlein, *Beethoven's Pianoforte Sonatas: Explained for the lovers of the musical art*, London: W. Reeves, 1898, p. 31 and pp. 32–3.

MANUEL DE FALLA

The Spanish composer expressed his views on several composers, including Beethoven, that were subsequently published as: *On Music and Musicians*, Marion Boyars (publisher), 1979. Concerning Beethoven, and his influence on him, he writes:

> 'Independently of the admiration owed to Beethoven and the greater or lesser coincidence of my sentiments and aspirations with his works, these offer three powerful examples which I have made an effort to follow:
>
> (1) The nobility and lack of self-interest with which he served music, convinced of its elevated social mission.

(2) His desire for rhythmic-melodic-tonal purity.

(3) Beethoven's resolute undertaking to Germanize his music; an undertaking which should serve us as a luminous example so as to make sure that the Latin character, in its divers forms, is reflected with the greatest possible intensity in the artistic production of our race.'

De Falla concludes:

'I believe that this sincere, simple and faithful declaration — made with love, good will and with the vehement desire that it be received with the same sentiments — is the best homage that I can offer to the genius whose centenary [1927] is celebrated universally by the Art of Music.'

Nancy Lee Harper, *Manuel de Falla: His life and music*, Lanham, Maryland; London: The Scarecrow Press, 2005, p. 185. See also: Gonzalo Armero, and Jorge de Persia, *Manuel de Falla: His life and works,* London: Omnibus Press, 1999, p. 185.

AMY FAY

Amy (Amelia) Fay was a pioneering American concert pianist and manager of the New York Women's Philharmonic Society. A measure of her standing is that when in Europe she studied with Theodor Kullak and Franz Liszt. She is remembered today for the recollections of her training and descriptions of the concerts and recitals she attended that were subsequently published as *Music Study in Germany* (1880). In January 1880 she wrote from Chicago to her friend the poet Henry Wadsworth Longfellow — of *The Song of Hiawatha* fame. A new concert hall had just been completed, news of which Fay was eager to share. She describes it as 'a gay and cheery place' and, with a feminine touch, she remarks how the foyer allows the ladies 'to show of their dress to advantage' and is 'a very nice place to promenade in'. She pronounced the acoustic to be 'admirable'. As Fay remarks, she had the privilege of giving the opening concert:

> 'I was the first person to sound a note of music in the new Hall. What composer do you think I played? Wagner. I had some prickings of conscience, as I thought Beethoven ought to be the presiding genius of the new Hall, but I finally got over it by saying to myself that Wagner is the composer who represents progress, and is therefore better suited to Chicago.'

Margaret William McCarthy, editor, *More Letters of Amy Fay: The American years, 1879–1916*, Detroit: Information Coordinators, 1986, pp. 6–7.

EDWIN FISCHER

The Swiss born Edwin Fischer was celebrated in his day as a conductor but is perhaps best remembered today for being a classical pianist of distinction who could count amongst his distinguished pupils such, no less distinguished pianists, as Alfred Brendel, Paul Badura-Skoda and Daniel Barenboim. Fischer is also remembered for his discerning writing about Beethoven's piano sonatas, from which we quote the following:

> 'Ludwig van Beethoven's work has the quality of
> true greatness. What world's he traversed from
> his simple beginnings to the sublimation that he
> achieved at the close of his life's struggle! None
> of us could bear the strain of the tensions that his
> spirit was able to endure. We have the result of
> these struggles before us and we can only say:
> "The sound is a reflection of the life".'

Edwin Fischer, *Beethoven's Pianoforte Sonatas: A guide for students & amateurs*, London: Faber and Faber, 1959, p. 15.

NIGEL FORTUNE
See: Denis Arnold and Nigel Fortune

ALAIN FROGLEY
The musicologist Alain Frogley contributed an essay to the *Cambridge Companion to music* (see below) titled *Beethoven's music in performance: historical perspectives*. He opens this with a reflection on the manner in which the composer's music is central to Western musical culture:

> 'The history of performing Beethoven is in
> essence the history of our entire Western culture
> of musical performance as it has evolved since
> the eighteenth century. One is even tempted to
> write "Western culture" tout court [with no
> addition or qualification]. The ways in which we
> have kept alive the creations of one of the most
> potent icons of our civilization, the written instruc-
> tions of the printed scores mediated by individual
> performance conventions, speak eloquently of

deeper issues – of cultural value, tradition, authority, the individual and society, written versus oral communication, intuition versus reason. At a more concrete level, Beethoven's music underpinned the formation both of the fundamental performance institutions of modern musical life, including the character and makeup of our public concerts and recitals, and of the very idea of a mass culture of "serious" music that elevates edification over mere entertainment.'

Frogley offers the following estimate of Beethoven's musical legacy in the context of performance:

'All Beethoven's major works were performed during his lifetime, and in most cases his direct involvement, either as pianist or conductor (and sometimes both), or as a consultant at rehearsal. Furthermore, since his death the bulk of his output has continued to be performed: there has never been a Beethoven "revival" or any need for one. This has ensured an unbroken lineage of performers descended from Beethoven, as it were, initially those who knew and worked with him or, in a handful of cases, were actually taught by him. Of the latter, Carl Czerny was the most influential; he published detailed instructions on the performance of Beethoven's piano works, and also taught the young Liszt, among others: the succession runs Czerny–Leschetitzky–Schnabel– and beyond [and] is a particularly impressive one.'

Alain F. Frogley, *Beethoven's Music in Performance: Historical perspectives*, In: Glen Stanley, editor: *The*

Cambridge Companion to Beethoven, Cambridge; New York: Cambridge University Press, 2000, pp. 255–71.

WILHELM FURTWÄNGLER

The universally recognised interpreter of Beethoven, Wilhelm Furtwängler, was fulsome in his praise of the composer:

> 'Scarcely any other German name has been accorded such veneration through the entire world as that of Beethoven. If it is not in the same sense national as the creations of Wagner or Schubert, Beethoven's work yet possesses a spiritual power that Germany does not possess elsewhere in the art of music. Through no one else is the force and greatness of German perception and being brought to such penetrating expression.'

Originally published in: Walter Riezler, *Beethoven,* Zurich, 1936, translated, G.D.H Pidcock, New York: Vienna House, 1972, p. 9. Quoted in: John L. Holmes, *Composers on Composers*, New York: Greenwood Press, 1990, p. 52.

For the years 1924–54, Furtwängler kept a notebook in which he recorded his thoughts about music. From these we cite the following extracts:

> 'What makes Beethoven and Goethe so great, so compelling? The fact that they had *both*, the natural strength of the earth, breadth and stature, "sublimation". Both in such a proportion that the one was able to *grow* out of the other. The liberal world, the intellectuals, need to be told repeatedly

that sublimation alone is not enough, and our contemporaries need to be told that folk-art and breadth alone are not enough.'

'In judging an artist one should differentiate between the intellectual superstructure that is pervasive and individual to him, and the substance itself. In Beethoven this superstructure is very small, the substance enormous, In Bruckner the discrepancy is even greater. In today's artist it is generally the other way around. A great "intellectual" attitude and great intellectual abilities can mask quite a weak and false substance (and generally do so).'

'The pernicious inheritance of Romanticism is the "art of inspiration". Overcoming it is a task that has been taken up anew by every individual artist since Beethoven.'

Michael Tanner, editor, *Notebooks, 1924—1954: Wilhelm Furtwängler*, London: Quartet Books, 1989, pp. 103—4 and pp. 150—1.

In his essay 'Beethoven, a world force', Furtwängler wrote:

'What is most evident in respect of Beethoven and exerts more influence than anything from other composers is what I would term the 'Law'. He strives like no one else after the natural law, and after what is definitive, as a consequence of which we have the extraordinary clarity that distinguishes his music. The kind of simplicity that prevails therein is not the simplicity of

> naïveté, nor is it a calculated effect like that, for instance, of a modern popular number. Yet at no time was music written that confronts the listener so directly, so openly and — one might say — so nakedly! We know from Beethoven's life that he never found his work as an artist easy, that the monumental and simple qualities of his themes did not simply fall into his lap. On the contrary: each of his works shows a concentrated essence of a whole world, and — from a limitless, chaotic life and experience — is given order, form, and clarity by means of the iron will of the artist. This particular kind of clarity signifies nevertheless the renunciation of all means — which exist in art as in life — of placing the subject in an advantageous light so that through kinds of colouring and through refinement it may appear as more profound and greater than it really is.'

This preceding quotation is derived from the writings of Santeri Levas who was the personal secretary to Jean Sibelius for twenty years. He considered the words quoted to be also appropriate to his master and the manner in which he evolved his own creations.

Santeri Levas, *Sibelius: A personal portrait*, London: J. M. Dent, 1972, p. 62.

HANS GAL

In his survey of *The Golden Age of Vienna*, the Austrian-British composer and author Hans Gal reserves a special position for Beethoven whom he describes as *The Master Builder*. He adds:

> 'Beethoven is the first representative of the modern intellectual type, whose range of interests is not confined to his art. Wherever one looks into his letters, subjects of general interest are touched. Though his scanty education is pathetically obvious in certain limitations of style and difficulties of spelling, a great mind, a wide, comprehensive conception assert themselves everywhere.'

Gal considered Beethoven's early achievements in composition:

> 'Beethoven was twenty-one when he became Haydn's pupil, and the most remarkable composition he brought with him, a Cantata on the death of Joseph II, already gives the impression of a fully asserted personality. But his technique as a composer was inadequate, more superficially acquired that systematically built up, the outcome of irregular studies with indifferent teachers, who obviously did their best, but could not give more than they had themselves. His Op.1, published three years later and with the unmistakable intention of discarding everything he had done before, the most remarkable first work a composer has ever published, shows him as a master of his art.'

The Cantata to which Gal refers was written when Beethoven was just twenty years old but was never performed in his lifetime – the Bonn orchestra available to him found the parts too taxing. It was only premiered in 1884, fifty-seven years after his death. However, echoes of the work can be heard in the composer's opera *Leonore*, or *The Triumph of Marital Love* – later reworked as *Fidelio*.

Gal reaffirms his view as Beethoven being an architect-like constructor:

> 'The fact is that no great master has ever regarded form as more than a principle, based on the common sense of musical construction, adapted to the peculiarities of the actual material and idea in every single instance. This is what Beethoven, the most clear-sighted architect of music who ever lived, seems to demonstrate in every single work. The main difference between his conception and his predecessors' is not the actual form but, so to speak, the voltage, the degree of tension between the component musical characters or ideas.'

Gal concludes:

> 'Beethoven — like Michelangelo, who offers the most obvious parallel among the great artists — is the prototype of such a living volcano. Like Michelangelo, he had the titanic power of moulding the eruptive material, of imposing on it his creative will. It is the most demoniac of all elements: Chaos, both the eternal source and eternal contradiction of Cosmos, the ordered world.'

Hans Gal, *The Golden Age of Vienna*, London: Max Parrish & Co. Limited, 1948, pp. 44–46 and p. 51.

GLEN GOULD
In an interview with the American writer, and Pulitzer Prize-winning music critic Tim Page, the Canadian pianist Glen Gould shared his views on the music of Beethoven —

known for being unorthodox if not somewhat eccentric:

> 'I have very ambivalent feelings about Beethoven. I'm absolutely at a loss for any reasonable explanation as to why his best-known works — the Fifth Symphony, the Violin Concerto, the *Emperor*, the *Waldstein* — ever became popular, much less as to why they have retained their appeal. Almost every criterion that I expect to encounter in great music — harmonic and rhythmic variety, contrapuntal invention — is almost entirely absent in these pieces. In this middle period — the period which produced those works — Beethoven offered us the supreme historical example of a composer on an ego trip, a composer absolutely confident that whatever he did was justified simply because he did it! I don't know any other way to explain the predominance of those empty, banal, belligerent gestures that serve as his themes in that middle period. The later years are another story — my favourite Beethoven symphony is the Eighth, my favourite movement in all of his sonatas the opening of Op.101, and, for me, the *Grosse Fuge* is not only the greatest work Beethoven ever wrote but just about the most astonishing piece in musical literature. But even the late works are remarkably inconsistent — for instance, I don't think that the remainder of Op.101 has much to do with the extraordinary first movement, except for that quotation right before the finale.'

Tim Page, editor, *The Glenn Gould Reader*, 1987, pp. 101–2.

*

PERCY GRAINGER

The Australian pianist, composer and arranger of folk music Percy Grainger gave his first public recital in Melbourne at the age of twelve — including works by Beethoven. In 1903 Grainger studied with the eminent pianist Ferruccio Busoni. Later, when performing in London, *The Times* critic reported Grainger's playing 'revealed rare intelligence and a good deal of artistic insight'. In a letter written in 1909 to Karen Holten, one of his pupils, Grainger — notwithstanding his success — seems to have been in a despondent mood disposing him to invoke the circumstances of other composers including Beethoven:

> 'Few folk have so little calamity happen to them as I, and few can afford to digest *inner* soul-sorrow more soundly than I. Most men of my talents have more "push" or yearning for activity and *realization* than I. Wagner with his schemes, his wars, his whole forcefulness was an army continually on the move. Beethoven too with his despair & bubbling joyousness had not the calm for clear cold *onlooking* sadness that I have. Men who have died young like Keats, Schubert, A. Beardsley, Dowson seem often to have been as publicly inactive as I.'

Kay Dreyfus, *The Farthest North of Humanness: Letters of Percy Grainger, 1901–1914*, South Melbourne; Basingstoke: Macmillan, 1985, p. 289.

In 1915 Grainger wrote an article for the magazine *Étude*, in which he expressed his delight in what he called 'new forms of pianism', as he considered to be found in the piano writing of Debussy and Ravel — amongst others. He expressed reservations though about the writing for piano of certain masters of the past:

> 'The great composers, such as Bach and Beethoven, thought of the piano as a medium for all-round expression, but perhaps they did not so often feel inspired by its specifically pianistic attributes as do several of the moderns. Many of Beethoven's sonatas could be orchestrated and a symphonic effect produced.'

Malcolm Gillies and Bruce Clunies Ross, editors, *Grainger on Music*, Oxford; New York: Oxford University Press, 1999, p. 66.

CECIL GRAY

The English composer and music critic Cecil Gray wrote for *The Daily Telegraph* and *The Manchester Guardian*. He reiterated some of his views about composers in his *Autobiography* from which the following extract is derived:

> 'A Bach fugue is the symbolic embodiment of the principle of predestination. Everything in it is latent, pre-ordained; nothing happens, nor can happen, that is not contained in embryo within the theme, as the oak is contained in the acorn. Beethoven, on the other hand, exemplifies the opposite principle of free-will. He is master of his fate, the captain of his soul. There is no element in his work of divine inevitability. The whole plot can be reversed at a moment's notice, and frequently is, as the outcome of pure wilfulness or caprice. The element of the unexpected is

paramount. Anything can, and generally does, happen with him. Bach, in fact, represents the element of fate, the divine, the pre-ordained; Beethoven is Promethean man, the rebel. The reconciliation of the two opposing principles is to be found in the music of Mozart, the mediator between God and Man, half deity, half human.'

Cecil Gray, *Musical Chairs, or, Between Two Stools: Being the life and memoirs of Cecil Gray*, London: Home & Van Thal, 1948, p. 31.

FRANZ GRILLPARZER
The Austrian writer, poet and dramatist Franz Grillparzer became acquainted with Beethoven when he was about seventeen years of age. At this time (the summer of 1808), he was living with his mother in rooms close by those occupied by Beethoven in a house in Heiligenstadt. Alexander Thayer reports:

> 'Mme. Grillparzer, mother of the poet, was a lady of great taste and culture, and was fond of music. She used to stand outside her door in order to enjoy Beethoven's playing [improvising], as she did not then know of his aversion to listeners. One day Beethoven, springing from his piano to the door to see if anyone were listening, unfortunately discovered her there. Despite her messages to him through his servant that her door into the common passageway would remain locked, and that her family would use another, Beethoven played no more.'

In 1823, Grillparzer discussed the possibility with Beethoven of collaborating with him in an operatic project on the fable of the fresh-water spirit *Melusine* but, like many other of the composer's putative operatic ventures, it came to nothing.

Elliot Forbes, editor: *Thayer's life of Beethoven*, Princeton, New Jersey: Princeton University Press, 1967, pp. 441–2 and pp. 843–4.

Grillparzer is perhaps best remembered in Beethoven musicology for his Funeral Oration that was read at the composer's graveside, from which we cite the following passage:

> 'Standing by the grave of him who has passed away, we are in a manner the representatives of an entire nation, of the whole German people, mourning the loss of the one highly acclaimed half of the fatherland's full spiritual bloom. There yet lives – and may his life be long! – the hero of verse in German speech and tongue; but the last master of tuneful song ... the organ of soulful concord, the heir and amplifier of Handel and Bach's of Haydn and Mozart's immortal fame is now no more, and we stand weeping over the riven strings of the harp that is hushed.'

A number of versions of Grillparzer's text exist. We have quoted from the following source:

Gerhard von Breuning: Oscar George Theodore Sonneck, *Beethoven: Impressions of contemporaries*, London: Oxford University Press, 1927, pp. 229–30.

*

Donald J. Grout and Claude V. Palisca

The American born Grout and the Italian born Palisca — both musicologists — consider the fascination that music held for the emerging Romantic generation bearing upon its 'revolutionary element, the free, impulsive, mysterious, demonic spirit, the underlying conception of *music as a mode of self-expression*' [their words and italics]. As evidence, they cite the pioneering essay (1813) by the German writer and composer E. T. A. Hoffman who remarks:

> 'Beethoven's music sets in motion the lever of fear, of horror, of suffering, and awakens just that infinite longing which is the essence of romanticism ... He is accordingly a completely romantic composer.'

Grout and Palisca comment:

> 'Hoffman was not unaware nor unappreciative of the importance of structure and control in Beethoven's music, nor in that of Haydn and Mozart, whom he also called "Romantic" ... Romantic or not, Beethoven was one of the great disruptive forces in the history of music. After him, nothing could ever be the same again; he had opened the gateway to a new world.'

Donald Jay Grout and Claude V. Palisca, editors: *A History of Western Music*, London: J. M. Dent, 1988.

George Grove

The name Grove is familiar to generations of music lovers through association with *Grove's Dictionary of Music and*

Musicians of which Grove was the inspiration and source. Sir George Grove, however, did not receive a formal education in music and trained as a structural engineer, being admitted as a graduate of the Institution of Civil Engineers. He worked in this capacity for the first thirty years of his life and it was while he was engaged on the Britannia Bridge that he became known to such luminaries of the age as Robert Stephenson, Isambard Kingdom Brunel and Sir Charles Barry. Through their influence, Grove made a change of career and was appointed in 1849 to the secretaryship of the Society of Arts — at the period of gestation of the Great Exhibition of 1851. When the exhibition relocated to Sydenham, in the guise of The Crystal Palace, it was as a result of the actions of Grove that the German-born August Manns was appointed, first as bandmaster and later as the conductor of a full-size orchestra. Manns presided over regular concerts for more than forty years, Grove providing numerous programme notes that later formed the basis for his *Dictionary*.

Many of Beethoven's works were performed at The Crystal Palace under the direction of August Manns including overtures, concertos, symphonies and choral works. *Fidelio* received a concert performance in 1859 and in 1866 the resident orchestra had to be augmented for a rendering of the *Eroica* Symphony that was billed as 'a special event'. The occasion of Queen Victoria's Diamond Jubilee in 1894 offered *The Musical Times* the chance to review some of the significant musical activities that had taken place at The Crystal Palace in its preceding forty-or-so years of concert life. Sir George Grove was singled out for being a 'very natural exhibitor' and for promoting the works of Beethoven amongst others including Mendelsohn and Schubert. The following year was the 125th anniversary of Beethoven's birth, an event that was commemorated in a special concert devoted entirely to works by the composer, namely: Overture *Prometheus*,

First Symphony, slow movement; *Emperor* Piano Concerto; *Ah! Perfido*, *Eroica* Symphony; a selection of songs; and to conclude the Overture *Leonora* No. 3. A detailed inventory of the works of Beethoven performed at The Crystal Palace, and the role played by Sir George Grove, will be found in:

Michael Musgrave, *The Musical Life of the Crystal Palace*, Cambridge: Cambridge University Press, 1995.

A more intimate portrait of Grove's musical associations, and his personal feelings about Beethoven's music, can be derived from the accounts he left in his letters — many of which have been published. The impression conveyed in these is that he was especially fond of the composer's piano sonatas. In his discussion of the craftsmanship that Beethoven expended on the first movement of Beethoven's Piano Sonata in E-flat major, Op. 7, Egerton Lowe urges the performer to take care and to observe the composer's expression marks. In so doing, he invokes one of Grove's characteristic observations:

'There is hardly a bar in his [Beethoven's] music
of which it may be said with confidence that it has
been rewritten a dozen times'.

C. Egerton Lowe, *Beethoven's Pianoforte Sonatas: Hints on their rendering, form, etc., with appendices on definition of sonata, music forms, ornaments, pianoforte pedals, and how to discover keys*, London: Novello, 1929, p. 22.

Grove particularly cherished the Piano Sonata in C minor, Op. 13, The *Pathétique*. Writing to a friend he remarks:

'[Isn't] Beethoven inexhaustible ... That sonata
[Op. 13] is one of my magic things ... so noble,
so peculiar, so *new*.'

*

Grove's correspondence sheds light on a long-forgotten young woman pianist, Arabella Goddard, who must have possessed extraordinary pianistic gifts. Despite her English-sounding name, she was born in France. An acknowledged child prodigy, Arrabella studied with Sigismond Thalberg and played before Chopin and Queen Victoria. She made her formal debut in London on 14 April 1853, when age 17, giving a performance of the *Hammerklavier* Sonata — no less. Some authorities, including Grove, considered Goddard's performance to be the first London performance of this work but the honour may go to Ignaz Moscheles. Be this as it may, Goddard can be credited with bringing performances of Beethoven's late piano sonatas — largely unknown at the time — before the London public, primarily through the series of recitals she gave at The Crystal Palace in the concert seasons of 1857 and 1858. At these she pioneered playing from memory, then still an innovation. Writing to his sister-in-law Emma Bradley [November?] 1862, Grove enthused about the *Hammerklavier* Sonata in the following terms:

> 'Why, my dear child, it's the most *awfully difficult* thing! You perhaps don't know what an event it is, having heard it at all. I recollect Miss [Arabella] Goddard played it ... and the extraordinary sensation it made. There is no doubt whatever, it is she we have to thank for Beethoven's latest and most difficult sonatas having become so popular as they now are.'

In the summer of 1895 (14 June), Grove had occasion to write to his pupil Louise Heath. In his letter he makes reference to Beethoven's E major Piano Sonata, Op. 109 remarking:

> 'Do things take *hold of you* sometimes? They do so of me quite absurdly. All yesterday from 6 a.m., I was humming, howling, shouting the first variation in the finale of Beethoven's Sonata in E, Op. 109. How lively it is! And also how bold! A variation? Wherein does the likeness to the theme consist? And yet there is no mistaking the resemblance. Look at the 6th and 7th bars. They are only a kind of *excursion* outside of the melody, and how beautiful they are — the A natural and then the A sharp, and then the G sharp further on. Oh dear, it is all magical, I think.'

Grove had occasion to write to his pianist sister-in-law Miss Emma Bradley sometime in 1862. In his letter he enthuses to Miss Bradley in the following terms:

> 'There is no doubt whatever, it is she [Arabella Goddard] we have to thank for Beethoven's latest and most difficult sonatas having become so popular as they are. But the gem of them all (and playable too) is the *Arietta* which is the subject of the last movement of Op. 111. You will find no difficulty in playing the *Arietta* itself and the first two variations, and if they don't make you cry I shall be astonished ... the tenderness of this little air is most overcoming.'

Charles L. Graves, *The Life & Letters of Sir George Grove, Hon. D.C.L. (Durham), Hon. LL.D.*, London: Macmillan and Co., Ltd.; New York: The Macmillan Co., 1903, p. 93, p. 368, p. 396, and pp. 421–2.

*

IVOR GURNEY

To commemorate the anniversary of Beethoven's Death Centenary in 1927, *The Musical Times* devoted what it described as a *Special Number* to an evaluation of Beethoven and his music. The British music critic and scholar John Fuller Maitland edited the many articles contained in this issue and he himself contributed an extended essay on the piano sonatas. The *Special Number* contained several poems celebrating the composer, including a contribution from the Gloucestershire poet and musician Ivor Gurney. His life was marred by poor health and mental instability but today he is recognized for being a War Poet of distinction and, in this capacity, is commemorated alongside several others in *Poet's* Corner in Westminster Abbey. Of Beethoven, Gurney Wrote:

> 'Beethoven I wronged thee undernoting thus
> Thy dignity and worth; the overplus
> Of one quartet would our book overweigh —
> Almost chosen out at random from your own day.
> You have our great Ben's mastery and a freer
> Carriage of method, spice of the open air ...
> Which he, our greatest builder, had not so —
> Not as his own at least but acquired to.
> May no false fashion put thy true fame away
> As in Vienna, when wantons laid all away
> Thy work Homeric for a soft Southern zephyr,
> And heroes were no other than as day's heifer
> Sacrificed on the altar of world's praise,
> The amusement or brittle heightening of drab
>   days;
> Whereas thy sinewed strength is by Aeschylus,
> Homer, Ben Jonson, Shakespeare, and a pillar
>   of us.

> Master! Such are out memories which do never
> betray
> Our own makings, thou so generous in they
> great-heart way.'

Ivor Gurney in: *Music & Letters: Beethoven: Special Number*, London: *Music & Letters*, 1927, Vol. VIII, No. 2.

WILLIAM HENRY HADOW

The educational reformer, and musicologist, Sir William Henry Hadow was invited by the British Academy to give its *Annual Master-Mind Lecture* in June 1917. Hadow took Beethoven as his subject:

> 'Historians have customarily distinguished [Beethoven's] music into three periods, a division which is really valuable if we do not insist too closely on lines of demarcation. They cannot be chronologically determined, partly because he did not master all his media simultaneously, partly because, like all great artists, he occasionally threw back to an earlier idiom or method. Still, allowing for some looseness and elasticity in the use of terms, the distinctions are not only intelligible but also illuminating. There can be no doubt that the first two symphonies are essentially different from the *Eroica*, the first six string quartets from the *Rasoumoffskys*: the three piano sonatas published as Op. 31 are described by Beethoven himself as "written in a new Style". An equally unmistakable frontier is crossed by the last pianoforte trio, the last violin sonata, and the

F minor Quartet, precursor and herald of the greatest achievements in all chamber music. It may be observed that the succession corresponds closely to the natural growth and development of Beethoven's character.'

Hadow concludes:

'[Beethoven's] music is not only a joy of beautiful sound and emotion nobly felt and nobly communicated: it is also a marvel of intellectual power and of deep spiritual insight; nor is it only a master of melody, but in very truth as a *Maestro di color che sanno* ['the colour master who knows' — Aristotle], that I ask you to place him among the master-minds of all humanity.'

William Henry Hadow, *Collected Essays*, London: H. Milford at the Oxford University Press, 1928, pp. 107–23.

CHARLES HALLÉ

Sir Charles Hallé was of German extraction and in his early years was renowned as a child prodigy — at the age of four, for example, he performed a sonatina in public. In his student days, in Paris, he associated with Frédéric Chopin and Franz Liszt. He moved to England in 1848, changing his name from Karl Halle to Charles Hallé, and became a favourite of the musical salons and a pioneer in the promotion of Beethoven's piano sonatas. Hallé was the first pianist in England to perform the complete series of the composer's piano sonatas, initially in recitals held at his own house and later in the St. James Concert Hall, Piccadilly. It has been said that it was due in great measure to Hallé's recitals 'that a knowledge of Beethoven's pianoforte sonatas became general in English society'.

Hallé recalls his initial experience of London recitals in 1848 when he made his début.

'I may consider my first public appearance in England ... was favourably received and criticised.'

As a consequence, Hallé was invited to play for *The Musical Union*, then the most important concert institution for chamber music in London. This was originated in 1845 by the English violinist John Ella and existed until 1880, helping to shape and inform the wider public appreciation of music, alongside its sister concert series known as the *Popular Concerts*. When Hallé stated to Ella that he wished to play 'one of Beethoven's pianoforte sonatas' Ella exclaimed, 'Impossible!' and endeavoured to demonstrate to Hallé:

'They were not works to be played in public; that, as far as he knew, no solo sonata had ever before been included in any concert programme, and that he could not venture to offer one to his subscribers.'

Hallé further recalls how he had to battle for several days before Ella consented and who 'was much surprised to find that the sonata I had chosen [was] Op. 31, No. 3 in E-flat major'. Ella's fears proved to be unfounded, as Hallé recounts:

'His performance pleased so much that several ladies who heard it arranged parties in order to hear it once more.'

Subsequently Ella made no difficulty about Hallé performing other Beethoven sonatas, but he still cautioned the young pianist 'to be careful in their selection, and to choose those that could more easily be appreciated'. Hallé duly acquiesced:

> 'I advanced therefore very cautiously, the second sonata I played being the one in D, Op. 28, commonly known as the *Pastorale*.'

Looking back on these years in 1896 when he wrote his recollections, he records:

> '*Then* the question was: "Can this or that [Beethoven] sonata be understood by the audience?" Nowadays the difficulty lies in finding one not too hackneyed.'

C. E. Hallé, *Life and Letters of Sir Charles Hallé: Being an autobiography (1819–1860) with correspondence and diaries*, London: Smith, Elder & Co., 1896, pp. 103–4. Hallé's account is also recalled by Charles Rigby, see: *Sir Charles Hallé: A portrait today*, 1952, p. 66 and Michael Kennedy, *Hallé Tradition: A century of music*, 1960, p. 18.

It so chanced that Louis Spohr was in London in 1855 and heard Hallé perform the D major Piano Sonata Op. 10. After the concert, Spohr made some flattering remarks about Hallé's performance and proclaimed the D major to be 'a fine sonata', adding, 'not antiquated'. The latter remark left Hallé somewhat perplexed. Was Spohr perhaps trying to say that he regarded the Piano Sonata Op. 10, No. 3 as modern sounding? At about this same period, George Bernard Shaw, in his capacity as a London music critic, also heard Hallé perform Beethoven's Sonata Op. 10, No. 3 at a recital in the City. He considered Hallé's artistry as being self-effacing, remarking — with characteristic wit:

> 'Sir Charles is not a sensational player ... The
> secret is that he gives you as little as possible of
> Hallé and as much as possible of Beethoven.'

Michael Kennedy, *Hallé Tradition: a century of music*, Manchester: Manchester University Press, 1960, p. 72. Kennedy also tells the same anecdote in his: *The Autobiography of Charles Hallé; with correspondence and diaries*, London: Paul Elek, 1972, p. 10. Shaw's own text, together with numerous other of his concert reviews, is published in: Bernard Shaw, *London Music in 1888–89,* 1937, pp. 41-2.

In 1853 Hallé moved to Manchester to direct what were known as the Manchester's Gentleman's Concerts. In due course Hallé enhanced their standing in the form of the *Hallé Orchestra Concert Series*, performed under his baton, and continuing to this day. During the concert season of 1870–1, by which time Hallé was better known to the public as a conductor, in fulfilment of a personal resolution, he gave a performance of the C-sharp minor Piano Sonata on the anniversary of Beethoven's death — which fell on 17 December 1870. In the event, the concert had to be given on 15 December and included so many other works of Beethoven's it did not finish until 11.00 p.m.

Hallé regularly took the family for their summer holiday on the Isle of Wight, where they had a cottage at Cowes. His son recalls, affectionately, the delight of sitting in the garden on summer nights 'hearing the *Moonlight* and other divine sonatas [of Beethoven] played as only my father could play them'.

Michael Kennedy as previously cited. The above quotation is taken from p. 81.

*

THE HARMONICON

The Harmonicon was a monthly music journal that was published in London for the period 1823 to 1833. For a time it was edited by William Ayrton, who is credited with the production of England's first performance of Mozart's *Don Giovanni* (1817). In the very first year of issue *The Harmonicon* published what was in effect, a (quite remarkable) contemporary pen-portrait of Beethoven, outlining aspects of his personal life and the character of certain of his compositions:

> '[Beethoven] has secured a name, and reached a height of renown, to which no other author, Handel, Haydn and Mozart excepted, has attained ... Beethoven is as original and independent in his modes of thinking as he is in his musical productions. A decided enemy to flattery, and an utter stranger to everything dishonorable, he disdains to court the favour of everyone, however wealthy or exalted in rank ... [Beethoven has] that deplorable calamity, the greatest that could befall a man of his profession, his extreme deafness, which we are assured is now so great as to amount to a total privation of hearing. Those who visit him are obliged to write down what they have to communicate.'

The passage that follows is of particular interest:

> 'To this cause [his deafness] may be traced many of the peculiarities visible in his later compositions.'

The challenges posed by many of Beethoven's works were considered attributable in his lifetime — and long afterwards— to his deafness. *The Harmonicon* continues:

> 'The last account we hear of this great man is that he has just completed a new grand mass [the *Missa Solemnis*]. The dark tone of his mind is in unison with that solemn style which the services of the church demand; and the gigantic harmony he knows so well how to wield enables him to excite feelings of the awful and sublime in a manner that none living can attempt to rival.'

Cited in: Piero Weiss and Richard Taruskin. *Music in the Western World: A history in documents*, New York: Schirmer; London: Collier Macmillan, 1984, pp. 329–31.

CHRISTOPHER HEADINGTON

The English composer and musicologist Christopher Headington affirms:

> 'No history of music can offer a simple answer. But it can draw attention to Beethoven, a composer whose work attracts experts and public alike. In this, his art resembles that of Shakespeare. Beethoven believed in the message of the choral finale of his last symphony, "Be embraced, ye millions!" For him, all men were brothers under God.'

Headington places Beethoven alongside Tchaikovsky:

> 'But when we think of Beethoven's Fifth Symphony beside Tchaikovsky's work we immediately sense a profound difference between these

two composers. Beethoven reaches out beyond himself to a universal ideal: he speaks to mankind at large, even to God. Music was for him "a higher revelation than all wisdom and philosophy", offering entrance to a spiritual world. He saw his work, quite consciously, as a humanitarian vocation in a religious sense. This is perhaps why he has been called "too great an artist to be left to the musicians".'

Christopher Headington, *The Bodley Head History of Western Music*, London: The Bodley Head, 1974, pp. 155–6.

GUSTAV HOLST

In 1903 the English composer and teacher Gustav Holst wrote to his life-long friend Vaughan Williams. As is apparent, his subject was Richard Strauss to whom he was given to referring as "Richard II"! He opens his letter self deprecatingly:

> 'I hope you bear in mind that all the rot I write is merely a collection of stray thoughts ... As I told you once before, Richard II seems to me to be the most "Beethovenish" composer since Beethoven. Perhaps I am wrong, but anyhow you will agree that, whatever his faults, he is a real life composer.'

Hans Gal, *The Musician's World: Great composers in their letters*, London: Thames and Hudson, 1965, p. 420.

*

ARTHUR HONEGGER

The French organist and musicologist Bernard Gavoty put a number of questions to the Swiss Composer Arthur Honegger. He first invited him to express his views on the nature of music and composition. The following are extracts from his extended response: 'Absolute originality does not exist.'

Honegger argued that each generation builds on what has gone before but acknowledged that the works of a powerful genius have revolutionary power. To the lay mind, Honegger believed 'the act of composing music remains an incomprehensible thing'. He identified with Beethoven's manner of working, stating 'musical construction must first be done in the mind, then be noted on paper ... Composing is a mental operation which takes place in the brain of the composer'. Honegger qualified this observation, and, in so doing, further identified with Beethoven's own way of working:

> 'However, I don't claim that to check certain passages at the piano is not useful, if only as an aid or guide in the linking of certain passages.'

Honneger's remark runs close to Anton Schindler's description of Beethoven testing at the keyboard what he had written, particularly in the case of the piano sonatas. Honegger's next passage could almost be a description of Beethoven when at the height of his powers as a virtuoso:

> 'Searching at the piano can be fruitful, especially when the composer is a skilful instrumentalist who gives himself to improvisation ... Thus chance becomes inspiration.'

Honegger turned his attention directly to Beethoven:

> 'What has always astounded people is the existence of the deaf composer. It is not improbable that a great part of the admiration bestowed on Beethoven stems from his infirmity. Actually, apart from the tragic aspect of this situation, the fact that a creator can never hear the *execution* of his work should remove great technical restriction for him. Beethoven had gradually forgotten the purely aural qualities of certain combinations of tones. We discover this in the vocal writing of the *Missa Solemnis* and the *Ninth Symphony*. We also observe it in the great interval between the right hand and the left in his piano writing and especially in the paradoxical harmonization of up-beats. However, this had no influence whatsoever on the essence of his thought. I should be tempted to say that his deafness, which immured him in himself, helped him in the concentration of his genius and detached him from the tastelessness and banalities of his time.'

John L. Holmes, *Composers on Composers*, New York: Greenwood Press, 1990, pp. 466–9. Honegger's responses to the questions put to him were initially published as *Je suis compositeur*. See also: Sam Morgenstern, editor, *Composers on Music: An anthology of composers' writings,* London: Faber & Faber, 1956, pp. 468–9.

VICTOR HUGO
The French poet and novelist placed Beethoven in the Pantheon of the very great human beings:

> 'The great Pelasgian is Homer; the great Greek is Aeschylus; the great Hebrew is Isaiah; the great Roman is Juvenal; the great Italian is Dante; the great Englishman is Shakespeare; the great German is Beethoven.'

Leo Schrade, Cited in: *Tragedy in the Art of Music*, Cambridge, Massachusetts: Harvard University Press, 1964, p. 38.

VINCENT D'INDY

The French composer and teacher Vincent d'Indy was considered to be a child prodigy. At the Paris Conservatoire he became a devoted student of César Franck and later in life returned to the Conservatoire where he taught until his death in 1931. An ardent admirer of Beethoven, d'Indy published a biography about him in 1911 that was translated into English and published as *Beethoven: A Critical Biography*. Boston Music Company, 1913. Writing of the composer he states:

> 'Beethoven, the noble outcome of classic force, who began by writing purely formal symphonic works, before he won the place of a genius in the upward progress of his art, marked out by the works of his third period (1815–1827) a new road, and although he himself did not travel far along it, he left it open for such of his successors as were endowed with a sufficiently robust temperament to force their way along it, knowing also how to avoid the dangers they might encounter.'

D'Indy considered Beethoven had transformed the very concept of sonata form — what he described as 'that admirable basis of all symphonic art which had been accepted by all musicians from the seventeenth century onward by virtue of its harmonious logic'. D'Indy was aware that Hector Berlioz was a passionate admirer of Beethoven but remarked:

> 'It would be difficult to find two artists more completely at the opposite poles of creative thought than the creator of the *Symphonie Fantastique* or *La Damnation de Faust* and the mind which planned the *Missa Solemnis* and the Twelfth Quartet [E-flat major, Op. 127].'

Vincent D' Indy, writing in: *César Franck*, New York: Dover Publications, 1965, pp. 84–5 and p. 87.

CHARLES IVES

The American modernist composer Charles Ives was an admirer of Beethoven and paid homage to him in his mighty Second Piano Sonata that he subtitled *Concord, Massachusetts, 1840–1860*. In this he quotes the opening notes of the Fifth Symphony as well as making quotations from *the Hammerklavier* Piano Sonata, Op. 106. He compared Beethoven's capacity for introspection with that of his fellow countryman, the essayist, poet and philosopher Henry Thoreau:

> 'Thoreau was a great musician ... The rhythm of his prose, were there nothing else, would determine his value as a composer. He was divinely conscious of the enthusiasm of Nature, the

> emotion of her rhythms and the harmony of her solitude ... In their greatest moments the inspiration of both Beethoven and Thoreau express profound truth and deep sentiment, but the intimate passion of it, the storm and stress of it, affected Beethoven in such a way that he could not but be forever showing it and Thoreau that he could not easily expose it.'

Henry Cowell, *Charles Ives and his Music*, New York: Oxford University Press, 1955, p. 84.

Ives wrote an extended article titled *Essays Before a Sonata* (1920). In this he takes as his subjects Beethoven and Richard Strauss. He elevates Beethoven for being a 'dreamer', and relegates Strauss for being a 'rememberer':

> 'A man may aim as high as Beethoven, or as high as Richard Strauss. In the former case this shot may go far below the mark; in truth, it has not been reached since that "thunderstorm" in 1827 [a reference to the occasion of Beethoven's death when a storm broke out], and there is little chance that it will be reached by anyone living today, but that matters not; the shot will never rebound and destroy the marksman ... This choice tells why Beethoven is always modern and Strauss always medieval — try as he may to cover it up in new bottles.'

Sam Morgenstern. *Composers on Music: An anthology of composers' writings*, London: Faber & Faber, 1956, p.394.

*

OTTO JAHN

The German philologist and writer on art and music is today perhaps best remembered for his pioneering biography of Mozart, an English translation of which was published in 1882. In this Jahn makes passing references to Beethoven and his estimation of him:

> 'There can be no doubt that Beethoven has struck chords in the human mind which none before him had touched — that he employs the means at his command with a power and energy of expression unheard before; that by him — the true son of his time — the strife of passions and the struggle for individual freedom are more powerfully and unhesitatingly expressed than by any of his predecessors.'

Otto Jahn, *Life of Mozart*, London: Novello, Ewer & Co., 1882, Vol. 3, pp. 40–1.

LEOŠ JANÁČEK

According to Janáček's biographer Zdenka Fischmann, the Czech composer was averse to being compared with his contemporaries, notably his older compatriot Smetana but including also such others as Debussy. In his defence, he declared:

> 'It is necessary (unfortunately) to grant a creative person the right to be unjust [critical] — without such an unjust attitude, an artist sometimes would be unable to create.'

More generally, Fischmann comments:

'[Janáček] disliked "old" counterpoint in general and during the Beethoven Centennial [1927] had the courage to write that he just did not care for Beethoven; neither did he care for Strauss or Mahler.'

Zdenka E. Fischmann, *Janáček — Newmarch Correspondence*, First limited and numbered edition, Rockville, MD: Kabel Publishers, 1986, p. 29.

JOSEPH JOACHIM

The Hungarian violinist, conductor and composer Joseph Joachim showed a remarkable gift for the violin. At the age of twelve he performed Beethoven's Violin Concerto under the direction of Felix Mendelssohn — for which he supplied his own cadenzas. He later collaborated with Johannes Brahms in the working out of the violin part of his Concerto. Writing on 17 April 1853 to the German composer and musicologist Woldemar Bargiel, half brother to Clara Schumann, Joachim gave expression to his views on music in relation to Beethoven:

'Music is the purest expression of feeling, only that which is superficial, unnatural or self-conscious is foreign to it ... Beethoven is the eternal example of this. He, more than any other, has a deep understanding of the human soul. He is the Shakespeare of music ... His themes are his only friends throughout his whole spiritual life: they accompany him everywhere as his intimates, and they inevitably bear the stamp of his rich and sensitive nature. Hence the variety

and vitality of the forms which entrance us in his
modulations, which ring in our ears like sounds
heard long ago.'

Later (March 1857), Joachim had occasion to write to Gisela
von Arnim, the German writer of fairy tales — she was the
daughter-in-law of Wilhelm Grimm (younger of the celebrated Brothers Grimm). In his letter he expresses his
dislike of Franz Liszt and then takes issue with a publisher
for not bringing out his transcriptions, for violin, of some of
Schubert's compositions [not identified]. He then vents his
spleen on the Russian biographer Alex Oulibicheff. He had
published a well-received study of Mozart but his subsequent
biography of Beethoven clearly upset Joachim and stirred
him to express his own views regarding the composer:

'I have read Oulibicheff's book on Beethoven. It
contains many a shred and useful attack on
Beethoven's spurious imitators, and on the arrogant commentators who put their own vain
constructions on that sublime and sacred life; but
the Russian has no understanding for Beethoven's
greatness, for the divine and ardent resignations
which distinguished the proud, lonely victim
through all his anguish, and which made of him
the most touching martyr Providence has ever sent
for the purification of the human race.'

Cited in, Nora Bickley, editor: *Letters from and to Joseph
Joachim*, London: Macmillan, 1914, p.19, and p.143.

During the London concert season of 1852, Joachim gave
a number of recitals that provided him with insights into the
state of musical taste then prevailing within the capitol. His

experience appears to have been somewhat bleak as he complained in a letter he wrote to Franz Liszt on 27 May:

> '[I] was playing here [London] for the first time, and it was Schubert's Quartet [*Death and the Maiden*], which was still unknown here. It made no impression; people consider that, as Schubert was a novice in instrumental composition, they can dispose of the subject by expressing polite doubt as to his talent for that branch ... Beethoven has long been established here, so that Op. 1 and the Ninth Symphony both produce an equally great effect! I feel so helpless here, having the desire but not the means to fight against such preposterous conditions!'

Hans Gal, *The Musician's World: Great composers in their letters.* London: Thames and Hudson, 1965, p. 215.

Clara Schuman was on familiar terms with Joachim and valued his opinion of her playing. Writing to him on 21 August 1857 she remarks:

> 'I am very angry with you about one thing: you listened to my (i.e. Beethoven's) *Pastoral Sonata*, disliked my reading, and said nothing about it to me, for fear I should be offended!'

Later in the letter she adds: 'Johannes [Brahms] has told me all his thoughts about the *Pastoral Sonata*, and now I play it differently.'

On another occasion, Clara wrote to Joachim: 'Nothing can teach me more than your comments, nothing can so stimulate me.'

She concludes her letter:

> 'Lately, I have been studying [Beethoven's] Sonatas Op. 109 and Op. 110, for the first time, with much enjoyment. The A-flat major, which used to seem to me chaotic in places, has now become clear.'

Berthold Litzmann, editor: *Clara Schumann: An artist's life, based on material found in diaries and letters*, London: Macmillan; Leipzig: Breitkopf & Härtel, 1913, Vol. II, pp. 150–1 *et. Seq.*

KARL AUGUST KAHLERT

In May 1864, the German historian and aesthetician Karl August Kahlert contributed an influential essay to the magazine *Allgemeine musikalische Zeitung* ('General music newspaper') — which was founded at about the same time that Beethoven was becoming established in Vienna (1798). Kahlert's article is recognized for being among the first to define classicism and romanticism, in music, in terms that are generally accepted today. The essay contains the following passage:

> 'Beethoven's music is tense with expectation; so much is pregnant with significance; magnificent themes emerge like beautiful chords, the sheer luxuriance of sound, the very melodic ideas which would have been condemned as boring in a previous age all proved to be just right at that time when people were plumbing the depths of nature's profoundest secrets. Interest in the miraculous supplanted a previous concern to

achieve a balance between intellect and emotion.
Yet a third romantic element manifested itself in
Beethoven's music: humour.'

Karl August Kahlert, In: Peter Le Hurray and James Day, editors: *Music and Aesthetics in the Eighteenth and Early-Nineteenth Centuries*, Cambridge: Cambridge University Press, 1988, p. 560.

EMANUEL KANT

From about 1800, Beethoven began to make use of bound sketchbooks in which to preserve his musical thoughts — before then he had recourse to single leaves. Later in life he kept a *Tagebuch* — a form of diary or daily journal. Occasionally, he imparted to these 'personal communings' by way of self-exhortation — to embolden himself, as it were, to make progress with his art or to identify himself with a particular cause or philosophical outlook. With the latter in mind, the American musicologists Scott Burnham and Michael Steinberg draw attention to the influence of the writings of the German philosopher Emanuel Kant on Beethoven's own philosophical outlook. Kant, they recall, argued 'the universe has divine purpose, wisdom, and reason behind it: that, in fact, are the very order and beauty of the world ... are the result of natural laws and also prove the existence of God'. Burnham and Steinberg argue that Beethoven embraced the spirit of these beliefs as is implicit in the extract from Kant's writings that he copied into his *Tagebuch* (entry 105), which reads:

> 'When in the state of the world order and beauty
> shine forth, there is a God. But the other is not
> less well founded. When this order has been able

> to flow from universal laws of Nature, so the whole
> of Nature is inevitably of the highest wisdom.'

G. Burnham Scott and Michael P. Steinberg, editors: *Beethoven and his World*, Princeton, New Jersey; Oxford: Princeton University Press, 2000, p. 82.

WILLIAM KINDERMAN

The American pianist and musicologist cites the British philosopher Isaiah Berlin's writings on early Romantic aesthetics together with his own reference to Beethoven:

> 'All creation is in some sense creation out of
> nothing. It is the only fully autonomous activity of
> man. It is self-liberation from causal laws, the
> mechanism of the external world, from tyrants, or
> environmental influences, or the passions, which
> govern me — factors in relation to which I am as
> much an object in nature as trees, or stones, or
> animals [Isaiah Berlin].'

Kinderman adds:

> 'Beethoven, a pivotal figure in this reassessment
> of artistic creation as original, autonomous activ-
> ity, left an incomparable documentary record of
> the process itself, in the form of thousands of
> pages of sketches and drafts for his musical works.'

William Kinderman, *Contrast and Continuity in Beethoven's Creative Process*. In: Scott G. Burnham and Michael P. Steinberg, editors: *Beethoven and his World*. Princeton, New Jersey; Oxford: Princeton University Press, 2000. p. 193.

Kinderman also gives expression to his views about Beethoven in the following: William Kinderman, *Beethoven*, Oxford: Oxford University Press, 1997; William Kinderman, *Beethoven's Diabelli Variations*, Oxford: Clarendon Press; New York: Oxford University Press, 1987; and William Kinderman editor: *The String Quartets of Beethoven*, Urbana, Ilinois: University of Illinois Press, 2005.

OTTO KLEMPERER

As a young man the widely acclaimed German-born conductor Otto Klemperer studied piano in Berlin with the intention of becoming a concert pianist. When age twenty he gave a performance of the *Hammerklavier* Sonata that his fellow student Ilse Fromm praised for what she described as Klemperer's 'sense of musical equilibrium'. In 1905, Klemperer entered the Anton Rubinstein piano competition held that year in Paris. The winner was the twenty-one year old Wilhelm Backhaus but opinions amongst the judges were apparently divided. A month later Klemperer entered for the coveted Mendelssohn Prize in Berlin, then the foremost music competition in Germany. On that occasion he was commended by a jury, which included the violinist Joseph Joachim — again for his performance of the *Hammerklavier* Sonata. Although this mighty work was judged to be in keeping with Klemperer's own physical stature — he was 1.96m. tall (six feet five inches), a later meeting with Gustav Mahler determined the young Klemperer's career as an orchestral conductor.

Peter Heyworth, *Otto Klemperer, His Life and Times*, 1983–1996, 2 Vols., derived from Vol. 1, pp. 16–17.

In the 1950s and 1960s Klemperer recorded many of Beethoven's orchestral works including entire cycles of the symphonies, pianos concertos (with Arrau and Barenboim),

Fidelio and the *Missa Solemnis*. In recognition of his international standing as an interpreter of Beethoven, in 1969 he was invited to participate in a Sudwest-deutscher Rundfunk radio programme that was intended to be broadcast in 1970, as part of the Beethoven Centenary celebrations, under the heading: 'Why do we still play Beethoven today?' Klemperer responded to the invitation in terms of heavy irony:

> 'I have thought a great deal about your question "Why do we still play Beethoven today?" Try as I may, I cannot think of an answer. Should I say: "Because of the unique music?" Surely everyone knows that. Or: "Because of the guaranteed box-office success?" That is also all too obvious. In other words, I really cannot think of an answer, and must therefore regretfully decline to take part in this inquiry.'

Martin Anderson, editor: *Klemperer on Music: Shavings from a musician's workbench*, London: Toccata Press, 1986, p. 101.

ZOLTÁN KODÁLY

In 1952 Kodály was invited to give the Opening Address at the Gala Concert of the Hungarian Academy of Music, in celebration of the 125th anniversary of Beethoven's death. He opened with a proposition:

> 'If I were to ask, "What have we got to do with Beethoven?" the majority of you present would be scandalised by the question. What, indeed? The same as we have to do with Shakespeare, Goethe, Michelangelo, and every other great figure in European culture. We have been part

> of this for a thousand years now. For this reason Beethoven's music is also the indispensable nourishment for, and an inseparable part of innumerable Hungarian lives.'

Kodály, however, recognised that many of his countrymen were still inclined to ask, "What is Beethoven to me?" and to believe "A good gipsy [melody] is worth more than any classic music." He wished to elevate the level of musical appreciation for all so that Beethoven would not remain:

> 'the property of the privileged [and] of the minority, if we do not want the millions to be further excluded from his life-giving, elevating, joyous influence'.

Kodály resolutely believed:

> '[There] is no other composer whose whole life-work is such a powerful expression of protest against tyranny, or of world freedom, and of the desire for brotherhood.'

Mindful of the Hungarian Academy's role in musical pedagogy, Kodály concluded his address:

> 'It is not enough merely to place Beethoven before the masses. It is also necessary to teach them how to approach him. It is the right of every citizen to be taught the basic elements of music, to be handed the key with which he can enter the locked world of music. To open the ear and heart of the millions to serious music is a great thing.'

Ferenc Bonis, editor: *The Selected Writings of Zoltán Kodály*, London; New York: Boosey & Hawkes, 1974, p. 76.

NIKOLAI RIMSKY-KORSAKOV

The Russian composer Rimsky-Korsakov was a member of the so-called Mighty Handful of the New Russian School of composers who were prominent in the late nineteenth century; others in the group included Balakirev, Borodin and Mussorgsky. Rimsky's friend and associate V.V. Yastrebtsev was in regular contact with him during the last years of his life and kept a record, in diary form, of his meetings with the composer and his circle of friends. An entry for 19 January 1897 reveals Rimsky's estimation of Beethoven:

> 'You can't imagine how I envy Beethoven that he could say to his friend Stephan Breuning, a few hours before he died, "I did have talent, didn't I." These days, I'm coming more and more to love the classics: Bach, Beethoven, Haydn, and the others, whose music is still so fresh and full of life.'

Rimsky continued:

> 'You may not believe this but Beethoven had such inexhaustible resources when it came to form and modulation that, in this regard, alongside of him all other composers are pygmies.'

An anecdote of a more general nature derives from a conversation amongst a circle of friends one afternoon on 23 March 1898. The key figure in the group was Rimsky-Korsakov; others included an art critic, a composer and a singer. The subject of Eduard Hanslick's theories of music-aesthetics came up in conversation; Hanslick had propounded these in his pioneering treatise on *The Beautiful in Music* (1854). Rimsky-Korsakov's biographer relates that after tea the attention of the group turned to the subject of programme music and Hanslick's contention that 'music is a tonal form, a tonal arabesque devoid of spiritual and extra-musical content', in support of which Beethoven's *Les Adieux* Piano Sonata came under scrutiny. The circle of friends was not disposed to agree with Hanslick, but their conversation reveals the extent to which the Op. 81a Piano Sonata was by then familiar to the intellectually-minded group and also indicates how pervasive was the influence of Hanslick's music theories.

V.V. Yastrebtsev, edited and translated by Florence Jonas, *Reminiscences of Rimsky-Korsakov*, New York: Columbia University Press, 1985, p. 32 and pp. 173–4.

Later in life Rimsky-Korsakov taught orchestration at the St. Petersburg Conservatory. Sergey Prokofiev was one of his students in the years 1902–3. He was fifteen at the time and recalls how Rimsky's classes could last for four hours. His assignment was to orchestrate passages of Beethoven sonatas and Schubert quartets, which were then criticised and corrected. Prokofiev clearly appreciated these classes that he describes as being 'unforgettable'.

Igor Stravinsky, *An Autobiography*, London: Calder and Boyars, 1975, p. 21 and Igor Stravinsky, and Robert Craft, *Memories and Commentaries*. London: Faber and Faber, 2002, p. 39.

Ernst Ludwig Kossak

On the occasion of the death of Felix Mendelssohn, at the untimely age of 38, the German writer and journalist Ernst

Ludwig Kossak wrote his obituary notice. In this he acknowledged Mendelssohn's gifts but considered they fell short of Beethoven's:

> '[Mendelssohn] possessed an uncommonly high conception of the essence of music and made it his life's aim to obtain the goal that floated before Beethoven as the musical artists' ideal. Nature does not, however, give anyone everything; she imparted to the soul of the deceased that addiction to reflection, arising perhaps from the modesty and inner humility that is only characteristic of great spirits, which he felt about his compositions coming so soon after the incomparable works of Beethoven.'

Ernst Ludwig Kossak, *Neue Berliner Musikzeitung*, 10 November 1847.

PAUL HENRY LANG

The Hungarian-American musicologist and music critic considers Beethoven's originality:

> 'Beethoven was the first among the great masters to divorce the creative from the performing artist, the first to whom composing was a bitterly relentless affair, "perhaps the only language of his soul," as [Adolph Bernhard] Marx says in his early biography. And the Beethoven of his last period attains to that degree of universality in which tendencies and forms lose their significance, melting into a vision that encompasses all that is human. Those who in the early nineteenth

century heard his agitated and yearning themes, who were struck by the irresistible propulsive force of the allegros, the majesty of the adagios, the menacing humour of the scherzos, and the wild rhythms of the finales, recognized that this music, compared to that of his predecessors, is somewhat raw, gnarled, even unfinished. There were some who were repelled, among them such able composers as Spohr and Weber; but many more, despite or perhaps because of these qualities, found Beethoven's music to be warmer, more intense, and more fulfilling that any other they had known.'

Lang considers Beethoven in the context of the emerging school of Romanticism:

'The new movement could not defend itself against Beethoven's invincible art; all its instincts of self-preservation ceased when confronted with him, for there was everything in this music that the Romantics desired and valued. "Terrible!" exclaimed the enervated Pope Leo X at the sight of Michelangelo's murals; it is this *terribilità* that the romantics saw in the *Sonata Appassionata* and the Fifth Symphony. But they saw only the means in this music, not its essence; they saw how Beethoven demolished the boundaries but did not see that he demolished only to force the unbounded into severe and logical unity.'

Lang reminds us that Beethoven reaches out in his music with both heart and mind:

'We tend to think that in Beethoven it is exclusively the heart that speaks to us, for we know about his deep interest in freedom and brotherly love, and our predecessors have already proclaimed him the liberator of music, or, as a book popular a generation ago was entitled, *The Man who Freed Music* [Robert Haven, 1929]. Even much earlier he was regarded as the first great composer who in his music withheld nothing of himself, and so was the first true romantic. And yet the voice of the intellect is never absent in Beethoven, even when he is rebellious, because he immediately proceeds to rebuild what he demolishes; he does not deny, he only contradicts. It was romantic anti-intellectualism in the arts that created the fashion of banishing from music logic of construction and procedure as inimical to poetry, thus creating the greatest impediment to true appreciation of Beethoven.'

Lang reflects on Beethoven's working method:

'Looking at the famous sketchbooks, one's first impression is that they are haphazard and sporadic; we also see that while Beethoven's imagination and inventiveness are inexhaustible he often struggles with his material, notably with his themes, and there is constant and ever-growing need to set things right, "order from disorder sprung". The approach is always analytical and synthetic; he raises questions and then answers them, often years later. He neither gives way to the impatience that characterizes the romantic, nor allows his expression to fail for want of craftsmanship. It seems as if the germ of every idea has been there in his soul from the beginning, growing slowly as Beethoven returns again and again, attempting to prune it down or extend it to the shape he desired. Indeed, the sketchbooks disclose the triumph of the *ars combinatoria* of old, or as [Wilhelm von] Lenz so engagingly says about the *Waldstein* Sonata: "In the development section Beethoven makes a nest from torn feathers".'

Lang concludes:

'The world needs rebels in order to be able to move and preserve its rhythm. Beethoven does not represent the highest heroism precisely because the revolutionary character of his music is kept powerfully within bounds; the mind of the classically schooled craftsman is always in command, ordering and organizing.'

Paul Henry Lang, *Musicology and Performance*, New Haven: Yale University Press, 1997, pp. 89–90, p. 93 and p. 98. Originally published in *The Creative World of Beethoven*, New York: W.W. Norton, 1971.

RAYMOND LEPPARD

In 1992 the composer Mark Grant interviewed the English conductor and harpsichordist Raymond Leppard. He asked him:

'Do you think what makes greatness in a composer is the ability of his or her music to withstand the greatest number of differing interpretations?'

Leppard responded:

> 'I think what matters is what we conceive of as being great now. Nevertheless, it certainly is true that someone like Beethoven has survived since ... he seems to have been such a towering person mentally that whatever he said in music, whatever the vitality he put into his music, has seemed apposite to every generation ever since, for 200 years now. And that's — I mean — I think that's jolly good. I wouldn't say it's more than that, but it is rather wonderful.'

Of Beethoven and his achievements he adds:

> 'He was a towering mind it served as an example, sometimes even as a threat to most composers who came after him in the nineteenth century, just as Shakespeare did to his successors. But at this distance and at this very point in time it seems important to stress that he was not, some would have us believe, writers and performers alike, the inventor of Brahms who, fifty years later, composed in a completely different style; nor was he the bedfellow of Mendelssohn, Schubert, Weber or Schuman and certainly not the musical progenitor of Siegfried, whose author claimed that he was.'

Leppard continues:

> 'Beethoven's compositions have never left the music scene and each generation, as with Shakespeare, has interpreted them differently. Lately

he was seen as a sort of musical Zeus on an Olympian high altar before which all must kneel respectfully and slowly. Now we are coming to see his genius through the eyes of his own time finding him no less wonderful, no less Olympian but dressed differently, revealing his greatness from within the musical style he inherited and made his own ... The middle years show this most clearly. It was a time of great achievement.'

Raymond Leppard, *On Music: An anthology of critical and personal writings*, Thomas P. Lewis, editor, White Plains, N.Y.: Pro/Am Music Resources, 1993, p. 367 and pp. 282–5.

FRANZ LISZT

As an interpreter of Beethoven's piano music, Franz Liszt may be regarded as being a direct descendant of the composer. He had been a pupil of Carl Czerny, who, in turn, as we have remarked (see above), learned Beethoven's pianos sonatas directly from the master. We know from Liszt's father, Adam, that his son begged him to be taught the piano from an early age and how he subsequently made astonishing progress. It is to Adam's credit that he taught his son how to read musical notation, to sight-read and to improvise. He also introduced the young Franz to a wide range of keyboard repertoire that included the works of Bach, Hummel and early Beethoven. Liszt soon became so proficient as to perform in public, revealing a special affinity for Beethoven. Liszt's biographer relates:

'Whenever Liszt was asked as a boy what he wanted to be when he grew up, he pointed to the wall where a portrait of Beethoven was hanging

[and remarked]:
"Ein solcher" – "Like him".'

Alan Walker, *Franz Liszt, The virtuoso years: 1811–1847*, New York: Alfred A. Knopf, 1983, Vol. 1, pp. 59–60.

On 2 October 1839, Liszt wrote to Hector Berlioz. He was staying in Rome at the time and was deeply affected by the artistic legacy he found all around him. He enthused:

> 'The Colosseum and the Campo Santo [Teutonic Cemetery (Italian: *Cimitero Teutonico*) – the burial site adjacent to St. Peter's Basilica] seem more familiar when one thinks of the *Eroica* Symphony and [Mozart's] *Requiem*.'

More generally he mused:

> 'Art showed itself to me in the full range of its splendour; revealed itself in all its unity and universality. With every day that passed, feeling and reflection brought me to a still greater awareness of the secret link between works of genius. Raphael and Michelangelo enabled me better to understand Mozart and Beethoven.'

A visit to the Sistine Chapel appears to have been particularly moving to Liszt. Years later he wrote about this to the Grand Duke Carl Alexander, Rome. Liszt was aware of the tradition that tells how the fourteen-year old Mozart had committed Gregorio Allegri's setting of the *Miserere* to memory – his subsequent transcription earning him praise from the Pope himself (Clement XIV). These recollections disposed Liszt to cite works of Beethoven:

> 'It was on Allegri's mode, and on the same interval — a stubborn dominant — that Beethoven's genius thrice alighted, to leave thereon, and everlastingly, its immortal imprint. Listen to the *Funeral March* on the Death of a Hero [Piano Sonata, Op. 26 — third movement], the *Adagio* of the *Sonata quasi Fantasia* [Op. 27, No. 2], and the mysterious banquet of phantoms and angels in the *Andante* of the Seventh Symphony. Is there not a striking analogy between these three motifs and Allegri's *Miserere*?'

Adrian Williams, *Portrait of Liszt: By himself and his contemporaries*, Oxford: Clarendon Press, 1990, p. 112 and pp. 387–388.

The reverence Liszt felt towards Beethoven is evident in a letter he wrote in 1852 to the composer's early biographer Wilhelm von Lenz. It was Lenz who first proposed, in his *Beethoven et ses trois styles* (1855), that the composer's music could be sub-divided musicologically and chronologically into three distinct periods. Resorting to Biblical imagery Liszt wrote:

> 'To us musicians the work of Beethoven parallels the pillars of smoke and fire which led the Israelites through the desert, a pillar of smoke to lead us by day, and a pillar of fire to light the night, so that we may march ahead both day and night. His darkness and his light equally trace for us the road we must follow; both the one and the other are a perpetual commandment, an infallible revelation.'

John L. Holmes, *Composers on Composers*, New York: Greenwood Press, 1990, p. 14. Also quoted in: George R. Marek, *Beethoven: Biography of a Genius*, New York: Funk & Wagnalls, 1969, p. 638 and Adrian Williams, editor and translator: *Franz Liszt: Selected Letters*, Oxford: Clarendon Press, 1998, p. 335.

It was Liszt's championing of Beethoven's piano sonatas, especially in his early years as a concert pianist, which did much to raise them from their relative neglect and to place them at the forefront of the pianists' repertoire. We learn something of this from Liszt's own recollections. In 1876 he wrote of the period, from about 1821, when he commenced his studies with Carl Czerny. Liszt, like Czerny, was ten years old when he began his studies although even by then his remarkable powers were much in evidence — in fact Czerny complained that Liszt had learned too much too soon. Liszt tells us:

> 'Many of Beethoven's sonatas were known and profoundly admired, especially the *Pathétique*, *Moonlight* and *Appassionata*, but it wasn't the custom to play them in public. Not until after Beethoven's death did his works circulate everywhere.'

As recalled in: William S. Newman, *The Sonata in the Classic Era*, Chapel Hill: University of North Carolina Press 1963, pp. 528–9.

A measure of the aloofness, if not downright hostility, to Beethoven's later piano music is conveyed in an account from the writings of Beethoven's early biographer Wilhelm von Lenz. He has this to say of his experience of the reception of the composer's late piano sonatas when Liszt was performing them in Paris in the 1820s:

> 'The last five [Opp. 101, 106, 109, 110 and 111] passed for the monstrous abortions of a German idealist who did not know how to write for the piano. People only understood Hummel & Co.'

Derived from: Harold C. Schonberg, *The Great Pianists*, London: Victor Gollancz, 1964, p. 92.

A further indication of the time it took for Beethoven's late piano music to reach the ears of even the musically informed, can be inferred from a diary entry of Giacomo Meyerbeer dating from 1862. He writes:

> 'With Cornelie [a friend] to Hans von Bülow's concert which was devoted to piano music [including] Beethoven's Sonata in A major, Op. 101 which I had never heard before, a gifted glorious work, particularly the first elegiac movement and the third or fourth, which is a fugue.'

In passing, we may observe that Hans von Bülow, now largely remembered as a conductor, was, together with Franz Liszt, a pioneer in promoting the awareness of Beethoven's late piano sonatas to the wider public in the nineteenth century.

Robert Ignatius Letellier, editor and translator: *The Diaries of Giacomo Meyerbeer*, Madison: Fairleigh Dickinson University Press; London: Associated University Presses, 4 Vols., 1999–2004, Vol. 4, p. 245.

*

In the autumn of 1839 Liszt gave a series of recitals in Vienna — he was twenty-eight at the time. Writing in the *Allgemeine Theaterzeitung* (30 November), the theatre and music critic Heinrch Adamai described Liszt's reception in the following terms:

> 'The enthusiasm which this great virtuoso is exciting in Vienna cannot be described ... No sooner is one of his concerts over than everyone is already longing for the next ... Not since Paganini has an artist made such a magical impression on the Viennese public.'

On 2 December, Liszt gave his third recital that included a performance of the *Appassionata* Sonata. Of this, Adamai wrote in the *Allgemeine Theaterzeitung* (4 December):

> 'Liszt began with the F minor Sonata of Beethoven [Op. 57]. The one which when played by Clara Schumann (see below) had given rise to such vehement debate in our newspapers ... For younger listeners in particular, who never had the opportunity of hearing Beethoven himself in his piano sonatas and concertos, Liszt's renderings are of exceptional interest, and from them are best able to study these works, often capable of so multifarious an interpretation, and to form a correct view for themselves.'

Liszt further demonstrated his remarkable powers on 5 December when he gave his fourth recital in Vienna's *Redoutensaal* — the 'fancy-dress' ballroom where Beethoven's Eighth Symphony was premiered. Liszt was billed to perform the composer's C minor Piano Concerto that was not then known to him. Despite feeling unwell, he learned the work and committed it to memory in a single day.

Adrian Williams, *Portrait of Liszt: By himself and his contemporaries*, Oxford: Clarendon Press, 1990, p. 115. An illustration of the interior of the *Redoutensaal*, where Beethoven had supplied music for the Charity Ball of 1795, is depicted in H. C. Robbins Landon, *Beethoven: A documentary study*, London: Thames and Hudson, 1970, p. 50, plate 33.

In his correspondence with the French writer George Sand, Liszt reveals how, in his youth, he would occasionally deceive an audience by passing off one of his own compositions as being by Beethoven. One such instance took place at a gathering of musical amateurs in Bordeaux in 1826 — Liszt was then fourteen years old. He played one of his own sonatas, telling them that it was by Beethoven. Liszt recalls how the assembly found the work to be "sublime". In Liszt's own words:

> 'I would play the same piece, presenting it at various times as one written by Beethoven, or by Czerny, or by myself ... At those times when I played it under Czerny's name, no one listened to me. But when I played it as a work of Beethoven, I could inevitably count on bravos from the entire hall.'

Franz Liszt, *An Artist's Journey. Lettres d'un bachelier dès musique, 1835–1841*, Chicago: University of Chicago Press, 1989.

Apart from revealing the prankish humour evident in Liszt's youthful personality, his anecdote illustrates how little known were Beethoven compositions, at the period in question, enabling the youthful prodigy to so deceive his audiences. In a letter to Dionys Pruckner, one of Liszt's piano pupils, Liszt recalled the piano playing of his teacher Carl Czerny. His brief observation casts light on Czerny's contribution to the promotion of Beethoven's works for piano:

> 'In the [eighteen] twenties, when a great portion of Beethoven's creations was a kind of Sphinx [the enigmatic Sphinx was at that period still largely shrouded in sand], Czerny was playing Beethoven *exclusively*, with an understanding as *excellent* as his technique was efficient and effective; and, later on, he did not set himself up against some progress that had been made in technique, but contributed materially to it by his own teaching and works.'

La Mara [pseudonym], *Letters of Franz Liszt*, London: H. Grevel & Co., 2 Vols. 1894. Derived from Vol. 1, p. 266.

Several anecdotes connect Franz Liszt with Beethoven's C-sharp minor Piano Sonata, Op. 27, No. 2 the *Moonlight*. By all accounts Liszt, ever the dazzling virtuoso and lion of the keyboard, was willing to condone the occasional taking of liberties with Beethoven's music — at least in his early years as a travelling virtuoso. For example, sometime around 1830 he gave a performance of the Op. 27, No. 2 Piano Sonata to which he added 'trills and tremolos and *impassioned chords* to the first movement'. On another occasion he combined the first movement of the Op. 26 Sonata, which he played on the organ, with that of the final movement of the *Moonlight* that he played on the piano.

*

Derived from Alain Frogley in: Glen Stanley, editor, *The Cambridge Companion to Beethoven*, Cambridge; New York: Cambridge University Press, 2000, p. 24.

At a concert in Paris, in 1835, the first movement of the Op. 27, No. 2 Piano Sonata was performed in an arrangement for orchestra that Liszt then completed unaccompanied on the piano. The occasion was considered so memorable it was later depicted in various paintings and lithographs.

As recalled by, William S. Newman, *The Sonata in the Classic Era*, Chapel Hill: University of North Carolina Press 1963, p. 518.

As Liszt's career as a virtuoso pianist progressed, so did his theatricality. Henry Reeve attended a recital given by Liszt when he was on a concert tour in Scotland in 1841; he performed in Glasgow and in Edinburgh's fashionable Assembly Rooms. Reeve was Editor of the *Edinburgh Review*, an intellectually inclined journal established in 1802 by men-of-letters — 'to gather all the rays of culture into one' (the Journal's motto). Reeve's account of the Concert records the hall being very full and Liszt's person as being 'slight and tall, a delicate frame ... perpetually strained by the flow of animated thoughts'. Liszt played a *Fantasia* of his own followed by Beethoven's C-sharp minor Piano Sonata. On completion of the Beethoven, Reeve took the platform, grasped Liszt's hand and 'thanked him for the divine energy that he had shed forth'. As the concert continued, as a consequence of the emotional stresses Liszt was suffering at the time — 'he fainted at the keyboard and had to be escorted from the hall'.

As recalled by, Adrian Williams, *Portrait of Liszt: By himself and his contemporaries*, Oxford: Clarendon Press, 1990. Details of Liszt's concert tour in Scotland are described in, *Liszt Society Journal* 13 (1988) pp. 65–9. Liszt fainting at the keyboard is worthy of the Hollywood biographical film-romance *Song Without End: The Story of Franz Liszt*, in which the matinee idol Dirk Bogarde portrayed the celebrated pianist-composer.

The French dramatist Ernest Legouvé has left an account of the emotional effect Liszt's playing could have on individuals. The occasion in question was a private soiree attended by a small, but highly select, audience of connoisseurs. Legouvé describes how Liszt took his place at the piano and, as he puts it, 'began the funereal and heart-rending *Adagio* of the Sonata in C-sharp minor'. He himself was seated in an armchair and was disturbed by 'stifled sobs and moans'. He turned to look, only to see they came from non other than Hector Berlioz.

As recalled in: Alan Walker, *Franz Liszt, Volume 1, The Virtuoso Years: 1811-1847*, New York: Alfred A. Knopf, 1983, p. 182.

Incompetent playing by his pupils could upset Liszt's equanimity and he was given to describing wrong notes as 'uninvited guests'. His biographer Alan Walker relates: 'It was mainly in the defence of Beethoven and Bach that he would display the greatest aggression.' A case in point occurred at a lesson in June 1882 — Liszt was then in his seventies. A young man had brought along a copy of the *Waldstein* Piano Sonata, Op. 53. Despite having received lessons from the distinguished pedagogue Theodor Kullak (himself a pupil of Liszt), he was inadequately prepared. His stumbling through the piece prompted Liszt to correct him at such frequent intervals that he finally flew into a rage, scattered the music and exclaimed:

'I do not take in washing here — do your washing at home!'

On another occasion the interpretation of a pupil who had just started to learn the *Waldstein* Piano Sonata also upset him; the young man's rhythm must have been all of a piece, prompting Liszt to exclaim:

'Do not chop beefsteak for us!'

Alan Walker, *Franz Liszt, The Final Years, 1861–1886*, London: Faber and Faber, 1997, Volume 3, pp. 246–7.

Franz Liszt is usually accorded the honour of giving the first public performance of the Op. 106 Sonata in two recitals that he performed in 1836 at the Salle Érard in Paris. There are many references to the early performances of the *Hammerklavier* Sonata by Franz Liszt; see for example; Edwin Fischer, 1959, p. 103 and Brian Rees, 1999, p. 29. Liszt himself tells us how he discovered the *Hammerklavier* Sonata at the unbelievably early age of ten. It is more probable that he *played with* the Sonata rather than having *performed* it, nevertheless for a mere child to have the maturity of outlook to engage with such a work is remarkable. Of this, Liszt says:

'My father [his first teacher] wasn't up to it and Czerny [his subsequent teacher] was afraid to put me on such a diet.'

Adrian Williams, editor and translator, *Franz Liszt: Selected Letters*, Oxford: Clarendon Press, 1998, p. 807.

A possible rival claimant to being the first to play the *Hammerklavier* Sonata, in public, is the Franco-Polish pianist Henri Mortier de Fontaine. History has now neglected him, but he is described in Grove's *A Dictionary of Music and Musicians* (1900) as being 'possessed of unusual technical ability'. De Fontaine was born in Warsaw in 1816. If we assume he performed the *Hammerklavier* Piano Sonata sometime, say, in the early 1830s, he must still have been only in his late teens.

Alan Tyson, *The Authentic English Editions of Beethoven*, London: Faber and Faber, 1963, p. 105. The reader is also referred to the website text *Henri Mortier de Fontaine* for an account of this remarkable artist's life and work.

An anecdote from the recollections of the American

pianist Amy Fay (1844–1928) connects us with Franz Liszt and the European musical scene of the 1870s. Fay was an accomplished performer who had travelled to Europe to study with Liszt; she also had lessons with two other lions of the keyboard, namely Theodor Kullak and Carl Tausig. On 19 June 1873 she heard a young student from Stuttgart perform the *Appassionata* Sonata for Liszt. Her diary entry reveals the impression the music made upon her — and that of Liszt's interventions:

> '[The student] had a good deal of technique, and a moderately good conception of the work ... It was a hot afternoon, and the clouds had been gathering for a storm. As the Stuggarter played the opening notes, the tree tops suddenly waved wildly, and a low growl of thunder was heard muttering in the distance.'

Fay adds that, with the storm breaking, Liszt remarked with his characteristic alacrity:

'Ah, a fitting accompaniment!'

It appears though that Liszt was not impressed by the student's performance; he interrupted him at intervals and played passages himself, prompting Fay to record in her diary how magnificent was the little he did play and how startling was the individuality of his conception. She was so transported by the experience she later wrote:

'I did not know whether I were in the body or out of the body.'

Amy Fay, *Music-Study in Germany: From the home correspondence of Amy Fay* [1880], New York: Dover Publications (reprint), 1965, pp. 229–30. See also: Adrian Williams, *Portrait of Liszt: By himself and his contemporaries,* Oxford: Clarendon Press, 1990, pp. 496–7.

Reflecting late in life on his relationship with the piano, Liszt remarked:

> 'My piano ... is to me what his frigate is to the sailor, his charger to the Arab; even more perhaps, for my piano has been until now my very self, my words, my life; it is the intimate repository of everything that stirred and tossed within my mind during the most ardent days of my youth; all my desires, dreams, joys, and sorrows were found in it. Its strings have shuddered under my passions, its submissive keys obeyed my every whim ... Perhaps I am deceived by this kind of mysterious feeling which attaches me to the piano, yet I consider its importance very great. It has, it seems to me, the leading place in the hierarchy of instruments. It is the most generally cultivated, the most popular of all; and this importance and this popularity it owes in part to the harmonic power which it alone possesses; and, as a consequence of this power, to the faculty of summarizing and concentrating within itself the whole of the art of music. In the span of seven octaves it embraces the range of an orchestra; and ten fingers of man suffice to render the harmonies produced by the concourse of more than a hundred instruments put together.'

Adrian Williams, *Portrait of Liszt: By himself and his contemporaries*, Oxford: Clarendon Press, 1990, pp. 92–3.

Heitor Villa-Lobos

On 10 June 1959 the Mexican composer Villa Lobos was in America. He was seventy-two at the time and agreed to an interview with the journalist Renatto Bittencourt. In this he reflected on his own music and that of America as he had experience of it. Of the latter he remarked:

> 'Ninety per cent of Americans like light music. The great number of concerts of serious music is explained by the fact that the population of the U.S. is great. But it is always the elite. Art is not of the people ... The distinction must always be made: there is spontaneous music, people-to-people music. Then there is art music, music for the aristocracy. The artist, thus, is forced to become an intellectual. This does not mean that I despise the masses, because it is from the masses that I receive the inspiration for my creations. I greatly appreciate jazz. If I have a choice between listening to a "jam session" or a Beethoven symphony, I will choose the "jam session" every time.'

This remark, though, may have to be taken with some caution since several years earlier, after hearing some jazz, Villa-Lobos had written to a friend:

> 'Alas! Jazz is a kind of accompaniment, now soft, now an orgy of sounds, of futile conversation between people.'

David P. Appleby, *Heitor Villa-Lobos: A bio-bibliography*, New York: Greenwood Press, 1988, p. 170.

*

EDWARD MACDOWELL

Edward MacDowell is primarily remembered today as a composer but he was also a pianist of considerably powers. He studied at the Paris Conservatory and was known to Clara Schuman and Franz Liszt. He once wrote:

> 'Beethoven is the first one who built a poem and brought poetic thoughts to a logical conclusion. His music expresses ideal things, not actual things, as previous music did.'

Notwithstanding this tribute, as MacDowell's biographer records, he also had reservations about Beethoven's music:

> 'Certain outwardly, and popularly regarded, peaks of Beethoven's opus were actually not paramount in MacDowell's mind as to the true genius of the man. The "Ode to Joy" from the Ninth Symphony, for example, MacDowell found "essentially obvious and commonplace, so that nothing could be done with it." The late sonatas and string quartets were "a matter for despair, penetrating to such subtleties and intricacies of the spirit that it was difficult to follow them".'

His biographer continues:

> 'MacDowell did not see this [the preceding remarks] as Beethoven's failure. To some extent the failure lay with limitations among listeners. But mostly it was indicative of how the spirit of genius could range to levels that need not but often do bypass those of others.'

Alan Howard Levy, *Edward MacDowell, An American master*, Lanham, Md. & London: Scarecrow Press, 1998, p. 196.

JOHN B. MCEWAN

Sir John Blackwood McEwen was a Scottish classical composer and educator. He was professor of harmony and composition at the Royal Academy of Music, London, from 1898 to 1924, and Principal from 1924 to 1936. It was probably for reasons of his acknowledged musicological standing that he was invited to contribute to the 'Special Issue' of the *Musical Times* that was published in 1927 to commemorate Beethoven's Death Centenary.

He structures his account along the lines of the so-called 'three periods' into which Beethoven's creative achievements are considered to fall. He wrote:

> 'In the first, which terminates about the thirtieth year of his age, Beethoven is regarded as imitating, more or less consciously, the methods and works of his predecessors. In the second, which lasted until his forty-fifth year, having consolidated his powers and perfected his equipment, he produces a series of works in which, while still conforming, more or less, to the methods of Haydn and Mozart, he adds to and modifies these methods and reaches a style which is really individual and personal. In his last period, however, having exhausted the old methods and idioms, he develops new ways of expression in a series of compositions, which when originally produced, not only appeared strange, bizarre and impracticable, but were regarded by some of his

contemporaries as the product of a mind which had reached decadence.'

McEwan posed the questions:

> 'What then, is the real significance of Beethoven's latest works? How are they to be regarded, both from the point of view of his artistic development and from that of the general progress of his artistic development and from that of the general progress of art?'

In response he remarked:

> 'Naturally, Beethoven's first works, based as they were on the example of his predecessors, approximate to that example both in manner and intention: but even in these first works there are intentions eloquent of a new outlook and objective. With regard to technical processes of composition, Beethoven's attitude was fundamentally different from that of his predecessors, and this difference illustrated both his methods and in the results of these methods. He seems always to have composed with difficulty — not because he was less able to manipulate structure and design than the other musicians, but because he could not regard design as an end in itself. His methods were laborious because he was unable to content himself with the unessential and the insignificant, and the search for the right and final expression of his thought did not proceed too easily. Lacking neither fluency nor facility, wisely he distrusted both.'

John B. McEwan, *The Significance of Beethoven's "Third Period", Music & Letters. Beethoven*: Special Number. London: *Music & Letters*, 1927, pp. 156–62.

GUSTAV MAHLER

During a conversation about Beethoven, Mahler is reported to have said:

> 'In order to understand and appreciate Beethoven fully, we should not only accept him for what he means to us today, but must realize what a tremendous revolutionary advance he represents in comparison with his forerunners. Only when we understand what a difference there is between Mozart's G minor Symphony and the Ninth can we properly evaluate Beethoven's achievement. Of geniuses like Beethoven, of such sublime and most universal kind, there are only two or three among millions. Among poets and composers of more recent times we can, perhaps, name but three: Shakespeare Beethoven and Wagner.'

When on a walk with a friend, Mahler once remarked:

> 'You ask me whether they understand Beethoven today? What an idea! Because they have grown up with his works, because he is "recognized", they listen to him, play him, and perhaps even love him — but not because they are able to follow him in his flight. With their bleary eyes, they will *never* be able to look the sun in the face.'

As a student Gustav Mahler heard Anton Rubinstein perform the complete cycle of Beethoven piano sonatas in Vienna and later in Leipzig and Hamburg. One of these series of concerts was spent in the company of the viola player, and devoted admirer of Mahler, Natalie Bauer-Lechner. She has left this reminiscence of that occasion:

> 'We began to talk about the playing of Beethoven's sonatas. Mahler said that this is particularly difficult because the sonata demands a freer, more improvisational style of performance than that of orchestral works. The latter have a firm structure; they are already held together by the necessary interaction of all the various instruments.'

Concerning Rubinstein's interpretation of Beethoven, Bauer-Lechner adds:

> '[Mahler] called Rubinstein a "man of the Steppes" ... by which he meant to indicate the elemental force, the boundless power and lack of cultivation — in the sense of nature, which needs no cultivation — of that magnificent artist.'

Natalie Bauer-Lechner, *Recollections of Gustav Mahler*, London: Faber Music, 1980, pp. 29–30, p. 149 and p.174.

When she was a mere eight or nine years old Gisella Tolney-Witt — known later in life as the musicologist Gisella Seldon-Goth — wrote to Mahler to ask 'why such a large apparatus as an orchestra should be necessary in order to express a great thought'. Mahler, by his own admission, was reluctant to enter into correspondence, but on this occasion he must have been motivated to respond by the musical insight implicit in the young fräulein's question. Mahler's reply is long, discursive and full of interest. We give a brief outline of its salient points — that eventually lead us to Beethoven. He first invited his young correspondent to think back to earlier times — he cites Bach in particular. Then, he explained, composers left questions of interpretation largely to the performer regarding, for example, determining the tempo of the music. He makes a distinction between the kind of orchestra Haydn required for the performance of his symphonies and the extended forces Beethoven demands in his *Choral* Symphony. Mahler then cites how chamber music, conceived to be played in a small space before a small audience, typically expressing feelings of joy or sadness. He adds:

> 'The musicians were confident that they knew their business, they moved within a familiar field of ideas and on the grounds of clearly delimited skill, well grounded within these limits ... It was taken for granted that everything would be rightly seen, felt and heard.'

Turning to the heart of the question he had been set, Mahler next remarked on the complexity of later music and the corresponding need, on the part of the composer, to give greater care in its presentation to ensure its correct interpretation. He explains:

> 'So a great system of sign-language gradually evolved, which — like the heads of notes indicating pitch — provided a definite reference for duration or volume. Together with this, moreover, came the *appropriation of new elements of*

> *feeling* as objects of imitation in sounds — i.e. the composer began to relate ever deeper and more complex aspects of his emotional life to the area of his creativeness — until with Beethoven the *new era* of music began: from now on the *fundamentals* are no longer mood — that is to say, mere sadness, etc. — but also the transition from one to the other — conflicts — physical nature and its effect on us — humour and poetic ideas — all these become objects of musical imitation.'

Mahler continues by explaining the need to enlarge the orchestra as music became more 'common property', with listeners and players becoming ever more numerous and the recital chamber being replaced by the concert hall.

Gisella wrote to Mahler in February 1893, by which time the composer was at work on his Third Symphony. The next passage in his response to her goes to the very heart of her original question and captures the essence of his own musical agenda:

> 'We moderns need such a great apparatus [orchestra] to express *our* ideas, whether they be great or small. First ... to distribute the various colours of our rainbow over various palettes; secondly, because our eye is learning to distinguish more and more colours of the rainbow ... thirdly, because in order to be heard by many in our over-large concert halls and opera houses we have to make a loud noise!
>
> 'With best wishes, Gustav Mahler.'

Knud Martner, editor, *Selected Letters of Gustav Mahler*, London; Boston: Faber and Faber, 1979, pp. 147–9.

FRANÇOIS MARTIN MAI

The medically trained physician François Martin Mai has made a study of the many illnesses that bore down on Beethoven during his lifetime. Alongside his well-documented deafness he experienced, tormented relationships, isolation, depression and the ineffectual, but well-intended, attempts by the clinicians of the day to seek to alleviate his condition. Some consider the composer's afflictions may have fed his genius and creativity as he resolutely emboldened himself to triumph over adversity. Mai writes:

> 'We can never understand all the reasons for Beethoven's creativity. He came to maturity at a critical time in political and musical history and because of his natural talent he was able to ride the crests of both these waves. In the final analysis, he possessed, probably like all those touched by the highest levels of creativity, an indefinable inner impulse that demanded expression, even in the face of seemingly impassable internal and external barriers. He possessed and expressed to the highest degree that intangible and ineffable quality that humankind shares with its Creator.'

François Martin Mai, *Diagnosing Genius: The life and death of Beethoven*, Montreal; London: McGill-Queen's University Press, 2007, p. 199.

DENIS MATTHEWS

Denis Matthews is remembered today primarily for being a concert pianist with a particular liking for the music of the first Viennese school — notably that of Haydn, Mozart, Beethoven and Schubert. His many writings on music, however, reveal his knowledge of, and affinity for, the keyboard music of their contemporaries such as Hummel and Clementi. Matthews outlined his thoughts about music in his Autobiography *In Pursuit of Music* (1968) and reached a wide audience in his study of Beethoven, published in the *Master Musicians* series (1985). In his role as professor of music at the University of Newcastle (1971–81) Matthews wrote extensively about Beethoven, inspiring a younger generation thereby. Writing of the greatness of Beethoven he remarks:

> 'Beethoven sought, above all, independence: his greatest teacher was to be his own experience. It taught him early on that enduring art must satisfy in opposite, complementary ways. There is the emotional impact of music — "from the heart to the heart" — but there is also the desire to satisfy the mind and to arrange ideas in their most potent form. Call it, if you like, the architectural quality of music. Even the unskilled listener senses when a piece is well made, because the composer's struggle with form forces him to channel and to crystallize his thoughts.'

Denis Matthews, *Beethoven, Piano Sonatas*, London: British Broadcasting Corporation, 1967, p. 11.

Writing of the central importance of Beethoven's piano sonatas in the history of the genre Matthew's writes:

> 'Think for a moment of the variety of [Beethoven's] sonatas and the width of their appeal. Even the most casual of music-lovers has been known to succumb to the strange, veiled

potency of the first movement of the so-called *Moonlight*. Is there a general-practising virtuoso who escapes carrying either the *Waldstein* or *Appassionata* in his repertoire? (And what companion works could be more different in their affirmation of major and minor keys?) The intellectual who confesses, to his loss, that middle-period Beethoven has nothing new to say to him will still turn to the *Hammerklavier* as one of the stiffest challenges for player and listener alike; yet for those who fight shy of the epic, titanic Beethoven there are sonatas in all periods that converse in intimate domestic tones. Even the youngest pianists can still find an entrance to Beethoven's world through the sonatas. As they mature in mind and fingers they may set their sights on the lofty pinnacles of the late works; but they will be constantly surprised at the unsuspected richness of the earlier slow movements. "Early", however, needs some qualification in Beethoven's case. He wrote three childhood sonatas in his Bonn days which are prophetic, maybe, but are not normally accepted into the self-approved cannon. [This is a reference to the so-called *Kurfürstensonaten* that Beethoven composed between the ages of twelve and thirteen that he dedicated to the Elector (Kurfüst) Maximillian Frederick.] Beethoven was twenty-five when he confirmed his readiness by publishing works with opus-numbers, a late-starter by Mozartean standards.'

Denis Matthews, *Beethoven, Piano Sonatas*, London: British Broadcasting Corporation, 1967, p. 5.

Of Beethoven in relation to the piano Matthews comments:

> 'Beethoven had watched the growing scope of the piano and utilized its resources to the utmost — beyond the utmost at times. Yet he can hardly be called a pioneer of piano technique in the sense that Chopin, or even Clementi and Czerny, were pioneers. The piano was a means to an end, not to be wooed for its own sake but a vehicle for expression — to be bullied, if necessary, into submission. There is scarcely a passage in Beethoven, early or late, that could be modified in the interests of technique, comfort or "effectiveness" without dissipation of the strength and willpower that made it. The artist thrives within his limitations and even the much-worked Alberti bass and the routine range of arpeggio formulas served Beethoven well.'

Beethoven was not strictly a 'harmonic composer' in Matthews' opinion:

> 'Neither could Beethoven be called a harmonic composer in the normal sense — in many instances Mozart was much more "modern" in his use of dissonance — and his frequent reliance on tonic-and-dominant patterns, on Neapolitan sixths and diminished sevenths, has been ridiculed by those who obstinately refuse to see the wood for the trees. Wherein lies his extraordinary strength, then? The answer lies in Beethoven's unique mastery of tonality and key relationships, the larger view of harmony; or,

putting it another way, in the architectural sense he could find more resources in the deployment of ordinary structural bricks than less enduring, though more alluring, decorative ones. Only a short-sighted view can find a commonplace in the *Waldstein*.'

Denis Matthews, *Keyboard Music*, Newton Abbot: London David & Charles, 1972, pp. 181–2.

Concerning performance from memory, Matthews observes:

'The tradition of playing from memory is comparatively recent and according to historians little more than a century old, but it is now almost a hard and fast rule that pianists in particular should habitually dispense with the music in public; and so expected is this feat that a rustle of disappointment can be heard running through the audience if the player brings the notes and a turn-over on the platform with him ... Reliance on memory may limit the repertoire, cramp the musicianship, and at its worst lead to sins of varying nature against the score.'

Dennis Matthews, *In Pursuit of Music*, London: Victor Gollancz Ltd., 1968, pp. 132–3.

WILFRID MELLERS

The English musicologist and composer Wilfrid Mellers places Beethoven as a figure in history and one who made history:

> 'No work of art can be "explained" by reference to its historical connotations. Every artist self-evidently "reflects" the values and beliefs of his time ... At the same time, any truly creative artist is also making those beliefs. It is true that we cannot fully understand Beethoven without understanding the impulses behind the French Revolution. It is equally true that we cannot fully understand the French Revolution without some insight into Beethoven's music. We can see in his music those elements which are conditioned by his time (for they could not be otherwise) and yet are beyond the topical and local. Beethoven is a point at which the growth of the mind shows itself. He is a part of history: and also of the human spirit making history.'

Wilfrid Howard Mellers and Alec Harman, *Man and his Music*, London, Barrie and Jenkins, 1988, pp. 575–6.

In his study *The Sonata Principle*, Mellers opens his observations:

> 'It is the essence of the personality of Beethoven (1770-1827), both as man and as artist, that he should invite discussion in other than musical terms. We cannot begin to understand him unless we recognize that for him music was not merely a pattern of sounds nor even merely an aural means of self-expression; it was also a moral and ethical power.'

Of Beethoven the revolutionary, Mellers writes:

> 'There *is* a connection between Beethoven's music and the French revolution, since even in so strikingly personal a work as the Fifth Symphony he was directly influenced by French revolutionary music.'

He adds:

> '[If] Haydn and Mozart were incipiently revolutionary composers, Beethoven is overtly so. The Fifth Symphony revolutionises the then accepted notion of symphonic form, and its technical revolution is inseparable from the fact that it conveys in musical terms a message — a new approach to human experience.'

Mellers considers Beethoven disturbed what he calls the 'equilibrium' of music:

> '[From] the start Beethoven desired change. He wanted to build a new world; and he thought of his music as a means to that end. Mozart's art, as we can see most readily from his operas, is based on acceptance, tolerance, and understanding. This does not preclude stringent criticism; but he has no ethical intentions. Beethoven was probably the first composer to be consciously animated by the desire to do good.'

In support of this contention, Mellers quotes words that Beethoven inscribed in a friend's album:

> 'To help wherever one can./Love liberty above

all things./Never deny the truth/ Even at the foot of the throne.'

In a summary passage, Mellers concludes:

> '[Beethoven] was born into a great musical tradition which he respected; for with his disrespect towards people and things he considered unworthy, he had the true humility of the great. So the subversive tendencies of his music are not immediately evident. He accepts the conventions which he inherited from Haydn and Mozart: but emphasises the revolutionary at the expense of the traditional features.'

Wilfrid Howard Mellers, *The Sonata Principle (from c. 1750)*, London: Rockliff, 1957, pp. 53–6.

FELIX MENDELSSOHN

In the autumn of 1825, Felix Mendelssohn completed work on his Octet in E-flat major, Op. 20 — he was just sixteen years old at the time. Conrad Wilson, writing of this achievement, remarkable even by Mozartian standards, remarks:

> 'Its youthful verve, brilliance and perfection make it one of the miracles of nineteenth-century music.'

Four years later, Mendelssohn paid homage to Beethoven, albeit indirectly, in his first string quartet that is also written in the same key of E-flat major. For Mendelssohn's views about Beethoven and his music, we are indebted to the reminiscences of the composer and music theorist Johann Christian Lobe. He recalls a walk one day with the composer that provided him with the opportunity to seek his opinions concerning 'originality' in Beethoven's music. Mendelssohn was cautious in conceding what was innovatory in music. For him, breaking new ground consisted of producing creations that obeyed 'newly discovered' and 'more sublime laws'. He was of the opinion:

> 'Never, in fact, did an artist break new ground. In the best case he did things imperceptibly better than his immediate predecessors.'

Mendelssohn accepted that Beethoven had opened up new ground but questioned if his early orchestral music departed so greatly from that of Mozart and Haydn. He questioned:

> 'Do Beethoven's symphonies proceed down completely new paths? No, I say. Between the first symphony of Beethoven and the last of Mozart I find no extraordinary [leap in] artistic value, and no more than ordinary effect. The one pleases me and the other pleases me.'

Mendelssohn acknowledged the moving forces at work in Beethoven's only creation for the lyric theatre, *Fidelio*, exclaiming: 'What an opera it is!'

But he qualified his enthusiasm:

> 'I do not say that every idea in it appeals to me completely, but I would like to know the name of the opera that could have a more profound effect, or offer more enchanting pleasures to the listener.'

He posed the question:

> 'Do you find in it a single number with which
> Beethoven broke new ground? I do not. I look
> at the score and listen to the performance, and
> everywhere I find Cherubini's dramatic style.
> Beethoven was not imitating it, but he had it in
> mind as a favourite musical model.'

Lobe then ventured to ask Mendelssohn about his views on the music of Beethoven's final period including his last string quartets, the Ninth Symphony and the *Missa Solemnis*. 'Here', Lobe reasoned, 'one cannot speak of a comparability with Mozart, or any other artist before him?' Mendelssohn responded:

> 'That may be, in a certain sense ... [Beethoven's]
> forms are wider and broader, the style is more
> polyphonic, more artificial, the ideas for the most
> part darker, more melancholy, even when they
> want to be cheerful; the instrumentation is fuller,
> and *he went somewhat farther along the path he
> had already embarked on, but he did not clear a
> new one.* And let us be honest; where did he lead
> us? To regions that are really *more beautiful?*'
> [Mendelssohn's emphasis]

Mendelssohn summarized his views about Beethoven with the observation:

> 'The fact that Beethoven's genius took the shape
> it did is a consequence of the sequence in which
> it appeared. In Handel's time he would not have
> become our Beethoven. Haydn and Mozart
> would have been different people if they had

come after Beethoven. And all this would most certainly have come about no matter how the world might have looked from a political or religious viewpoint.'

Roger Nichols, *Mendelssohn Remembered*, London: Faber and Faber, 1997, pp. 99–103 and p. 108.

When the youthful Mendelssohn was resident in Paris, he had occasion to write on 14 February 1832 to his former music teacher Carl Friedrich Zelter. His remarks provide insights into the state of musical performance in Paris and of the reception of Beethoven's symphonies:

'[It] is the Paris Conservatoire that gives the concerts; but more than that, it is the most perfect performance to be heard anywhere ... The general arrangements, too, are very appropriate and sensible ... Moreover, the hall is a little one, so that for one thing the music makes twice the effect and we hear every detail twice as clearly and for another thing the audience is small, very select, and yet seems a large gathering.'

Beethoven's orchestral music was clearly finding favour:

'The musicians themselves delight in Beethoven's great symphonies; they have made themselves thoroughly familiar with them, and are happy to have mastered the difficulties. Some of them, including Habeneck himself, undoubtedly have a perfectly genuine love of Beethoven; but as for the others, who are the loudest in their enthusiasm, I do not believe a word they say about it; for they make this an excuse for decrying the other masters — declaring Haydn was merely a fashionable composer, Mozart an ordinary sort of fellow; and such narrow-minded enthusiasm cannot be sincere. If they really felt what Beethoven meant, they would also realize what Haydn was, and feel small; but not a bit of it, they go briskly ahead with their criticism. Beethoven is uncommonly popular with the concert public, as well, because they believe that only the connoisseur can appreciate him; but only a small minority really enjoy him, and I cannot abide the disdainful attitude towards Haydn and Mozart; it infuriates me.'

François Habeneck, the French violinist and conductor to whom Mendelssohn makes reference, was the first conductor to introduce French audiences to the Symphonies of Beethoven in the late 1820s.

A few weeks later, Mendelssohn attended a rehearsal of Beethoven's *Pastoral Symphony* and found himself unexpectedly the centre of attention. The rehearsal over he left his seat to greet some friends. To his pleasure and surprise the full orchestra exclaimed 'There is Mendelssohn'. He wrote to his father:

'I shall never forget that, for it meant more to me than any distinction.'

Cited in: Hans Gal, *The Musician's World: Great composers in their letters*, London: Thames and Hudson, 1965, pp. 163–5.

Dorothea von Ertmann was one of the most gifted pianists of her day and one of the foremost interpreters of Beethoven's piano sonatas. She received lessons from the composer, earning from him the affectionate soubriquet

'Dorothea Cecilia' — a thinly disguised reference to Sancta Caecilia, the patroness of musicians. When her only child died at a young age, Beethoven sought to console her by improvising at the piano for more than an hour. In July 1831, Mendelssohn heard Dorothea play when he visited her in Milan during his tour of Italy. Writing to his sister Fanny he gave the following account of her playing and its influence upon him:

> 'She plays Beethoven's works [the piano sonatas] admirably, though it is so long since she studied them she sometimes rather exaggerates the expression, dwelling too long on one passage, and hurrying the next; but there are many parts she plays splendidly, and I think I have learned something from her.'

Bartholdy Mendelssohn, *Letters from Italy and Switzerland,* London: Longman, Green, Longman, and Roberts, 1862, p. 203.

A further recollection from the past connects us to an evening when two great artists were brought together in a performance of Beethoven's Piano Sonata Op. 57. The evening in question was sometime in 1874 when several friends had been invited to hear Mendelssohn perform — one of them being Clara Schumann. At one point in his recital, Mendelssohn played the F minor Piano Sonata. At the end of the Andante he deliberately held the final chord for a long time, by way of securing the attention of the audience. At this he rose, and turning to Clara said:

'You must play the Finale.'

The composer-pianist Ferdinand Hiller, a close friend of Mendelssohn, was among the invited guests, and records how at first Clara 'strongly protested' but finally yielded to Mendelssohn's entreaties and performed the Finale. In Hiller's estimation:

> 'The end was worthy of the beginning, and if the order had been reversed it would no doubt have been just as fine.'

Ferdinand Hiller, *Mendelssohn: Letters and recollections*, New York: Vienna House, 1972, p. 167.

YEHUDI MENUHIN

Although Yehudi Menuhin will be forever associated with the legendary recording he made of the Elgar Violin Concerto (HMV 1932), performed at the age of sixteen, it is for many with his association of the Beethoven Violin Concerto that his lasting fame endures. One of his first teachers, Louis Persinger — first violin of the San Francisco Symphony Orchestra, — recalls that at the age of eight the young Yehudi begged to be allowed to work on the D major concerto. Later in his career Beethoven's Violin Concerto came to be something of a talisman for Menuhin. For example in 1947, in the wake of the Holocaust, he returned to Germany to play concerto concerts, including the Beethoven, with the Berlin Philharmonic Orchestra under Wilhelm Furtwängler. Menuhin saw this as an act of reconciliation, remarking to his Jewish critics that 'he wanted to rehabilitate Germany's music and spirit'. Similarly, the present writer recall's Menuhin's response to the events subsequent to the emergence of the so-called 'Prague Spring' when the reformist Alexander Dubček was elected First Secretary of the Communist Party of Czechoslovakia. Following its ruthless suppression, later in the year by the Soviet Union, Menuhin, then taking part in the Edinburgh International Festival, dedicated his performance of the Beethoven Violin Concerto to the oppressed people of Prague.

The thirteenth-century Persian poet and scholar Rumi wrote:

'The voice of the violin is the sound of the opening gate of paradise.'

Menuhin reflected this in his own writings, saying:

'The violin, through the serene clarity of its song,
helps to keep our bearings in the storm, as a light
in the night, a compass in the tempest, it shows
us a way to a haven of sincerity and respect.'

Menuhin was more than a violinist of course. He has been described as a philosopher, visionary, humanist, music's ambassador to the world – he was nominated 'UNESCO Ambassador of Goodwill, 1992' – and, amongst his numerous other honours, was the recipient of more than twenty honorary doctorates. Perhaps the most significant tribute paid to Menuhin was the estimation of him as:

'An artist who believed the music he played to
be, quite literally, a form of human healing, out
of which we might make peace with ourselves.'

The spirit of the preceding remarks pervades much of Menuhin's recorded conversation and writing about music, of which the following is a selection of texts.

When in conversation with the author and writer on music Robin Daniels, Menuhin outlined his views about music, making occasional references to Beethoven:

'Music can penetrate all one's defences. The combination of music and an especially poignant occasion can be unbelievably potent ... We all have joys and tragedies, ecstasies and struggles, but we may not have enough experience of life to draw the full measure of emotional depth or rational analysis or philosophical meaning from what has happened to us. We need elucidation, and so we go to the great creative artists whom we can trust, such as Bach or Beethoven or Shakespeare. The experience of the most evolved people — whether artists or religious leaders or people from any profession or background — opens our eyes, broadens and matures us, and unlocks our repressed feelings, giving them shape, sound, form, and meaning. A great work of art *re-presents* human beings to themselves ... Music, unlike the visual arts, lives in time. The music of Bach or Beethoven captures our vibrations, compels co-living. I am prepared, without reservation, to live through Beethoven and his depth of experience, but what I cannot accept is the almost total subservience that cheap entertainment demands. I want to be informed, enlightened, enhanced, by art; I am not willing to be presented with the crudest sensations — fear, cruelty, bizarre behaviour.'

Turning to his interest in eastern music, Menuhin remarked:

'The music of the east is totally different: it selects one mood or atmosphere to express, and can then maintain this for hours. There may be a certain rise in tension as the rhythms become more complex, but this is quite unlike western music's fast changes of mood. In a Beethoven symphony or quartet you experience, within only a few minutes, sudden and wide contrast, from power to tenderness, from joy to sorrow. In life, joy and sorrow can and do alternate in close sequence; but much of western music tends to be very swift in its juxtaposition of emotions.'

Robin Daniels, *Conversations with Menuhin*, London: Macdonald General Books, 1979, p. 65 and pp. 119—120.

Menuhin collaborated with the television producer Curtis W. Davis in a television series called *The Music of Man*. In their resulting publication, Menuhin writes of Beethoven's struggle to achieve perfection — in the context of similar creative efforts made by contemporary composers:

'The emerging doctrine of egocentric, personal self-realization [at the opening of the nineteenth century] could not have found a more vigorous expression than it did in Beethoven, which may be due in part to his eventual deafness and isolation. This tendency has continued to our day when every literate composer feels obliged to invent a new style, rather than simply evolve a distinctive personality. The result has been a great number of disappointments and blind alleys. No composer has ever refined his raw material to the degree of purity Beethoven achieved. Wrestling with it until he transformed it into concentrated statement of intense meaning, he focused his fire in the process. Today, when composers so often

> begin with their raw material already in an advanced state of abstraction, there can be no such process of distillation, of self-immolation, in the creative act. In Beethoven, more than in almost any other creative artist, we are allowed to witness the struggle for the ideal of beauty, purpose and truth.'

Menuhin directed his attention to more personal aspects of Beethoven:

> 'Beethoven's tragedy has been compared to blindness in a painter. That is only a half-truth; the blind painter may no longer be able to paint, but blind musicians compose and perform, like Cabezon in Spain. And while the deaf performer cannot play, the deaf composer can still write, creating by a process of inner conception, drawing on aural images etched onto his mind and heart; for music is finally an inner experience, a happening occurring within ourselves. Beethoven needed only his eyes and his hand, and they continued to serve him well. And yet, how are we to assess the depth of tragedy in the monumental despair of this colossus, facing so fateful and shattering a curse? It was as if Beethoven were Prometheus, who stole fire from the gods and gave it to man; then, like Prometheus, the gods punished him by chaining him to a rock, the rock of his deafness.'

Menuhin discusses Beethoven in the wider context of mankind's musical heritage:

'By nature man is an explorer, one of the most consistent characteristics of the human race. Beethoven is an explorer in search of first causes. His nature was not an accepting one, but challenging, defiant and questioning. Indeed, his incomparable stretches of utmost serenity were very dearly bought, and so often were followed by bucolic festivity, as the celebration of inner creative struggle leads to serenity, thanksgiving and celebration. Nowhere in his volcanic temperament can we see this more clearly than in his sketchbooks, of which hundreds survive. These are like the sketchbooks of Leonardo da Vinci, only without their neatness and precision. Beethoven was too impatient, struggling constantly to reinvent music itself, working under pressure, to make form emerge from recalcitrant material. Beethoven started as a disciple of Haydn and Mozart, but soon he no longer quoted others, as a scientist like Darwin might quote ideas and techniques learned in the course of setting forth an argument. In the final analysis, Beethoven is like Moses, an intermediary between Divine Will and human recalcitrance, leading us out of bondage into the Promised Land, a mortal become immortal, no longer quoting others. God perhaps said it first and Beethoven was content to quote God.'

Menuhin concludes:

'Beethoven's greatness of soul transcends craft while illuminating it. As he became increasingly locked inside his deafness, he devised elaborate hearing aids so that he could pick up vibrations from his piano directly, applying a stick against the sounding board and pressing the other end directly against the side of his head. Beethoven's isolation emphasizes something new in Western music: the separation between composer and performer that had begun at the turn of the nineteenth century ... Beethoven's achievement is that universality of utterance which partakes alike of the rigours of mathematical equation and the emotions of human experience.'

Yehudi Menuhin and Curtis W. Davis, *The Music of Man*, London: Macdonald and Janes, 1979, p. 147 and pp. 150—4.

OLIVIER MESSIAEN

The French composer, organist and ornithologist Olivier Messiaen is known for his exploration of sound worlds and sonorities inspired by bird song. Aware of this, fellow Frenchmen and composer Claude Samuel, in conversation with Messiaen (in the early 1990s), put to him the question:

'Western music is played regularly in the concert halls of Tokyo. How does a Japanese person experience a Beethoven symphony?'

Messiaen replied:

'I'll answer you with an anecdote. My pupil, Gerald Levinson [American composer of contemporary classical music], who lived in Bali to learn the technique of the gamelan, one day played two European pieces for his Balinese teacher: an excerpt from Mozart's Symphony No. 40 in G minor and a fragment of my *Transfiguration*. Now, it was my music that the Balinese musician appreciated more readily, doubtless because he recognized the sound of tam-tams and gongs, which reminded him of his metallophones. The music of Mozart left him indifferent. I think the Japanese find reminders of their own music in certain Western works, but Beethoven naturally is very far removed from their sensibility.'

Olivier Messiaen, *Music and Color: Conversations with Claude Samuel*, Portland, Oregon: Amadeus, 1994, pp. 102–3.

In an essay, primarily in defence of Igor Stravinsky, Messiaen opened his account with the question:

'What did Beethoven do to be the greatest of all?'

And his response:

'He loved, he suffered, and his music speaks from the heart.'

Peter Hill, *The Messiaen Companion*, London: Faber and Faber, 1995, p. 154.

DARIUS MILHAUD

In the early 1920s, the French composer Darius Milhaud undertook to write articles of music criticism for the Paris Journal *Courrier musical*. Reporting on the Sunday concerts held in Paris at this time, he likened them 'to the display of *old masters* to be seen at the Louvre's *Salon Carré*. Regarding Beethoven and Wagner, Milhaud considered it was possible to have too much of a good thing:

> 'The Sunday concerts were a sort of musical *Salon Carré,* an exhibition of the masters of past centuries. I loved classical music, but protested in my articles against the excessive number of Beethoven-Wagner and Wagner-Beethoven programmes. It was very tiresome. Every Sunday, the *Fifth,* the *Third,* the *Leonora Overture.* And Wagner every Sunday ... Apart from one or two of his overtures, his works should never be performed in the concert hall.'

Mihaud then turned his criticism to music festivals that he considered also to be over-representative of the works of Beethoven and Wagner. He concedes in a final outburst — and not without a sense of humour — that these are inevitable:

> '[Our] criticisms are wasted, and we shall always have to put up with festivals of this kind, I may say I am prepared to shout, "Long live Beethoven!" even after the hundred-thousandth performance of the *Fifth,* but — oh, yes! Certainly — always to cry, "Down with Wagner!"'

Darius Milhaud, *My Happy Life*, London: Boyars, 1995, p. 95.

ANTON NEUMAYR

The physician and musician Anton Neumayr studied the medical histories of Haydn, Mozart, Beethoven and Schubert. His many observations concerning Beethoven include the following:

'He who has been seized by Beethoven's inspiration has gained a clear view of the highest elevations, of the mountain chain connecting the summits of religion, ethics, philosophy, and the arts; he inhales the essential unity of their atmosphere and, in that unity, enjoys the most complete harmony and the greatest dignity of man's existence.'

'Beethoven's music fills us with the reverence we feel on entering a holy shrine, whether we consider ourselves religious or not. And because our intellect does not enable us to fully understand his language, which came as if from another, more exalted world, we sense the divine character of his music all the more, music that has probed to the farthest reaches of art'.

'It will always seem miraculous that Beethoven's total commitment to discipline and his powerful, single-minded striving to reach the most exalted heights of art that man is capable of scaling were possible in a body that was plagued by intestinal disease form the early years of his maturity and until he died, and which, in the last years of his life, was increasingly tormented by the effects of his fatal liver disease.'

Anton Neumayr, *Music and Medicine*, Bloomington, Illinois: Medi-Ed Press, 1994–1997, p. 225 and p. 335.

ERNEST NEWMAN

The English music critic and musicologist Ernest Newman has been described as 'the most celebrated British music critic in the first half of the 20th century' (*Grove's Dictionary of Music and Musicians*). He was Music Critic for *the Sunday Times* for almost forty years. In his many writings and articles he makes occasional reference to Beethoven, including the following:

> 'Fate seems to have shaped [Beethoven] with the conscious and deliberate hand of an artist bending a mass of inchoate material to the realization of his own. It pruned him as an horticulturist prunes a tree, destroying a dozen shoots that one may bear richer fruit. [A reference to Beethoven's tireless rejection of one musical idea in search of a superior one.] We can only dimly speculate on what would have become of him had not disease laid her ugly and terrible hand on him.'

Newman continues:

> 'I fancy we have, by a sort of paradox, another evidence of the clairvoyant nature of Beethoven's genius — genius that was simply the medium through which a power beyond himself delivered oracles — in the very slowness of some of his conceptions. His sketch books show us that his themes were, as a rule, arrived at by a series of experiments: as first set down they are often incredibly commonplace: then they are altered by a touch here and a touch there, until, after a score of hackings and hewing, they take the shape in which we know them.'

Ernest Newman, *Testament of Music: Essays and papers*, London: Putnam, 1962, p. 279. Originally published as *Beethoven* in 1917.

Writing in the *Sunday Times* (17 Feb. 1929), Newman discussed Beethoven in the context of prevailing music criticism:

> 'The only composer who has been at all adequately studied is Beethoven the reason being that only in his case have we sufficient documents (his sketch books are particularly valuable) that throw light on the structure of his musical faculty. But even the mind of Beethoven still holds mysteries for us. Personally I have no further use for the kind of Beethoven criticism that ranges in merely literary fashion over his music, telling us, with more-or-less eloquence, how that music affected the writer, which philosophy, of course he innocently proceeds to attribute to Beethoven himself. My contention is that three-fourths of what is written about Beethoven is "literature", not music. Misled by this or that story from his life, our writers read something into the music that is not really there. They would never have discovered, or thought they had discovered, these things had all the records of Beethoven's life perished the day he had died. They form a certain conception of him from the story of his life, and then innocently proceed to foist that conception upon his music.'

Ernest Newman, *From the World of Music: Essays from "The Sunday Times"*, London: J. Calder, 1956, pp. 24–5.

Later in his career (1950) Newman contributed to *The Atlantic Monthly*. His articles belonged to a series, the object of which formed part of the study of a great thinker or man of action in a period of crisis in his life. Newman's subject was Beethoven. Of the composer's later works he writes:

> 'On one point ... everyone is agreed — that in the works unmistakably of his third period, of which the last two piano sonatas and the last five quartets (with the Great Fugue) constitute a definite unity, a territory with a spiritual climate and a flora and fauna entirely its own, we are confronted with what seems to be virtually new Beethoven: such music had never been heard in the world before, and we may doubt whether its like will ever be heard again. All who have fallen under its spell agree that here music explores the profoundest depths of the spirits and soars to the loftiest mystical heights.'

Newman's reference to 'the last two piano sonatas' may be an oversight since Beethoven's final sequence of Piano Sonatas, namely, Op. 109. Op. 110 and Op. 111, is generally considered to be a majestic and unified trilogy that can be, and on occasions has been, performed as single work.

At the close of his article, Newman reflects:

> 'Of all the mystics of art, the Beethoven of the last few years is the greatest: one has to go back to the thirteenth-century Persian poet Rumi to find his parallel, and we can only be grateful for the tremendous inner change, whatever its hidden origins may have been, that took place in him in his final years. But he was hardly more than fifty-six when he died; and inevitably we ask ourselves what his next phase might have been. Is a "next phase" conceivable? He could hardly have travelled further along the mystical road than

he had done already; and we may ask ourselves whether, on the other hand, it was within the bounds of human possibility for him to have gone back once more to the outer world. Has any born mystic ever made that backward journey after ... he on honey dew hath fed?'

Ernest Newman, *Testament of Music: Essays and papers*, London: Putnam, 1962, p. 242, and p, 251.

CARL NIELSEN

The Danish musician, conductor and violinist Carl Nielsen, writing about his own life and music, makes the following remarks concerning Beethoven and the influence on the composers who followed him:

> 'Who would deny that Beethoven, the man and the musician, was highly subjective? What better ways are there of understanding the idiosyncrasies of the lifework of a great man than studying the man and the circumstances of his life? ... In doing so we of course run the risk of prompting men of lesser stature to claim subjective treatments. It is a claim which cannot be entertained. Only in the case of the supremely great will we submit to it, and one of these, in truth, is Ludwig van Beethoven.'

Nielsen was less than complimentary in his estimation of the influence of the composers who followed him:

> 'It is safe to say that it was Beethoven who, for all his sureness of form and magnificent attainment, led succeeding musicians into the quagmire of

Romanticism, where some sank in up to their knees and others up to the neck, while others, again, vanished altogether. Schubert was the only one to get home dry-shod. But, then, he was the confirmed Viennese, a completely happy character, never assailed by doubts, but dancing and singing in the sublimest, most delightful unawareness of all danger — a singing bird that made men stand still and listen entranced ... Beethoven was the reverse of happy; a fact not, of course, wholly due to the — at times — unfortunate circumstances of his life and tragic deafness, but also, and perhaps especially, to his entire contemporary position as a creative artist. A great period had just ended with the death of Mozart. It looked as if there was nothing more to achieve. Mozart had grappled with and overcome the most varied, difficult, and involved musical problems with miraculous ease, and everything seemed to have been raised to the highest pitch of artistic perfection in a romp. It would not surprise me if this phenomenon irritated young Beethoven into wanting to toss something, like a young bull. At least he must have had some feeling that it was necessary to begin again at the beginning, while yet unable to free himself from his predecessors.'

Carl Nielsen, *Living Music*, Copenhagen, Wilhelm Hansen, 1968, pp. 63–4.

LUDWIG NOHL

Ludwig Nohl was a German music scholar and writer whose legacies to Beethoven musicology are his pioneering studies of the composer's life (biography), his letters and his contemporaries. Nohl may have been encouraged to undertake the latter aspect of his work by his reading of Anton Schindler's biographical study of Beethoven, first published in 1845. In this, Schindler intimated that a collection of contemporary impressions of the composer would 'be one of the most interesting publications of the day'. Nohl duly published such a collection of writings in 1877 that appeared in English translation in 1880 under the title *Beethoven: Depicted by his Contemporaries*. In his Preface, Nohl remarks on his surprise that it had not occurred to any lover of Beethoven to make such a collection before. He remarks:

> 'I took a broad survey of the rich artistic nature depicted [in the writings about Beethoven], and the importance, not to say necessity, of a compilation like the present flashed upon me, and I saw, if chronologically arranged and carefully elucidated, how wonderfully it would enhance the value of the biography and published letters of Beethoven'.

The following is a selection of the individuals that Nohl included in his survey, presented in the chronological sequence to which he makes reference: Carl Czerny, Ignaz von Seyfried, Johann Friedrich Reichardt, Ignaz Moscheles, Louis Spohr, Giacomo Meyerbeer, Aloys Weissenbach, August von Kloeber, Dr. W. C. Müller, Friedrich Starke, Sir John Russell, Friedrich Rochlitz, Wilhelmine Schröder-Devrient, Franz Grillparzer and Ludwig Rellstab.

Ludwig Nohl, *Beethoven Depicted by his Contemporaries*, translated by Emily Hill, London: Reeves, 1880.

TIA DE NORA

In her roles as Professor of Sociology of Music and Director of Research, in the Department of Sociology/Philosophy at the University of Exeter, Tia de Nora has made a study of what she describes as 'the construction of genius' in relation to Beethoven. She considers how his reputation was first established in Vienna, how his renown was established and its social-musicological consequences. She examines how Beethoven's identity as 'an extraordinary musician' was communicated initially to a small circle of aristocratic admirers and then beyond to the wider musically minded public — we recall that at the composer's death an estimated 10,000 people followed his funeral cortege.

In the introductory remarks to her study as to how Beethoven became such a culturally authoritative figure, de Nora remarks:

> 'The image of Beethoven — haughty, scowling, and disheveled, as he is depicted in numerous portraits and busts — has been a part of the popular iconography of genius since the early nineteenth century. These images, and at least some of Beethoven's works, are familiar to many people who are otherwise unacquainted with the world of "high culture" music. As a part of our cultural common sense, Beethoven's identity as an exceptional musician appears transcendent. Beethoven is the quintessential genius of western culture, and the history of how his reputation became established should interest sociologists, social psychologists, and cultural historians, because that history cannot be addressed fully by conventional musicological discourse alone.'

Tia de Nora, *Beethoven and the Construction of Genius*, Berkeley, University of California Press, 1997, p. Xi.

HUBERT PARRY

Sir Charles Hubert Hastings Parry was a former pillar of the English musical establishment, occupying the professorship in music at the University of Oxford and later the headship of the Royal College of Music where his pupils included Vaughn Williams, Gustav Holst, Frank Bridge and John Ireland. From his substantial musical output, Parry is best remembered today for his choral song *Jerusalem* and his setting for the coronation anthem 'I was glad when they said unto me'.

In his undergraduate days at the University of Oxford, Parry was co-founder of *The Music Club* and it was at this period when Beethoven's pianos sonatas 'cast a powerful spell' upon him. His diary for 27 December 1866 records:

'Practised all morning — Beethoven mostly'.

The work he studied intently was the Piano Sonata in F, Op. 10, No. 2. When Parry succeeded Sir Charles Grove as Director of the Royal College of Music, of necessity he devoted much of his time to college administration but not to the neglect of composition and musicology. In the latter capacity he published a study of Beethoven (1886) that includes an evaluation of his works, including the piano sonatas. In this he writes:

> 'The imagination and the reason must both be satisfied, but above all things the imagination.'

C. Hubert H. Parry, *Beethoven* in: David Ewen, *From Bach to Stravinsky: The history of music by its foremost critics*, New York, Greenwood Press, 1968, pp. 105–131.

*

Aware that his technique in piano had many shortcomings, Parry took lessons from his music teacher Professor James Taylor — remembered today for establishing Oxford's chamber music recitals. According to Parry's diary (27 December 1866), 'Taylor soon had him tackling the Op, 57 Piano Sonata — The *Appassionata*.' Writing of Parry's student days, Anthony Boden recalls:

> 'He had discovered the music of Beethoven and begun to explore the sonatas, and with Taylor's guidance was soon scaling the peaks of the *Appassionata*, but only after the ending of the Trinity term would the full impact of Beethoven's genius take him like a flood.'

It was then that Parry heard Beethoven's Fifth Symphony for the first time, prompting him to enthuse:

'Words cannot express the hopeless gloriousness of this old ruffian! Such a whacker! So tremendously massive!'

Parry was to put his knowledge of the *Appassionata* to good effect years later when he guided his young protégé Vaughn Williams through his own music studies. In his estimation of the Op. 57 Piano Sonata Parry wrote the moving words:

'Here the human soul asked mighty questions of its God and had its reply.'

And of the composer more generally he remarked:

> '[Beethoven] is one of the few great creators of art whom a man, though he be ever so blessed with musical intelligence, may study for a lifetime and never exhaust.'

Jeremy C. Dibble, *Hubert H. Parry: His life and music*, Oxford: Clarendon Press, 1992, pp. 50–1 and Anthony Boden, *The Parrys of the Golden Vale: Background to genius*, London: Thames Publishing, 1998, pp. 120–1.

GIORGIO PESTELLI

The Italian musicologist Giorgio Pestelli is perhaps most notable for his 1967 edition of the 555 keyboard sonatas of Domenico Scarlatti. However, his musical interests were wide-ranging as is evident in his *The Age of Mozart and Beethoven*. In this he discusses Beethoven's musical language and the means he adopted in conveying his intentions to the performer of his works:

> 'More regular than Mozart in his use of two-bar phrases, which also dominate many works by other composers, Beethoven made up for this with constant changes of tempo in fits of acceleration and relaxations that give his language a distinctly anthropomorphic character. A few anthropological metaphors inserted above the stave are in themselves significant: "exhausted, plaintive", "reviving by degrees" (Op. 110), "oppressed" (Op. 130) and "feeling new strength" (Op. 132); but more indicative than anything else is the question of tempo in general. Bach, almost without using markings concerning movement, does not leave the performer in any real doubt concerning his contrasts of tempo, and even for Mozart, *allegro*, *adagio* and *presto* were sufficient opening instructions, since they fell within the performing tradition without any substantial variation. But for Beethoven, even when he uses detailed indications in his own

language or trusts in the mathematical time of the metronome, tempo is a problem that is always a matter of question, and generations of conductors and pianists will imagine afresh each time, watch in hand, the tempo of the *Eroica*, the Fifth Symphony, or Op. 106 with different results, giving the concert-going public a great deal to think about.'

Pestelli concludes:

'There is, in fact, nothing beyond the notes of Beethoven's music, yet one cannot conceive of the questions being asked; and within this tantalising situation lies the reason for the rhetoric devoted to Beethoven, and at the same time for his immense and consistent popularity.'

Giorgio Pestelli, *The Age of Mozart and Beethoven*, Cambridge: Cambridge University Press, 1984, p. 230.

ILDEBRANDO PIZZETTI

The Italian composer, musicologist and music critic Ildebrando Pizzetti wrote an appreciation of the music of Maurice Ravel but included a passing reference to Beethoven.

'Beethoven's Nature is calm yet not dead; there is always something that lives in it, vibrating, singing for all men.'

Ferruccio Bonavia, *Musicians on Music*, London: Routledge & Kegan Paul, 1956, p. 244.

*

ANDRE PREVIN

The German-American pianist, conductor, and composer (Sir) Andre George Previn became well know to audiences in the United Kingdom through his television appearances, notably with the entertainers Morecambe and Wise who would refer to him irreverently as 'Mr. Preview'. The irony of such levity is underlined when set against Previn's numerous international awards that include an honorary knighthood and recognition for his services to both classical and popular music. On one of his visits to the United Kingdom, he had an extended exchange of views about music with the composer, pianist, broadcaster and author Anthony Hopkins. He should not be confused with his namesake Sir Anthony Hopkins who, before achieving celebrity in film, was himself a practicing musician and composer. Hopkins endeared himself in the late 1950s to many radio listeners – the present writer included – when he discussed classical music in his BBC Third Programme broadcasts *Talking About Music*. In these he explored a particular piece of music with what has been described as 'a judicious mix of analysis and vivid metaphor', nothing less than 'a listener's *Baedeker*'. In his interview with Previn, Hopkins made reference to contemporary music and the manner in which he considered some composers seemed determined to disassociate themselves from the past.

Previn responded:

'Beethoven accepted the inheritance of Haydn and Mozart gladly enough until he could make something more of it.'

Expanding this thought he continued:

'Even the revolutionaries who really started to break away at the beginning of this [twentieth] century, leading figures like Stravinsky, Bartók and Debussy, each one started by trying to continue the traditions of the nineteenth century.'

Hopkins considered it was not healthy for contemporary composers to set aside their musical inheritance too readily and invited Previn to comment. He duly responded:

'I really have very little to add to that except the following: never before has the composer seemed to want to alienate the audience as much as he does now. Now, I think it is admirable in the highest sense when a composer, a serious composer, says: "I don't care who likes this and who doesn't, because I know that what I am writing is the essence of me." That is the Beethoven creed and it is beautiful; but I think that there are several of the more militant new composers who have gone one step beyond that. They say, "I don't want anybody to like it." Now that is a different story altogether.'

Antony Hopkins, *Andre Previn, Music Face to Face*, London, Hamish Hamilton, 1971, pp. 118–19.

SERGEI PROKOFIEV

Reflecting on his early piano lessons, Prokofiev recalls:

'[There] was always music in the home ... When I was put to bed at night, I never wanted to sleep. I would lie there and listen as the sound of a Beethoven sonata came from somewhere far off,

> several rooms away. More than anything else, my mother played the sonatas of Volume I [of Beethoven].'

Prokofiev soon commenced piano lessons and by the age of five composed his first piano composition — written down by his mother. By the age of eleven, Prokofiev received piano instruction from the distinguished Soviet composer, conductor, and teacher Reinhold Glière. Of this period he writes:

> 'A born teacher, Glière skillfully combined instruction in harmony with free composition and a study of the elements of form and orchestration ... Playing a Beethoven sonata Glière would give me a rough outline of sonata form, and whenever we came across a phrase characteristic of one or another instrument in a symphony orchestra, he would say: "Now this melody could be played by a flute; the fanfare could be given to the trumpet, and in the lower register to two French horns, etc." '

An anecdote from Prokofiev's memoirs is of related interest. At the age of fourteen he was a student at the Conservatory at St. Petersburg and wished to be considered for entry to the 'special piano class' — an endeavour known to be demanding. His teacher at the time was Alexander Winkler who asked his youthful protégé if he knew Beethoven's Piano Sonata Op. 22. 'By heart', was the youthful Prokofiev's reply. He subsequently performed the piece before eight or nine examiners — 'all grim-faced' — but, two hours later, they told him he was accepted. Winkler's response was to say:

> 'To start with we'll work on techniques to strengthen your fingers. It'll be a bit boring at first, but there's nothing we can do about it.'

Later in his mature years Prokofiev wrote:

> '[The] thinking of one and the same composer can be both complex and simple. Take the second volume of the piano sonatas [of Beethoven]. No one would go so far as to claim that the simple sonatas in that volume are better or more necessary than the complex ones.'

Later in life Prokofiev's prowess as a pianist earned him unwanted praise — insofar as he wished to be recognised as a composer. This is evident from a diary entry of his from 31 January 1927:

> 'An anonymous letter arrives signed "a Russian woman". She advises that when the dust settles and I am able to concentrate in peace and quiet, I will realize that my true metier is not composition, but the performance of Beethoven, with all his passion and titanic power; whereupon the whole world will prostrate itself in front of me. That's just what I need! Thank you, Russian woman!'

When in America in the 1920s, Prokofiev was engaged to perform several piano recitals. Inevitably he found his technical virtuosity being compared to that of Rachmaninov — who was blessed with hands so large hands he could span an octave with ease between his thumb and index finger. Of Prokofiev's playing, one music critic wrote he had 'steel fingers, steel wrists, steel biceps and steel triceps' and likened his rendering of the finale of his Piano Sonata No. 2 to 'a herd of mammoths charging across an Asiatic plateau'! For his part, Prokofiev was not impressed by the American musical scene:

> 'I roamed New York's Central Park and looked up at the skyscrapers facing it, I would think with cold fury of all the wonderful orchestras in America that cared nothing for my music; of the critics who never tired of uttering platitudes such as "Beethoven is a great composer", and who balked violently at anything new; of the managers who arranged long tours for artists playing the same old hackneyed programme fifty times over. I had come here too soon; the child (America) was not old enough to appreciate new music.'

Christopher Palmer, editor, *Sergei Prokofiev: Soviet diary 1927 and other writings*, London: Faber and Faber, 1991, p. 23, p. 44, p. 232, p. 267 and p. 286; and Sergey Prokofiev, *Prokofiev by Prokofiev: A composer's memoir*, London: Macdonald and Jane's, 1979, pp. 89–90.

Prokofiev provides an insight into the challenges faced by modern composers in the Soviet Union during the 1920s. This was a period when an aesthetic debate concerning Russian music took place between the Russian Association of Proletarian Musicians, founded in 1924, and the Association for Contemporary Music, founded in 1923. In short, contemporary music was held to be incompatible with 'the proletarian spirit'. This state of affairs prompted Prokofiev to reflect:

> 'What is closer to the proletariat, the pessimism of Tchaikovsky, and the would-be heroic spirit of Beethoven, a century out of date, or the chiselled rhythm and the excitement of *Rails* by [Vladimir] Deshevov?'

Following a particular concert, Prokofiev observed:

> 'During the performance of Beethoven, the workers were utterly bored, and patiently, with polite endurance, waited for the music to end. But music by contemporary Soviet composers aroused a contagious emotion among the audience.'

David Gutman, *Prokofiev*, London: Omnibus Press, 1990, p. 109.

PHILIP RADCLIFFE

The English musicologist and composer Phillip Radcliffe places Beethoven's music in its evolving time-context:

> 'Like the work of many great artists, Beethoven's music has produced very different reactions at different times. For many years the approach to it was dominated by the picture of a tragic rebel, perpetually shaking his fist at destiny; great emphasis was laid on the works of his middle period, especially those associated with some kind of extra-musical programme or message, the early works being patronized as immature and the latest dismissed as incomprehensible. A reaction against this attitude led to a tendency to

regard him as a much over-rated composer who, towards the end of his life, somehow contrived to write some fine quartets. The division of his creative life into three periods is helpful up to a point, but it has sometimes led people to refer to early, middle and late Beethoven as though they were practically three different composers. It is perhaps easier for us now to see how Beethoven's style could at the same time develop immeasurably and yet continue to be the expression of a highly independent personality.'

Radcliffe exemplifies the merits of Beethoven's music by making reference to various compositions:

'Beethoven, like Bach, had many facets to his musical personality, and this is true not only of his last works but of his whole output. His first period has been described as the period of imitation, but does not take into account the independence and imaginativeness of its best works. Similarly the second period is usually associated with the familiar large-scale works, heroic and spacious in manner, but it has ... been suggested that their more intimate and lyrical contemporaries, such as the Fourth Piano Concerto, the Piano Sonata in F-sharp major, Op. 78, the Violin Sonata in G major, Op. 96, and many others show an entirely different but equally important aspect of Beethoven's personality. In the works of his last period there is an element of bareness and austerity which, partly owing to the nature of their medium, finds particularly full expression in the posthumous quartets ... The style of his third period can show the most monumental spaciousness in such works as the Ninth Symphony, the Mass in D and the Piano Sonata in B-flat major, Op. 106, and the richest and mellowest lyricism in the sonatas Op. 109 and Op. 110 ... Since Beethoven's death his music has been appreciated, sometimes for this quality and sometimes for that; perhaps, at long last, it has now become possible for us to get a clearer and more comprehensive view of it all.'

Philip Radcliffe, *Beethoven's String Quartets*, Cambridge: Cambridge University Press, 1978, pp. 20–1.

MAURICE RAVEL

As a student at the Paris Conservatoire, Maurice Ravel showed great promise as a pianist, winning the Conservatoire's first prize in piano. He soon realised, however, that his true vocation was in composition and that his idol was Mozart. His writings bear testimony to this, generally to the detriment of Beethoven:

'For me it is Mozart. Mozart is perfection: he is Grecian, whereas Beethoven is Roman. The Greek is great, the Roman is colossal. I prefer the great. There is nothing as sublime as the third act of Mozart's *Idomeneo*.'

Ravel was given to proclaiming:

'My music is unequivocally French. Anything except Wagnerian. And just as little like that of Richard Strauss or the modern Viennese. That's

> why I hope it may please the Viennese, since it's so different from their own! Frenchmen, in turn, enjoy Viennese music. I personally feel particularly close to *Mozart*. My admirers exaggerate when they compare me with him. Beethoven strikes me as a classical Roman, Mozart as a classical Hellene. I myself feel closer to the open, sunny Hellenes.'

Ravel's biographer Arbie Orenstein reminds us that the music of Beethoven and Wagner was performed regularly in France during the composer's lifetime. He suggests that Ravel's response to this was complex and somewhat contradictory. Ravel considered Wagner and Beethoven to be "philosophical" composers and his response to them,

> 'combined elements of respect, awe, and jealousy, coupled with a marked rejection of their influence on French composers'.

In March 1911, Ravel gave an interview in which he expressed his opinions on contemporary French music; Ravel was by then considered to be one of France's leading composers. His views were subsequently published under an anonymous hand. Passages of his text more-or-less reiterate the thoughts quoted above:

> 'Beethoven can be considered a decadent Mozart from the point of view that he brought to its height and to its close the life which Mozart's music expresses, just as the Byzantine Art can be called a decadent Greek art because it brought to a close the Greek Art. Mozart in music, like Raphael in painting, possessed a certain perfection which was

> marked, nevertheless, by a certain dryness. Beethoven, who was less perfect, was also less dry.'

Twenty years later Ravel gave a further interview, a synopsis of which was subsequently published. By then Ravel was at the height of his fame and had just completed work on his piano concerto for the left hand, written for the pianist Paul Wittgenstein who had been seriously injured in the Great War. Time had clearly not weakened its hold on Ravel's musical opinions. With his own piano concerto in mind, he remarked:

> 'One should not make pretentious assumptions about this concerto which it cannot satisfy. What Mozart created for the enjoyment of the ear is perfect, in my opinion, and even Saint-Saëns achieved this goal, although on a much lower level. Beethoven, however, overacts, dramatizes, and glorifies himself, thereby failing to achieve his goal.'

Arbie Orenstein, editor, *A Ravel Reader: Correspondence, articles, interviews*, New York: Columbia University Press, 1990, p. 378, p. 409, p. 433, p. 473 and p. 488.

A further anecdote bears testimony to Ravel's antipathy to Beethoven. The fashionable portrait painter Jacques-Emile Blanche was a good amateur pianist who enjoyed playing piano duets. He initially persuaded Ravel to be his duet partner, but the planned enterprise foundered as Blanch explains:

> 'We agreed ... that [Ravel] would come twice a week to my studio to play duets. These meetings were planned, postponed and finally abandoned,

for the curious reason that Ravel asked me to exclude Beethoven, Wagner, Schumann and any other "romantics" from our repertoire and indicated we should stick to the numerous works of Mozart. I was not very happy with the idea and roused in him a mixture of disdain and pity.'

Roger Nichols, *Ravel Remembered*, London: Faber and Faber, 1987, pp. 15–16.

HANS RICHTER

As with Maurice Ravel (see above) the Austro-Hungarian conductor Hans Richter clearly preferred the music of Mozart to that of Beethoven. He revealed this, albeit in a somewhat backhanded and amusing manner, when he was once asked to name the composer who, in his opinion 'was the greatest of them all'. Without hesitation he responded, 'Beethoven, undoubtedly'. The questioner expressed surprise at a reply so positive: 'Undoubtedly, Herr Doktor? But I thought you might have considered Mozart.' 'Oh', replied Richter, 'I didn't understand that you were bringing Mozart into the argument; I thought you were referring to the rest!'

As told in: Neville Cardus, *Talking of Music* (brief description), London: Collins, 1957, p. 69.

FERDINAND RIES

The German composer and pianist Ferdinand Ries was a pupil of Beethoven from 1801 to 1804, the period when he made his public debut as a concert pianist playing the composer's C minor Piano Concerto, Op. 37 – with his own cadenza. In 1838 Ries published a collection of reminiscences of Beethoven, co-written with the composer's life-long friend the distinguished physician Franz Wegeler. These appeared under the original title *Biographische Notizen über Ludwig van Beethoven* and are considered to be an important and reliable source of information. They are available in English as: Franz Wegeler and Ferdinand Ries, *Remembering Beethoven: The biographical notes of Franz Wegeler and Ferdinand Ries*, London: Andre Deutsch, 1988. Perhaps the most repeated anecdote told about Ries relates to the occasion of the first rehearsal of the *Eroica* Symphony. During this, Ries mistakenly believed the horn player had come in too early and said so to Beethoven — incurring his displeasure. It is also from Ferdinand Ries that we learn of the deterioration of Beethoven's hearing. When out walking in the countryside one day Ries heard a shepherd playing his pipe — possibly a shawm. It was apparent to him that Beethoven was quite unaware of its sound and so he discreetly made out that he too could not hear anything.

Recalling his days in Vienna, when he received piano instruction from Beethoven, Ries states:

> 'If I missed something in a passage, or played wrongly the notes and leaps he often wanted me to bring out strongly, he rarely said anything; but when I fell short as regards expression, crescendos, etc., or the character of the piece, he got exasperated because he said, the first was an accident, but the other was a lack of judgement, feeling or attentiveness. The former happened to him quite often too, even when he played in public.'

Wegeler-Ries, 1988, p. 94 et seq. See also Ferdinand Ries cited in: Alfred Brendel, *Alfred Brendel on Music: Collected essays*, Chicago, Iliinois: A Cappella Books, 2001, p. 48.

Despite possessing a fiery temperament, Ries's recollections suggest Beethoven was a patient teacher. Writing to the publisher Nikolous Simrock, Ries remarks:

> 'Beethoven takes more pains with me than I shall ever have believed possible. I have three lesson a week, usually from one o'clock till half past two.'

It is at this period that Ries studied the *Pastoral* Sonata, Op. 28 with the composer that he later transcribed for string quartet.

For an account of Ferdinand Ries and his relationship with Beethoven, see: Peter Clive, *Beethoven and his World*, Oxford University Press, 2001, p. 285.

Ries left the following account of Beethoven's style at the piano:

> 'In general he played his own compositions in a very capricious manner, but he nevertheless kept strictly accurate time, occasionally, but very seldom, accelerating the tempo. On the other hand, in the performance of a crescendo passage, he would introduce a retard, which produced a beautiful and highly striking effect. Sometimes, in the performance of specific passages, he would infuse into them an exquisite but altogether inimitable expression. He seldom introduced notes or ornaments not set down in the composition.'

Ferdinand Ries cited in: Harold C. Schonberg, *The Great Pianists*, London: Victor Gollancz, 1964, p. 78. See also: Hans Conrad Fischer and Erich Kock, *Ludwig van*

Beethoven: A study in text and pictures, London: Macmillan; New York, St. Martin's Press, 1972, p. 14.

A possible source of influence on Beethoven, in deciding to include a funeral march in his Piano Sonata Op. 26, may have been the opera *Achilles* by the composer Ferdinand (Ferdinando) Paer. This work, a melodrama, celebrates the central character Achilles, Homer's renowned hero of the Trojan Wars. It was premiered on 6 June 1801 at the *Kärntnertor-Theater* where Paer was then Music Director. Writing about this Ries states:

> 'The Funeral March in the A-flat minor Sonata dedicated to Prince Lichnowsky (Opus 26) originated in the great praise Paer's funeral march in his opera *Achilles* received from Beethoven's friends.'

Carl Czerny, who had become a pupil of Beethoven at the time of the premiere of *Achilles*, also makes brief mention of Paer's opera with regard to Beethoven's Op. 26. It is probable Beethoven did not have a particular hero in mind for the subject of his Funeral March; doubtless he was intent upon giving more generalised musical expression to the feelings of loss associated with mourning.

Wegeler-Ries, 1988, p. 70.

Sometime late in 1806 Ries felt an obligation to acknowledge the debt he felt he owed to his teacher and duly wrote to Beethoven informing him of his intention to dedicate to him his own two Piano Sonatas Op. 1:

> 'I shall take this occasion to express my gratitude to you publicly; the sincere and the more ardent

for the intimacy that you have allowed me, and for the friendship with which you have honoured me. The memory of pleasant hours spent near you will never fade from my heart, and if my efforts are rewarded by any success, it is to your counsel that I shall be indebted.'

Derived from Theodore Albrecht, translator and editor, *Letters to Beethoven and other Correspondence*, Lincoln, New England: University of Nebraska Press, 1996, Vol. 1, Letter No. 121, pp. 189–90.

Ries played an important role in establishing Beethoven's works in England, particularly in connection with the Philharmonic Society of London – later the Royal Philharmonic Society. He took up residence in London in April 1813 and was elected a Director of the Society two years later. He was active in the promotion of his own compositions that included eight piano concertos, eight symphonies and 26 string quartets. These works reveal a style, not unsurprisingly, owning a debt to his teacher – Beethoven was once disposed to remark: 'Ries is the crow who follows my plough!' Ries maintained contact with Beethoven to the end and was instrumental (no pun intended) in bringing before the English public several of Beethoven's piano sonatas and other compositions. Perhaps Ries's most significant contribution in this context was the role he played, in 1822, in the Philharmonic Society's commissioning of Beethoven's Choral Symphony.

Ries once said of his master:

'Without wanting to hurt the feeling of any composers living or dead, I must reaffirm my belief that no one else showed such a wealth and

variety of ideas, nor such originality, as Beethoven
did in his works.'

Franz Wegeler and Ferdinand Ries, *Remembering Beethoven: The biographical notes of Franz Wegeler and Ferdinand Ries*, London: Andre Deutsch, 1988, p. 113.

ROMAIN ROLLAND

Notwithstanding his celebrity as a philosopher, dramatist, novelist, essayist, art historian and Nobel Laureate (prize for literature in 1915) Romain Rolland wrote extensively on music and was appointed to the first chair of music history at the Sorbonne in 1903. His passion for music – he was an accomplished pianist – found expression in several studies of Beethoven who for Rolland was 'the universal musician above all the others'. His writings about the composer and his works include: *Beethoven and Handel* (1917); *Goethe and Beethoven* (1930); and *Beethoven the creator* (1937). His *Essays on Music* (1915) also includes a study of Beethoven in his thirtieth year.

Typical of Rolland's word-imagery is:

'The music of Beethoven is the daughter of the same forces of imperious Nature that had just sought an outlet in the man of Rousseau's *Confessions*. Each of them is the flowering of a new season'.

Rolland is here making reference to the autobiographical work *The Confessions* of his fellow countryman Jean-Jacques Rousseau – published in 1782.

Cited in: David Ewen, *Romain Rolland's Essays on Music*. New York: Dover, Publications, 1959, p. 262.

*

In his study of the composer *Beethoven the Creator*, written shortly after the horrors of the Great War, Rolland had to confront not only its divisions and the new musical horizons that were dawning but also the challenge to the supremacy Beethoven and his music had held through the nineteenth century. We recall, for example, the stir that Igor Stravinsky's *The Rite of Spring* (*Le Sacre du printemps*) had created at its first performance in 1913; the police had to be summoned to quell the ensuing riot amongst the audience. Unshaken in his admiration for Beethoven, Rolland wrote:

> 'Alter a life of combat, Beethoven, from his tomb, continued the fight for half a century in the kingdom of the spirit, where, high above our heads, our gods wage their eternal warfare ... We know that everything must pass — we and you, all that we believe in, all that we deny. The suns themselves are mortal. Yet the beams they gave out thousands of years ago still bear their message through the night; and thousands of years later we see by the light of these extinct suns.'

Rolland continues:

> 'I will refresh my eyes, a last time, at the sun of Beethoven. I will say what he was for us — for the peoples of a century. What that is I know now better today than I did when, as a young man, I poured out my song to him. For at that time his light, unique as it was, penetrated us, Today the shock of the meeting of two epochs of humanity — of which the war [the Great War] has been not so much as the separation as the landmark at the crossroads, where so many runners have come

to grief — has had the advantage, that it has forced us to come to full conscience of ourselves, of what we are, of what we love ... I love, therefore I am. And I am which I love.'

Rolland movingly concludes:

'We had become so accustomed to living in our Beethoven, to sharing with him from our infancy the bed of his dreams that we had failed to perceive to what degree the tissue of his dreams was exceptional. Today, when we see a new generation detaching itself from this music that was the voice of our inner world, we perceive that the world was only one of the continents of the spirit. It is nonetheless beautiful for that, nonetheless dear to us; nay, it is dearer still. For only now do our eyes clearly perceive its delimiting lines, the definite contours of the imperial figure that was our *Ecce homo*. Each great epoch of humanity has its own, its Son of God, its human archetype, whose glance, whose gestures, and whose word are the common possession of millions of the living. The whole being of a Beethoven — his sensibility, his conception of the world, the form of his intelligence and of his will, the laws of his construction, his ideology, as well as the substance of his body and his temperament — everything is representative of a certain European epoch. Not that that epoch modelled itself on him! If we resemble him, it is because he and we are made of the same flesh. He is not the shepherd driving his flock before him; he is the bull marching at the head of the herd.'

*

Romain Rolland, *Beethoven the Creator*, Garden City, New York: Garden City, 1937, derived from the Introduction pp.19–21.

Mindful of Beethoven's many bodily afflictions, Rolland writes:

> 'The strong and pure Beethoven himself hoped in the midst of his sufferings that his example would help to give other unfortunate ones ... After years of battling with almost superhuman efforts to rise superior to his suffering and accomplish his life's work – to breathe a little more courage into poor weak humanity, this Prometheus observed to a friend who called too much on God, "O man help thyself". May we be inspired by his noble words. Animated by the example of this man's faith in life and his quiet confidence in himself, let us again take heart.'

Romain Rolland, *Beethoven and Handel*, The Waverley Book Company Ltd, 1917, pp. Vii–viii.

EUGÈNE RONTEIX
PSEUDONYM FOR F. R. DE TOREINX

Eugène Ronteix is considered to be one of the first French historians of romanticism, as demonstrated in his pioneering study *L'Histoire du romantisme en France* (Paris 1829). This is recognised for its perception and insight on many subjects, consistent with the author's belief that 'outworn conventions are being swept away and new vitality, new realism [is being] achieved: in literature, painting, music, historical method ...

and medicine'. In the section dealing with music, Ronteix considered the achievements of Beethoven. In the year when he published his book, Rossini had just composed Guillaume Tell — William Tell — with nearly forty other operas besides. Not surprisingly, therefore, given the Italian composer's widespread fame, Ronteix's remarks about Beethoven make reference to Rossini but are, nonetheless, discerning:

> 'Before Rossini had ever appeared, Beethoven was already a celebrity. Beethoven was one of those phenomena to whom nature declares, as they are brought forth, "There you are; create!" (*Te voilà, crée!*)'.

> 'I can say, without contradicting myself in any way, that original genius as he was, Rossini owed much to Beethoven.'

> 'And when we come to think of it, is not the human mind made in such a way that one idea sparks off another, the latest always being dependent on the penultimate one?'

> 'Would Beethoven himself have become what he is had he not followed Joseph Haydn and Mozart?'

> 'But it is to [Beethoven] alone that we owe those unprepared modulation of the third and minor sixth and the gigantic sounds that accompany them, and which so powerfully grip the listener's imagination.'

> 'It is to Beethoven that we must attribute those extremely repaid movements, in which the

accompaniment marks out every beat of the measure, while the melody graphically weaves its design overhead.'

Peter Le Huray and James Day, editors, *Music and Aesthetics in the Eighteenth and Early-Nineteenth Centuries*, Cambridge: Cambridge University Press, 1988, p. 418.

CHARLES ROSEN

The American pianist and musicologist Charles Rosen has made an intensive study of Beethoven's piano sonatas and their interpretation from which the following extracts are derived:

'The pianistic repertoire supplied by the Beethoven sonatas was one of the principal causes of the shift of the balance of music-making from the private house to the public hall. Intended for the more intimate surroundings, many of the sonatas were seen to be wonderfully apt for virtuoso performance in large halls. Some of the earliest sonatas already presented difficulties resented by the average amateur, and the technical obstacles became harder to surmount with the "Waldstein", the "Appassionata", and "Les Adieux". Later still, it was the "Hammerklavier", Op. 106, which appeared to shut out the amateur completely. Nevertheless, most of the sonatas remained just within the grasp of the amateur who could still make something of them: their difficulties, indeed, gave a sense of contact, however tenuous, with the professional that one could get from almost no other set of serious works. They were a challenge which could be taken on, an ideal to which one could aspire, even if they could not in the end be fully mastered — not even, as Artur Schnabel remarked, by the consummate professional: "No performance of a Beethoven sonata", he claimed, "could be as great as the work itself".'

Concerning Beethoven's expression marks, Rosen observes:

'The changes in phrasing and touch [in Beethoven's sonatas] are integral to the scenario, the concentration of dramatic development. We can find precedents for Beethoven's procedures, particularly in the early work of Haydn, but the transformations of a musical idea by touch, dynamics and phrasing had never been seen before Beethoven on such a scale or with such concentrated intensity. Nor was it ever seen again. This is one of the many reasons the sonatas remain so fascinating to play.'

Concerning tempo, Rosen remarks:

'It is not illegal to play a piece of music at the wrong tempo: we risk neither a jail sentence nor even a fine. A certain school of aesthetics considers it immoral to contravene the composer's intentions, but sometimes it may even be a good idea. We have all heard performances at clearly inauthentic and even absurd tempos which turn out to be revealing, instructive, moving or brilliantly effective. The wrong tempo might be still more effective than the right one. This leads some

> musicians to conclude that there is no correct tempo, and this may be true for certain styles of music in some periods. Nevertheless, Beethoven evidently thought there was a right tempo for each of his works, although it is not entirely clear that he himself always knew or had correctly decided on what that tempo should be.'

Rosen concludes:

> 'It is a fundamental mistake to think that a tempo with which we are comfortable today is bound to be correct. Instruments have changed, concert halls are different, habits of listening have altered. Sensibilities have changed as well. It is true that the majority of tempos at which we now perform Beethoven raise few problems. However, when we study the way Beethoven employed tempo indications, there will be some surprises. We have a bad habit of dismissing a tempo which goes against the grain which makes us ill at ease — claiming that Beethoven must be in error, or that a copyist was at fault. If, like all composers, Beethoven did on rare occasions make mistakes, we would always need some evidence to be able to claim this — an instinctive reaction is not enough.'

Charles Rosen, *Beethoven's Piano Sonatas: A short companion*, New Haven; Connecticut: London: Yal University Press, 2002, pp. 6–7, p.41 and p. 43.

Concerning modern-day performance on period instruments, Rosen comments:

'Above all, playing the ancient instruments with their weaker, subtle, and more fragile tone in a large space with modern acoustics only exacerbates the problem of revealing the music to the public. Reviving the sonority of an eighteenth-century piano is defeated when it is played in a hall that seats more than two or three hundred people even when it is completely audible, which is not always the case: it may be the same instrument, but it is not at all the same sound. Recordings are a more successful means of transmission, but more than anything else, the emphasis on the recorded performance has only reinforced the modern delusion that music is intended more for listening than playing. Nevertheless, the "Authenticity" movement has been salutary and beneficial. Few pianists today would want to perform a Beethoven sonata without at least taking into account the sonority it might have had during the composer's time.'

Charles Rosen, *Critical Entertainments: Music old and new,* Cambridge, Massachusetts; London: Harvard University Press, 2000, p. 300.

When asked if he felt the urge to perform on the fortepiano, Rosen replied:

'No. I don't really find that attractive at all; basically it seems to me that most composers' imaginations — Beethoven's particularly — always exceed the instruments of their time. In one respect a fortepiano is a kind of fraud because

> one assumes there was a kind of instrument in the eighteenth century called the fortepiano which had a certain sound. But in fact there were lots of different types of fortepianos, each having different kinds of sounds. A Viennese piano was so different from an English piano of the time that you might as well have given them different names. Certainly Beethoven expected his music to be played on a great variety of pianos and the music was intended to meet that requirement ... For instance, there are passages in Beethoven which are easier to play on an old piano, while other passages don't "come off" on the old piano at all. Beethoven must have known what would work and what wouldn't, but he still wanted to write them. In other words, there are advantages to both. On the whole, I think the balance is in favour of the modern piano, particularly since the old pianos only work in halls that seat less than 200 people, and you can't make a living playing to audiences of that kind anymore.'

Charles Rosen in conversation with the pianist and musicologist David Dubal in, David Dubal, *The World of the Concert Pianist*, London: Victor Gollancz, 1985, p. 274.

Discussing the last sonatas, Rosen states:

> 'The last sonatas are more radical ... as if the writing of Op. 106 had given Beethoven new confidence. The experimental works of the preceding years shared some of the ideals of Beethoven's younger contemporaries; they were close to the music of the next generation, above

> all the works of Schumann and Mendelssohn. The increase in Beethoven's deafness made him withdraw into himself in greater isolation. The last piano sonatas needed a much longer time to enter the mainstream of musical influence. Even the last quartets were easier for later composers to assimilate.'

We conclude our selection of extracts from Rosen's writings about Beethoven's piano sonatas with his observations:

> 'For all the consternation that the works of the middle period had aroused in critics and musicians, the Sonatas of Op. 31 and the *Waldstein* and *Appassionata*, revealed themselves fairly quickly to be respectable concert pieces. They are deeply serious works, but they do not seem to have, at first hearing, the forthright moral earnestness of the sonatas from the *Pathétique* to *Les Adieux*, largely because they make few concessions to the listener. Understanding them, taking pleasure in hearing them, requires an active participation from the listener never demanded before from the piano sonata. They have understandably inspired a good deal of pretentious interpretation in both writing and performance. This was inevitable: the composer clearly intended these works as exemplars of great spiritual experience. It is less evident that Beethoven's ideas of transcendence is the same as ours.'

Charles Rosen, *Beethoven's Piano Sonatas: A short companion*, New Haven, Connecticut: London: Yale University Press, 2002, p. 229.

Discussing Beethoven more generally, Rosen reflects:

> 'He was perhaps the first composer in history to write deliberately difficult music for a great part of his life. Not that he ever set his face against popular success, or lost hope of achieving it despite the uncompromising difficulty of his work. The fame and the love that his music inspired during his lifetime were, in any case, considerable; but the ovations he received at the premieres of the Ninth Symphony and *Missa Solemnis* — works apparently difficult enough to understand even today and which must have been almost disastrously executed when first played, to judge by the reports — are more a testimony to the respect in which the elderly composer was held than to a genuine acceptance of the music itself.'

Charles Rosen, *The Classical Style: Haydn, Mozart, Beethoven*, London: Faber and Faber, 1976, pp. 385–6.

GIOACHINO ROSSINI

It had long been the wish of the Italian composer Gioachino Rossini to meet Beethoven whose music, although so radically different to his own, he so much admired. The opportunity finally came in 1822 when Rossini was in Vienna — where his operas were all the rage. (Their success was to stir the young Franz Schubert to write his *Overture In The Italian Style*.) Rossini was finally able to arrange a meeting with Beethoven through the help of his fellow countryman Giuseppe Carpani — who knew Beethoven and before him Salieri and Haydn, to all of whom he had served as poet and translator. At the time when the meeting between the two composers took place, Beethoven was 51 and in poor health.

Rossini later recalled his meeting with Beethoven on the occasion when he, in turn, was visited in 1860 by Richard Wagner – an ardent admirer of Beethoven and eager to learn first hand what the Italian could tell him of the encounter. Rossini was then living in Paris and was long into his retirement as a composer for the lyric theatre. Edmond Michotte, a wealthy Belgian amateur composer-pianist, claimed to have been present at the meeting between Rossini and Wagner and later (1906) published an account of his recollections of what took place under the title *La Visite de R. Wagner À Rossini* – subsequently published in translation as *Richard Wagner's visit to Rossini* (see below). It requires an act of trust to believe all that Michotte has to say, but, writing of his recollections (*Preface* to the translation) Herbert Weinstock remarks:

> 'Michotte's dignified and completely honourable character, finds no doubt possible that the Belgian was a reliable, truth-telling witness.'

In that sprit, we relate the following extracts from Rossini's reminisces.

Rossini recalls how he had first heard string quartets by Beethoven performed when he was in Milan and of his admiration for them. He was also familiar with some of the composer's piano compositions. But it was hearing a performance of the *Eroica* Symphony that resolved Rossini to see Beethoven in person:

> 'That music bowled me over. I had only one thought: to meet that great genius, to see him, even if only once.'

*

Of the meeting itself, Rossini recalls:

> 'As I went up the stairs leading to the poor lodging's in which the great man lived, I had some difficulty in containing my emotions. When the door opened, I found myself in a sort of hovel, so dirty as to testify to frightening disorder.'

Rossini recognised Beethoven from the portraits he had already seen of him. He refers to:

> 'the indefinable sadness spread across all his features' but whose eyes 'though small appeared to pierce you'.

Beethoven congratulated Rossini for being the composer of *Il Barbiere di Siviglia* and encouraged him to work at his chosen vocation: 'You Italians. Your language and your vivacity of temperament destine you for it.'

Rossini's conversation with Wagner turned to composers more generally. He conceded his efforts were slight, when compared with those of Haydn and Mozart, adding:

'If Beethoven is a prodigy of humanity, Bach is a prodigy of God!'

When he eventually took leave of Beethoven, Rossini records:

> 'I felt such a painful impression of my visit to that great man — thinking of that destitution, that privation — that I couldn't hold back my tears.'

Edmond Michotte, *Richard Wagner's visit to Rossini* (Paris 1860): and, *An Evening at Rossini's in Beau-Sejour* (Passy),

1858, English translation: Chicago; London: University of Chicago Press, 1982, pp. 40—4, p. 49 and p. 52. See also: Ferruccio Bonavia, *Musicians on Music*, London: Routledge & Kegan Paul, 1956, pp. 215—6 and p. 235.

ANTON RUBINSTEIN

As a pianist, the Russian born Anton Rubinstein is regarded as one of the foremost keyboard virtuosos of the nineteenth century. His contemporary Hans von Bülow, himself a pianist of formidable accomplishments, described him as 'The Michelangelo of Music' and the German music critic Ludwig Rellstab was equally fulsome in his praise of Rubinstein, calling him 'The Hercules of the piano'.

Harold C. Schonberg, *The Great Pianists*, Simon & Schuster, 1963, p. 269.

Rubinstein's contemporaries were struck by his physical resemblance to Beethoven. His virtuosity at the keyboard also called to mind that of Beethoven when he was at the height of his powers. It was said that when Liszt went on recital in Paris, every Érard piano was heard to grown and when Rubinstein performed they would erupt volcanically! Audiences were known to leave after one of Rubinstein's recitals in a state of near mental exhaustion as though they had experienced a force of nature. In these recitals he promoted Beethoven's piano sonatas that included programmes of formidable length and pianistic challenge. For example, on one occasion he played the *Moonlight*, *Tempest*, *Waldstein*, *Appassionata*, the A major (Op. 101) the E major (Op. 109) and the C minor Op. 111!

Harold C. Schonberg, 'The Hercules of the piano'. The Belgian violinist and all-round musician Eugène Ysaÿe – known in his day as 'The God of the violin' – heard Rubinstein perform during a house party sometime in 1876 at which none other than Liszt was also a guest. Writing of Rubinstein's playing, Ysaÿe comments:

> 'He was truly my master of interpretation ... His power over the piano is something undreamt of; he transports you into another world; all that is mechanical in the instrument is forgotten. I am still under the influence of the all-embracing harmony, the scintillating passages and the thunder of Beethoven's Sonata Op. 57, which Rubinstein executed for us with unimagined mastery.'

Antoine Ysaÿe, *Ysaÿe: His life, Work and Influence*, London: W. Heinemann, 1947, p. 24.

Ten years later, it was the turn of Sergei Rachmaninoff – renowned for his own pianistic attainments – to have occasion to be captivated by Rubinstein's playing. Recalling his student days, from the period January–February 1886, Rachmaninoff informs us that Rubinstein was alternating between St. Petersburg and Moscow giving recitals. Rachmaninoff was so in thrall to the legendary interpreter of Beethoven that he heard him perform as often as he could. He enthuses:

> 'It was less his magnificent technique that held one spellbound than the profound, spiritually refined musicianship that sounded from each work he played. I remember how deeply I was

affected by his playing of Beethoven's *Appassionata*, and Chopin's Sonata in B flat minor.'

On one such occasion, Rubinstein was so dissatisfied with his rendering of the short closing crescendo in the Chopin Sonata he promptly repeated the entire work.

Sergei Rachmaninoff, *Rachmaninoff's Recollections told to Oskar von Riesemann*, London: George Allen & Unwin, 1934, pp. 12–13.

It was during one of his visits to Paris that Rubinstein heard the French Pianist Alfred Cortot play the first movement of the *Appassionata* Piano Sonata. Cortot's interpretation did not please Rubinstein, disposing him to proclaim the maxim by which he himself approached the composer's music:

> 'My boy, don't you ever forget what I am going to tell you. Beethoven's music must not be studied. It must be reincarnated.'

Schonberg *op. cit.*, p. 406.

ARTHUR RUBINSTEIN

The Polish-American pianist Arthur Rubinstein is universally admired and remembered for being one of the greatest interpreters of the music of Frédéric Chopin. However, his repertoire embraced works by many other composers including Beethoven. Rubinstein's recollections of his student days connect us to the Piano Sonata Op. 106 and give a hint of his views of the music and his thoughts about its performance.

In the summer of 1910, when he was twenty-three years old, Rubinstein took part in a piano competition held in St. Petersburg; the competition was named in honour of his namesake, the great Beethovenian Anton Rubinstein. Notwithstanding Rubinstein's endeavours, the first prize went to a fellow student by the name of Alfred Hoehn. Rubinstein generously acknowledged Hoehn's achievement; his programme had included the arduous *Hammerklavier* Piano Sonata. Of Hoehn's performance he says:

> 'He played this great work magnificently, as a mature master. This music was in him – it sounded as spontaneous as if he had just composed it. I was deeply impressed by the noble conception of the first movement and moved by the simply and beautifully played *Adagio*. The final difficult fugue was splendid; the whole Sonata was a masterly performance.'

Two days after the competition, Rubinstein and Hoehn performed together, each including the *Hammerklavier* Sonata in his programme. The critics found Rubinstein's interpretation too romantic and that of Hoehn too correct and less exciting. In conversation with his friend, André Diederichs, Rubinstein later declared:

'The truth is we were both right.'

When asked to defend this apparent contradiction, Rubinstein replied:

> '[If] you ask ten famous artists to paint you, your face will be *different* on each picture but the painters will assure you they *interpreted* your face exactly as they see.'

Elaborating his views, he added:

> '[Each] creative work becomes a part of the universe, just like a flower, or human being. Consequently, a sonata sounds *different* to each gifted interpreter. This is the real mission of our particular talents.'

Arthur Rubinstein, *My Young Years,* London: Jonathan Cape, 1973, p. 339 and p. 355.

Rubinstein recalled his time in Paris during the Great War. He visited a hospital where soldiers were being treated. He recounts how his eyes caught sight of an upright piano in the corner of the room. It was abominably out of tune and two or three keys were mute but he sat down and began to play:

> 'I played the Sonata *Pathétique* of Beethoven; I had never played it like that before. It was not how it sounded it was how I felt. I was ready to cry, and so was everyone present.'

Arthur Rubinstein, *My Young Years,* London: Jonathan Cape, 1973, p. 437.

Reflecting more generally on the nature of Beethoven's music, Rubinstein declared:

> 'One seems to forget that Beethoven was the first composer that one could call "romantic," which means simply that he used his creative genius to bring out in his music his despair, his joys, his feeling for nature, his outbursts of rage, and, above all, his love. With his unique mastery, he

expressed all these emotions in perfect forms. Nothing is more foreign to me than the term "classic" when speaking of Beethoven.'

Arthur Rubinstein, *My Many Years*, London: Jonathan Cape, 1980, p. 159.

STEPHEN RUMPH

The American musicologist and academic Stephan Rumph identifies Beethoven in the context of politics:

> 'Beethoven was a political composer. Like few other musicians in the Western canon, he stubbornly dedicated his art to the problems of human freedom, justice, progress, and community. Beethoven found his voice with a cantata memorializing the enlightened reforms of Joseph II, and he crowned his public career in Vienna with the Ninth Symphony's hymn to universal brotherhood. No intervening work drew more labour or revisions from him than *Fidelio* (née *Leonora*), the first political opera to remain in the permanent repertory ... The political note in Beethoven's music echoes the cataclysmic times in which he lived ... While Napoleon was gathering laurels in Italy and Egypt, Beethoven was conquering the salons and halls of Vienna, undertaking a deliberate campaign to annex all current musical genres.'

Rumph reflects on the origins of the estimations of Beethoven the romantic:

> 'For two centuries the evolving image of Beethoven has taken shape in the passionate echolalia of critical prose, no less than in the concert hall, the classroom, or the sculptor's studio. E. T. A. Hoffmann stands at the head of this line as its first great genius. His reviews, literary rhapsodies translated the heroic style into Romantic terms, bequeathing the nineteenth century a compelling portrait of Beethoven as mystic visionary and conquistador of the spirit of the world. Hoffmann's was, of course, a distorted image; like any interesting critic, he brought strong prejudices to his material. In particular, his allegiance to the transcendent metaphysical realm blinded him to the enlightened aspects of the heroic style. Yet even this distortion proves illumination. As we watch Hoffmann tailoring the Fifth Symphony to his specifications, we see a fascinating preview of the way Beethoven himself would rework his style as he fell under the Romantic spell.'

Hoffmann wrote a critical appreciation of Beethoven's Fifth Symphony in 1810 to much subsequent acclaim.

Rumph provides the reader with detailed commentaries on the writings of the following Beethoven authorities: Walter Riezler, Heinrich Schenker, Joseph Kerman, Charles Rosen, Maynard Solomon, and Theodor Adorno. He concludes by turning to the works of Beethoven's final period:

> 'Studying late Beethoven ... means coming to terms with the modern legacy. Our understanding of this repertory is twisted up at the roots with the

axioms of a bygone age. It seems telling that the most vital new studies of Beethoven have turned to the *Eroica* and the heroic works, resuscitating modes of interpretations the earlier critics disdained. The late works await the same kind of research by critics who will not shy away from paradoxical and contingent aspects of this music. Mythology will have to give way to history, the cultic Beethoven to a more human figure. Then perhaps these fascinating works can tumble from their pedestal of absolute music into the melee of real human discourse.'

Stephen C. Rumph, *Beethoven after Napoleon: Political romanticism in the late works*, Berkeley; London: University of California Press, 2004, pp. 1–2 and p. 222.

CAMILLE SAINT-SAËNS

The French composer, organist, conductor and pianist Camille Saint-Saëns was one of the most remarkable musical child prodigies in history. At the age of five he performed to private audiences and when age ten made his public debut in Paris at the Salle Pleyel. His programme included Mozart's Piano Concerto in B flat, K450 and Beethoven's Third Piano Concerto. Most remarkably, Saint-Saëns played from memory. At the close of the concert he offered to give as an encore any of the Beethoven Piano sonatas! At over the age of sixty he repeated the offer at a concert to the musical elect of Madrid. Towards the end of his long life (86), Saint-Saëns maintained diligent morning practice by performing scales and arpeggios – relieving what he considered to be the tedium by simultaneously reading the morning newspaper that he placed on the piano's music rack!

*

Adapted, in part, from James Harding, *Saint-Saëns and his Circle*, London: Chapman & Hall, 1965, p. 18.

Saint-Saëns paid homage to Beethoven in his Variations on a Theme by Beethoven, Op. 35. These take the form of a duo composed for four hands on two pianos. The main theme is taken from Beethoven's Sonata in E flat, Op. 31, No. 3. Saint-Saëns' ten variations are lively and technically demanding. Throughout the piece the two pianos trade-off between playing and waiting in a manner that is exciting to observe in performance. The two protagonists exchange rapidly alternating chords that are shared between the two pianos, much as they alternate between the lower and upper registers of the keyboard in Beethoven's original Menuetto. An amusing anecdote recalls the occasion when Saint-Saëns himself took part in a performance of his Variations, and, quite uncharacteristically, lost his nerve in the 'diabolical finale'.

> '[He] rushed headlong at the *Presto* — with his partner gallantly following — and won the breathless race with only a bar's difference between them.'

As recounted by James Harding, *Saint-Saëns and his Circle*, London: Chapman & Hall, 1965, pp. 129–30.

The Polish-American virtuoso pianist, composer, and teacher Leopold Godowsky was one of the most highly regarded virtuosi of his time. Something of his performance-style can still be appreciated today since he was a pioneer in the art of the piano-roll recording. Godowsky was on close terms with Saint-Saëns and played for him regularly. In turn, Saint-Saëns also performed — almost anything from his prodigious repertoire that included not only piano music but keyboard reductions of symphonies, overtures, chamber music and operas. Even Liszt held Saint-Saëns in high regard, as a recollection from Godowsky's memoirs confirms:

> 'Saint-Saëns could talk most delightfully about music, and many an interesting séance have I had with him in his Paris apartment, climbing four flights of stairs to reach it. Liszt gave him a photo of himself inscribed "Au Beethoven français", which seems not altogether appropriate; but then Liszt had a tendency to exaggerate when he praised.'

Jeremy Nicholas, *Godowsky: The pianists' pianist; A biography of Leopold Godowsky*, Hexham: Appian Publications & Recordings, 1989, p. 23.

ANTON FELIX SCHINDLER

Anton Felix Schindler was an associate of Beethoven and acted as his secretary, assistant and spokesman in the latter period of the composer's life. He was by training a lawyer although his vocation was in music; he was appointed leader of the violins in the Josephstadt-theatre. Schindler's claim to Beethoven fame is his early study *Biographie von Ludwig van Beethoven* that was published in Münster in 1840 and again in 1860 in two volumes with extensive revisions and additions. English-speaking readers know this work as *Beethoven as I Knew Him*, edited with commentaries and emendations by Donald W. MacArdle in a translation by Constance S. Jolly, London: Faber and Faber, 1966.

Throughout the nineteenth century, and well into the twentieth, Schindler's *Life* had a considerable influence on the perception of Beethoven and Beethoven biography.

Unfortunately for posterity, it is believed Schindler destroyed some of the composer's Conversation Books — although not as many as the 400 that has been previously suggested. In addition, his reliability as a credible chronicler of Beethoven has been called into question. It is now considered he may have inserted spurious entries into a number of the composer's surviving Conversation Books and that his accounts of alleged conversations with the composer, notably about the nature of his music, may have been exaggerated or even invented.

See: Peter Stadlen, *Schindler's Beethoven Forgeries*, The Musical Times, Vol. 118, No. 1613, July 1977, pp. 549–552.

The Beethoven scholar Barry Cooper discusses the problem of Schindler's alleged falsifications in his *The Beethoven Compendium: A guide to Beethoven's life and music*, London: Thames and Hudson, 1991. Others have attempted to exonerate Schindler, at least in part, from some of the more extreme accusations charged against him. See, for example, Theodore Albrecht, translator and editor, *Letters to Beethoven and other Correspondence*, Lincoln, New England: University of Nebraska Press, 3 vols., 1996. Notwithstanding Schindler's indiscretions, as Donald W. MacArdle, the editor to the 1960 edition of Schindler's text remarks:

> 'The Beethoven who steps forth from these pages is indeed the Beethoven of the *Eroica* and last Quartets ... [and] will give much that cannot be found elsewhere.'

Anton Schindler (1966), p. 19.

Beethoven had a number of nicknames for Schindler including *Papageno*. The musically inclined reader will recall *Papageno* is the bird catcher in Mozart's opera *The Magic Flute* whose mouth was padlocked to dispose him to greater circumspection. Schindler, somewhat vainly, let it be known the composer also knew him as *Samothracian Lumpenkerl* an allusion to the ancient ceremonies of Samothrace — taken to imply Schindler was one of the initiated to have privileged insights into the inner workings of Beethoven's life and work.

Elliot Forbes, editor, *Thayer's Life of Beethoven*, Princeton, New Jersey: Princeton, University Press, 1967, p. 858 and footnote 78.

It is considered Schindler's commentaries to Beethoven's piano sonatas are reliable and it is from these that we have selected the following extracts. Schindler enthuses:

> 'The [piano] sonatas alone claim the position of true poetry; they alone are portraits of the heart in the truest meaning of the expression, and therefore are confined within a narrower framework than any other medium performed in public. With the sonata the lover of musical poetry separates himself from all external influences or intrusions upon his feelings, and finds himself alone with his most intimate friend or beloved. Should the work fall false upon his outer ear, the heart will hear it otherwise, for his fantasy, awakened by the tones and harmonies, will correct any technical defects. The sonata is best able to inspire reverence in the soul, and often lifts it to prayer.'

Schindler, 1966, p. 403.

*

Typical of Schindler's effusive style and the manner of endorsement of his master's work is the following passage:

> 'Consider the form of the first movement of the first Sonata in F minor, how different it is from the form of the first movement of the Sonata in E-flat major, Op. 7! And how different again are the first movements of the Sonata in C minor Op. 10 and the *Pathétique* Op. 13, and so on through the wonderfully inspired Sonatas Op. 57 (F minor), Op. 90 (E minor), right up to the last! Each one different, and yet the master leads us by way of his form along such a sure, clear path that requires little imagination, provided the performance is adapted to the content, to retain the thread of poetry without losing it for even at instant!'

Schindler, 1966, p. 405.

Concerning the mood prevailing in the two Piano Sonatas Op. 14, Schindler gives an account of a conversation with Beethoven that he states took place sometime in 1823. He describes how he raised the question with the composer of the 'inner meaning' of his piano sonatas — a subject upon which the composer is known to have been particularly reticent. Regarding the Op. 14 Sonatas, Schindler alleges Beethoven said they embodied a form of dialogue between two principles whose meaning was inherent within the music and which required no interpretive words to be written above the score.

Schindler, 1966, p. 406.

In our desire for a better understanding of Beethoven, we want to believe in the veracity of such remarks as the forgoing. On this occasion it has to be conceded some commentators have reservations Schindler's conversation ever took place, or, if it did, that he may have elaborated the account to suit his own ends. Harold Truscott is one authority who considers Schindler's remarks to be somewhat fanciful, given Beethoven's reluctance to give detailed interpretations of his compositions.

Harold Truscott, *The Piano Music* [of Beethoven], in: Denis Arnold and Nigel Fortune, editors, London: Faber and Faber, 1973, p. 102.

Konrad Wolff gives Schindler the benefit of the doubt. He discusses Schindler's interpretation at some length and considers his views may have some 'inner truth'. He cites the manner in which, from the start, 'right hand and left hand are brought into rhythmic and melodic opposition – "pleading" and "resisting".'

Konrad Wolff, *Masters of the Keyboard: Individual style elements in the piano music of Bach, Haydn, Mozart, Beethoven, Schubert, Chopin, and Brahms*, Bloomington: Indiana University Press, 1990, p. 157.

William Newman also remarks on the 'personified conflict', thought by some to be inherent within the Op. 14 Piano Sonatas. He then observes, in more everyday terms, how much they differ from their dramatic predecessor the Sonata *Pathétique*:

'[They] are relatively quiet and intimate, distinguished by their charm, wit, and craftsmanship.'

William Newman, *The Sonata in the Classic Era*, Chapel Hill: University of North Carolina Press 1963, p. 515.

The D minor Piano Sonata, Op. 31, No. 2 bears the designation *The Tempest – Der Sturm* in Beethoven's native language. The origins of this sobriquet may be traced to an anecdote recalled by Schindler. According to his account, he told the composer what a great impression this piece had made upon him when he heard it played by the composer's pupil Carl Czerny (see above). When asked to reveal the meaning inherent in the composition, Schindler states Beethoven gave the laconic reply: 'Just read Shakespeare's *Tempest.*' He was no more explicit.

Schindler 1966, p. 406.

The reader will recall Shakespeare's play opens in the midst of a violent storm that rages about an enchanted isle, and contains such memorable lines as: 'The isle is full of noises, sounds and sweet airs.' Little wonder then, with such implicit musical associations, belief in Schindler's claims seized the imagination of later writers and artists. For example, the German scholar and musicologist Arnold Schering constructed an entire book that purported to establish relationships between Beethoven's piano music and Shakespeare's text.

Paul Henry Lang, *Musicology and Performance*, New Haven: Yale University Press, 1997, pp. 238–9.

In response to these romantic imaginings, the German illustrator Alois Kolb depicted Beethoven as a robed figure — probably the play's principal character Prospero — standing before tempestuous winds within which hapless maidens are tossed about. A reproduction of Kolb's illustration can be viewed on the Beethoven House Digital Archives, Library Document Ley, Band VIII, No. 112.

It is now considered Schindler's anecdote is probably apocryphal.

Barry Cooper, *Beethoven and the Creative Process*, Oxford: Clarendon Press, 1990, p. 42.

Wilfrid Mellers offers a carefully balanced judgement here. He reminds us how, throughout the nineteenth century — a period, let us remember, when Beethoven was being deified — a dominant strand in the estimation of his work 'was founded on the belief his music could best be elucidated by colourful poetic imagery'. Not surprisingly, such an outlook has nurtured the adoption of sobriquets, such as *The Tempest*, and has served as cues for 'elaborate extra-musical programmes'. As Mellers points out, even those 'predisposed to acknowledging a poetic dimension in music criticism have mistrusted their usefulness, viewing them as either too general, or as only selectively appropriate'.

Wilfrid Howard Mellers, *The Sonata Principle* (from c. 1750), London: Rockliff, 1957, p. 44.

We close our selection of extracts from Schindler's writings, by recalling the circumstances that have led to the two movements of the Op. 90 Piano Sonata being characterised, respectively, as a contest between the head and the heart (first movement) and a form of dialogue with a loved one (second movement). Beethoven dedicated the composition to his friend Count Moritz Lichnowsky. He had a relationship with a singer-actress by the name of Josepha (Johanna) Stummer; she is frequently, and mistakenly, described as being a dancer. Johanna was not of noble birth but must have been a singer of some accomplishments; for example, she sang the role of Donna Elvira in Mozart's *Don Giovanni* and was a member of the Gesellschaft der Musikfreunde. Schindler claims Beethoven had set the Count's love-story to music and that the two movements could be described as: 'Conflict between head and heart' — Moritz wrestling with his uncertainty and 'Conversations with the Beloved' — Moritz and Johanna united in their mutual affections.

Schindler, 1966, p. 210.

Thereby, Schindler set in motion a body of programmatic interpretation, bearing on the alleged inner meaning of the E minor Piano Sonata, that endured throughout the nineteenth century and beyond.

*

JOHANN ALOYS SCHLOSSER

Johann Aloys Schlosser is significant to Beethoven musicology for being the composer's first biographer. His *Biographie* was written in the year of Beethoven's death (1827) when it may also have been published — although the Title Page gives 1828. The work's full title reads, in translation: *Ludwig van Beethoven, A biography, together with assessments of his works, published with the aim of erecting a monument to his teacher, Joseph Haydn.* Of interest here is the regard in which Beethoven's teacher Haydn was held, and the value already being attached to Beethoven's correspondence as a source of information about him.

In his introduction to Richard G. Pauly's modern-day translation of Schlosser's text (1996), Beethoven authority Barry Cooper remarks how little of Schlosser himself is known. He was a partner in a publishing firm in Prague and may have become aware of the young Beethoven when he performed there in 1796 and 1798. Cooper remarks how Schlosser's brief biography 'satisfied an immediate need' about a composer whose funeral cortege was witnessed by several thousand spectators — an honour normally reserved for emperors. Although subsequent research has corrected errors and flaws in Schlosser's text, it is still held in high regard for providing a contemporary view of Beethoven and what was believed about him in Vienna and Prague in 1827.

Schlosser opens his account:

> 'Beethoven's death has been noted with more grief, in Germany and throughout Europe, than anyone else's for a long time. His art reached a level far above what others will attain. We therefore grieve not only because of our loss but also

because there is no one able to take his place. Beethoven was not only a great artist but also a great human being.'

Later Schlosser pays tribute to Beethoven the virtuoso:

'People marvelled at the facility with which he executed difficult passages. His playing may not always have been delicate, and at times may have lacked clarity, but it was extremely brilliant. He excelled particularly at free improvisation. Here it was really quite extraordinary with what ease, and yet soundness in the succession of ideas, he would improvise on any theme given to him.'

Of the composer's working method, Schlosser observes:

'Beethoven liked to compose outdoors: there he could best find ideas. When they came he treasured them as the inspirations of the moment but did not concern himself with developing them immediately. While still outdoors, however, he would commit them to paper and would continue them on his way home ... Only the working out of these ideas in score was carried out in his room ...'.

Schlosser remarks on the public acclaim Beethoven received at the period of the Congress of Vienna when his so-called Battle Symphony was performed — Wellington's Victory, or, The Battle of Vitoria (Wellingtons Sieg oder die Schlacht bei Vittoria). This work, now faded from the concert repertoire, together with the Seventh Symphony, elevated Beethoven's public reputation to a greater extent than he had ever previously enjoyed — or would ever again experience.

Writing about Beethoven's Op. 1, the set of three piano trios that were first performed in 1795, Schlosser remarks:

'They display extraordinary deep sentiments, which have not yet found their true outlet. This has caused some to complain of disorder in these and some subsequent compositions, and not without reason. In these and some later works Beethoven revels his heart, in a great surge of feeling. With this music we enter a new world, which he was to conquer triumphantly.'

Of Beethoven's first venture into writing for the medium of the string quartet, namely the six quartets Op. 18, Schlosser comments prophetically:

'[These] are works of a maturing artist, so that not surprisingly they contain many hints of the later period.'

Remarking on Beethoven's later compositions he adds:

'The works of the last period are shaped by inner necessity. Everything follows organically from what preceded, so that everything accidental, uncertain, or extraneous is excluded. Thus each composition is meaningful, coherent, and unified whole. In the same way, the fruit emerges from the blossom, which itself owes its life to the living tree: that is the mysterious law of life, in nature and in art.'

Of Beethoven himself, Schlosser concluded:

'He was an artist, but also a man – a human being in the word's most perfect sense.'

Johann Schlosser, *Beethoven: The first biography, 1827*: translated by Richard G. Pauly and edited by Barry Cooper, Portland, Oregon: Amadeus Press, 1996, pp. 9–34, pp. 70–80, p. 116, p. 138 and p. 141.

*

ARTUR SCHNABEL

In his music-making, the Austrian pianist Artur Schnabel is remembered for his high-mindedness and intellectual seriousness. His interpretations, particularly of the works of Beethoven and Schubert, have been described as 'displaying marked vitality, profundity and spirituality'. He was the first pianist to record the complete cycle of the 32 piano sonatas of Beethoven that he accomplished between 1932 and 1935 on the British HMV label. This achievement prompted the musicologist Harold C. Schonberg to dub Schnabel as 'the man who invented Beethoven'.

Harold C. Schonberg, *The Great Pianists*, London: Victor Gollancz, 1964.

Schnabel's first performance of the Beethoven piano-sonata cycle was in 1927 for an organisation called *The People's Stage*. The architect Oskar Kaufmmann, who designed the title pages for some of Schnabel's own early compositions, also designed their auditorium. Reflecting on his performance of the Beethoven piano sonatas Schnabel recalls:

> 'I played the complete cycle of the thirty-two Beethoven sonatas (each time in recitals) only four times in my life: twice in Berlin, once in London and once in New York. In Berlin I repeated the cycle, this time at the *Philharmonie*, the hall where all the orchestral concerts of the Berlin Philharmonic Orchestra took place, during the winter season of 1932–3.'

In the meantime, the National Socialists came to power. Of this Schnabel recalls:

> 'The right to broadcast my seven concerts – the cycle of the thirty-two Beethoven sonatas – had

been bought by the state-controlled German Broadcasting Company. Apparently, when Hitler took over they were commanded to stop broadcasting these concerts, for the last three recitals of my series, from February on, were not broadcast. I found out about this only from the people who wanted to hear my concerts on the radio (the hall was a sell out) because the Broadcasting Company never notified me.'

In 1945, with the ending of the war, Schnabel gave an address at the University of Chicago. At its conclusion, he took questions from the audience. One student asked if the difference between Beethoven's pianos and those of today should be considered in performance. Schnabel replied:

'It should. But the result will not be to disavow Beethoven's very daring and revealing use of the pedal. I have had access to the marvellous collections in Vienna and in Berlin. I have played Bach's, Beethoven's, Weber's and other pianos. In Beethoven's case the effect of the pedalizations demanded by him was exactly the same on the old instruments as on the new ones. In all his compositions for piano Beethoven made only thirty or a few more pedal marks ... The markings by Beethoven have to be observed under all circumstances, in every room or mood or company, because they are an inseparable part of the music as such, and if one does not observe these pedal marks, the music is changed.'

Artur Schnabel, *My Life and Music*, London: Longmans, 1961, p. 105 et seq.

Schnabel is remembered for his performing edition of the Beethoven sonatas. Commenting on this, the pianist Leon Fleisher remarked:

> 'His edition of the Beethoven sonatas is so instructive because his ideas and suggestions are in a different print than what Beethoven wrote; you can always distinguish between Beethoven and Schnabel. But that kind of dedication, that kind of musical integrity to the desires and instructions from the composer, gave it an authenticity that was irresistible, and that was combined with his level of inspiration.'

In his 1945 interview with the music students at the University of Chicago, one student remarked:

> 'You have edited many of the compositions of Beethoven. How do you go about editing the music of a man who is dead?'

Schnabel replied:

> 'I edited Beethoven's thirty-two sonatas in the twenties. Maybe I would proceed differently now. When I first tried my hand at editing, in 1912, I was not yet as conscientious, and much less experienced than in the twenties. For the Beethoven edition which, as a whole, I think to be still usable, I tried to get hold of as much original material as possible — manuscripts, first and second editions of which Beethoven had seen the proofs. In the case of different versions

in manuscripts and in the printed editions which Beethoven had seen the proofs, I decided on the printed version, because Beethoven was not always too careful in his manuscripts, knowing that he would see the proofs ... The metronome markings — with the one exception of Opus 106 where Beethoven has provided them — are my choice and responsibility, but are never intended to be more than suggestions.'

Artur Schnabel, *My Life and Music*, London: Longmans, 1961, pp. 130–1.

Schnabel's playing has not always found favour. In March 1944, he gave an all-Beethoven recital in the Carnegie Hall comprising the Piano Sonatas Opp. 10, No. 2, 31, No. 2, 110 and 111. The reviewer (unnamed but probably Virgil Thomson — see below) felt disposed to remark:

'Artur Schnabel, who played last night in the Carnegie Hall the second of three recitals ... devoted to the piano music of Beethoven, has for some thirty or forty years made this composer the object of his special attention. He passes, indeed, and with reason, for an expert on the subject ... His ideas about Beethoven's piano music in general, whether or not one finds his readings convincing, are not to be dismissed lightly. Neither need they, I think, be taken as the voice of authority. For all the consistency and logic of his musicianship, there is too large a modicum of late-nineteenth-century Romanticism in Mr. Schnabel's own personality to make his Beethoven — who was, after all, a child of the late eighteenth — wholly convincing to musicians of the mid-twentieth. No one wants to deny the Romantic elements in Beethoven, but I do think that they are another kind of Romanism from Schnabel's, which seems to be based on the Wagnerian theories of expressivity.'

Cited in: Virgil Thomson, *The Musical Scene*, New York: Greenwood Press, 1968, p.192.

Arthur Rubinstein was not always impressed by Schnabel's playing. He is on record as remaking:

'I was never convinced by the intellectual and almost pedantic conception of Artur Schnabel, the acknowledged specialist in these works. He sounded to me as if he were giving lessons to us in the audience.'

Arthur Rubinstein, *My Many Years*, London: Jonathan Cape, 1980, p. 159.

Schnabel was one of the few artists to perform the *Hammerklavier* Sonata at Beethoven's original tempo indications. Writing of his performance, Martin Cooper states:

'Artur Schnabel decided to take Beethoven at his word and to play the first movement of Op. 106 at the tempo so long considered impossible. He did not wholly convince listeners by his own performance in which the fullness of the fast chordal passages and the wealth of detail in inner parts were not ideally clear, and his example has not been generally followed by subsequent performers, even those with larger hands and greater facility than Schnabel's.'

A less generous commentator than Cooper condemned Schnabel's adherence to Beethoven's stipulations as an act of 'mistaken piety'.

Martin Cooper, *Beethoven: The last decade, 1817–1827*, London: Oxford University Press, 1970, p. 159.

It is now universally acknowledged — with the possible exception of Artur Schnabel — that Beethoven's tempo indications to the Piano Sonata Op. 106 are unrealistically too fast. In the words of Alfred Brendel:

> 'The metronome marks ... with one exception ... are all hurried, not to say mechanically overdriven. In the first movement particularly, the prescribed tempo cannot be attained, or even approached, on any instrument in the world, by any player at all, be he the devil incarnate, with grievous loss of dynamics, colour and clarity.'

Alfred Brendel, *Alfred Brendel on Music: Collected essays*, Chicago, Iliinois: A Cappella Books, 2001, p. 33.

An anecdote connects us with Artur Schnabel and the last of Beethoven's piano sonatas. In his recollections he relates:

> 'A friend of mine in Frankfurt-am-Main was the famous Louis Koch. I mention him because he had one of the finest collections of musical and other precious manuscripts. Each time I went to Frankfurt he invited me to spend hours in his house alone. His housekeeper had instructions

to open to me whatever I was interested in. So in
that house, quite by myself, I read or played from
manuscript works like some of the last Beethoven
Sonatas and the last three Schubert sonatas. It
was an inestimable experience.'

Artur Schnabel, 1961, p. 63.

Schnabel is known for his sense of humour. While on a tour
of Spain, he wrote to his wife saying that during a performance of Beethoven's *Diabelli* Variations he had begun to feel
sorry for the audience:

'I am the only person here who is enjoying this, and I
get the money; they pay and have to suffer.'

On another occasion he remarked:

'The notes I handle no better than many pianists. But the
pauses between the notes — ah, that is where the art resides.'

Comparing composers he once stated:

'Mozart is a garden, Schubert is a forest in light and
shade, but Beethoven is a mountain range.'

There were times when even Schnabel's sense of
humour must have been severely tested, as, for example, on
an occasion when he was performing Beethoven's Piano
Sonata Op. 101. The circumstance in question relates to a
period, just before the outbreak of the Great War, when
Schnabel was on a concert tour of what was then East
Prussia. We let him take up the tale:

'I remember one place where I played
Beethoven's Sonata Op. 101 as the first item. As
you know it opens with a very delicate movement.
The retired sergeant, who had been selling
programmes and tickets at a table behind the last
row, counted his takings during this delicate

> movement, throwing copper and sliver coins onto
> a china plate which he had ready on his table.'

The clatter of the coins proved too much, even for the equably disposed Schnabel; he had to request the sergeant to stop counting and to start all over again. He magnanimously reflected that the sergeant was only doing his job and no one had forewarned him.

Artur Schnabel, 1961, pp. 48–9.

The American composer and music critic Virgil Thomson heard Artur Schnabel perform on March 28, 1944. His programme included the Piano Sonata Op. 110. By then Thomson had earned a reputation for his wit, candour and independent-minded judgement in his capacity of music critic for the *New York Herald-Tribune*. Notwithstanding that by then Schnabel had also earned a reputation for his interpretations of the piano works of Beethoven, and, we may add, for the 'rediscovery' from years of neglect of the piano sonatas of Franz Schubert, Thomson was clearly not in awe of Schnabel's performance. In his review of the concert, Thomson reflected on Schnabel's many years of study of Beethoven and of his standing as an artist of distinction:

> 'He passes, indeed, and with reason, for an expert
> on the subject, by which is usually meant that his
> knowledge of it is extensive and that his judge-
> ments about it are respected ... His readings about
> Beethoven's piano music in general, whether or
> not one finds his readings convincing, are not to
> be dismissed lightly.'

We should add here, by way of amplification of Thomson's remarks, that, as remarked above, in 1932 Schnabel had completed the first recoding ever of Beethoven's complete set of piano sonatas and at about the same time had published a meticulously thorough performing edition of these works.

Of Schnabel's interpretation, Thomson considered the master unduly emphasized what he regarded as the composition's 'secondary material':

> 'Mr. Schnabel does not admit, or plays as if he did not admit, any difference between the expressive functions of melody and passage work. The neutral material of music — scales, arpeggiated basses, accompanying figures, ostinato chordal backgrounds, formal cadences — he plays as if they were as intense communication, as if they were saying something as important as the main thematic material. They are important to Beethoven's composition, of course; but they are not directly expressive musical elements. They serve as amplification, as underpinning, frequently as mere acoustical brilliance. To execute them all with climactic emphasis is to rob the melodic material, the expressive phrases, of their singing power.'

Virgil Thomson, *The Musical Scene*, New York: Greenwood Press, 1968, pp. 192–3.

In his *Autobiography*, Artur Schnabel recalls the occasion when, in 1945, he was invited to address a group of music students at the University of Chicago. He had remarked on the 'unevenness' in the quality of works of the great masters and was invited to amplify his meaning. Schnabel responded by conceding that such a circumstance was 'a mysterious problem' and how, indeed, it was very rare for the works 'created by one man [to be] equal in quality to his greatest creations'. Turning his attention to Beethoven he added:

> '[The] case of Beethoven is most amazing, as nearly *all* his works are of equal greatness. His nine symphonies, his sixteen quartets, almost all of his thirty-two piano sonatas are actually *of the same quality*, even in spite of the fact that they were composed throughout his whole life. Why is it so? Perhaps because he composed fewer works than others? I think that one explanation can be found in the fact that in each new work he wrote, he also faced — or was made by his creative disposition to face — a new formal problem. Each one of his quartets, symphonies and sonatas is decidedly different, very definitely different in form, while in that respect Mozart and Bach were rather less varied: unless you investigate their works very closely, it will seem to you that you find the same patterns, the same procedures quite often. Beethoven, I think, was the precursor of all the attempts towards more and more freedom from accepted procedures.'

Artur Schnabel, *My Life and Music*. London: Longmans, 1961, p. 218. See also: John L. Holmes, *Composers on Composers*, New York: Greenwood Press, 1990, p. 15.

ARNOLD SCHOENBERG (SCHÖNBERG)

Writing in February 1931 about national music, the Austrian composer and music theorist Arnold Schoenberg revealed the sources that had influenced his own understanding of music. He states:

> 'My teachers were primarily Bach and Mozart, and secondarily Beethoven, Brahms, and Wagner.'

With reference to Beethoven, he elaborates that he had learned:

> 'The art of developing themes and movements. The art of variation and of varying. The multifariousness of the ways in which long movements can be built. The art of being shamelessly long, or heartlessly brief, as the situation demands. Rhythm: the displacement of figures on to other beats of the bar.'

Leonard Stein, editor: *Style and Idea: Selected writings of Arnold Schoenberg*, London: Faber and Faber, 1975, pp. 173–4.

On 31 January 1949, Schoenberg had occasion to write to a Mr. Bud Behrens, a resident of Stockton, California, on the nature of emotion in music. He first acknowledges:

> 'Generalization produces too often the ridiculous. Whether music should arouse emotions or whether it does arouse emotion, whether it derives from emotion or not — all this depends on the two factors: the sender and the receiver.'

He then elaborates:

> 'No doubt composers like Beethoven and Schubert and Schumann were emotionally moved

when they composed. No doubt, also, that their music arouses emotion, or at least in those people who are the proper receivers of this kind of music. Of course there are also people who are not receivers of emotional music. In them, there is not the ability to arouse emotional reaction.'

Erwin Stein, editor: *Arnold Schoenberg: Letters*, London: Faber and Faber, 1964, p. 268.

Writing to Ferruccio Busoni on 24 August 1909, Arnold Schoenberg expressed his views about music in the following cryptic terms:

'Bach's contrapuntal art vanishes when Beethoven's melodic homophony begins. Beethoven's formal art is abandoned when Wagner introduces his expressive art.'

Turning to creation in the art world — we recall that Schoenberg was an accomplished artist — he comments:

'Unity of design, richness of colouring, working out of minutest details, painstaking formation, priming and varnishing, use of perspective and all the other constituents of older paintings simply die out when the Impressionists begin to paint things as the *appear* and not as the *are*.'

Joseph Henry Auner, *A Schoenberg Reader: Documents of a life*, New Haven Connecticut; London: Yale University Press, 2003, p. 72.

*

On another occasion Schoenberg wrote to Busoni about some recently composed piano pieces of his own:

> 'There can be no doubt that the piano-style of a period bears a certain resemblance to its orchestral style. I find that one can even see this in Mozart and Beethoven. All those for whom expression was the principal concern *composed for the piano* in that they *composed* according to the instrument's needs and demands. Composition is the dominant factor; one takes the instrument into account. Not the contrary.'

Antony Beaumont, editor, *Ferruccio Busoni: Selected letters*, London: Faber and Faber, 1987, pp. 135–6.

LEO SCHRADE

Leo Schrade was an American musicologist of German birth. In 1963 he was invited to give the Charles Eliot Norton Lectures in poetry held annually at the University of Harvard. C.C. Stillman (Harvard 1898) endowed these and encouraged the term 'poetry' to be interpreted in its widest sense — to include reflections on the fine arts and music. In Lecture VI of his series, Schrade calls to mind Prometheus who, in Greek mythology, defied the gods by stealing fire and giving it to humanity, thereby to assist the progress of human civilization. In 1801 the Prometheus myth had seized Beethoven's imagination as he expressed in his music *The Creatures of Prometheus* (*Die Geschöpfe des Prometheus*, Op. 43) — the composer's only full-length ballet score. Schrade first makes the generalization:

> 'If the gift of fire set mankind upon the road of civilization, the artist who creates his beneficial work in testimony to human culture, is — like Prometheus — the benefactor of mankind.'

He then draws a parallel between Beethoven and Prometheus — one made by other writers. Prometheus it will be recalled was punished by Zeus by having an eagle gnaw out his liver, only for it to be rejuvenated so that the torment could be repeated. Schrade, mindful of Beethoven's many bodily afflictions and tribulations, compares his fate with that of Prometheus remarking:

> 'It is Beethoven whom we behold as Prometheus.'

He adds how, far from submitting to his misfortune,

> 'Beethoven, in his quest for the shape of composition, persistently sought out the meaning of his work for the world at large, and from this meaning he gleaned the mission of his art.'

Turning to the circumstance of Beethoven's impending deafness, when the composer was in self-imposed exile in the village of Heiligenstadt, Schrade writes:

> 'When Beethoven was stricken by the affliction of deafness, he drew up the *Heiligenstadter Testament*, a document without parallel, addressed to mankind and written in defiance of a frightful fate. There he revealed for the first time, but not for the last, that despite all suffering inflicted upon him, suffering which for a moment set before him the alternative of suicide he — like a Prometheus — would for ever defy adversities and agonies. But the tragedy of life, the physical

affliction, did not assuage the tragedy of art. Even
the victory in the struggle with his destiny did not
acquit the artist from creative suffering until his
work had been completed.'

Leo Schrade, *Tragedy in the Art of Music*, Cambridge,
Massachusetts: Harvard University Press, 1964, pp. 120–19.

FRANZ SCHREKER

Franz Schreker was an Austrian composer, conductor,
teacher and administrator. In March 1920 he was appointed
director of the Berlin Hochschule für Musik, a position he
occupied for the period 1920–32 combing composition with
musical tuition. Following his appointment, he published
an article in the May issue of the *Berliner Tageblatt* in which
he outlined his goals for the institution. The spirit of his
discourse has been likened to that envisaged for the fledgling
German Republic:

> 'It is for [our youth] that I, we, who have the
> future, the development of Art in our hearts and
> in our keeping, are here. All else is a means to
> an end, work on behalf of an idea.'

With the Great War a recent memory, Schreker continued:

> 'These past awful years will not pass without
> leaving their mark on humanity's senses and
> psyche. But those who come after us will already
> see the bridge that will take us to our goal without
> which I cannot imagine the flourishing of true
> Art: total and comprehensive love ... One cannot
> make music with hate in one's heart.'

Schreker concluded his text, so resonant with impassioned humanism:

> 'The doors of the Hochschule must be open to all who are gifted and capable of enthusiasm. Are we to fear that the strong, healthy nature of our art could suffer from this enrichment? Haven't we always been the *providers*? We want to remain so and sow the seeds in the hearts of the youth of all peoples, the seeds from which a mighty blossoming tree may one day grow in whose shade all can be gathered: Reconciliation of all peoples through Art, the last testament of the greatest of the great, Beethoven: "*Seid umschlungen Millionen* — !" "Be embraced Millions — !", from Beethoven's Ninth Symphony-setting of Friedrich Schiller's *An die Freude*.'

Christopher Hailey, *Franz Schreker, 1878–1934: A cultural biography*, Cambridge: Cambridge University Press, 1993, pp. 119–20.

GUNTHER SCHULLER

Among his many accomplishments, the American Gunther Alexander Schuller was a composer, conductor, horn player, author, historian and jazz musician. In October 1980, he was invited to deliver an address to signal the opening of the sixteenth annual Nobel Conference that was held at Gustavus Adolphus College in St. Peter, Minnesota. This conference is the only formal Nobel programme in the world held outside of Sweden and Norway. Schuller took as his theme *The aesthetic dimension of science* — a measure of his polymath attainments. Beethoven featured prominently in his words to the assembled congress:

> 'We, who belong more-or-less to that same culture that spawned Beethoven, like to think that his music contains some profound truth and communicative ability that transcends all people of whatever rank, class or education or race. We ascribe to it "universality." And above all, we torment ourselves today with the notion that somehow Beethoven was on to something that we in the twentieth century (or for that matter musicians in the fifteenth century) cannot today and could not then achieve, right? No, wrong! For even that widely held belief of Beethoven's universality is not altogether true. It is again conditioned by all kinds of inconclusive evidence and debatable assumptions, Upon close inspection it turns out that, while *some* non-Western cultures, such as Japan's, have accepted Beethoven with open arms, just as they have obviously accepted Western technology and now excel in it, other cultures such as the Javanese or Indian or Arabic, cannot relate to Beethoven's music at all, even when all conditions for such acceptance appear to be propitious. All we can really say with certainty is that, *for the moment* and probably for some foreseeable amount of time, Beethoven's music seems to have a deep appeal, both potential and actual, for a wide segment of the population in *certain* cultures and *certain* human societies. But that's as far as one can go. One can neither prove nor disprove that Beethoven's popularity is universal, is permanent

and invariant. It is, as the mathematicians would say, undecidable.'

Gunther Schuller, *Musings: The musical worlds of Gunther Schuller*, New York: Oxford University Press, 1986, p. 287 and pp. 290–1.

MARION SCOTT

Marion Scott studied violin and piano at the Royal College of Music and after graduating founded *The Marion Scott String Quartet*. Her great enthusiasm was to introduce contemporary music to London audiences, particularly that of Frank Bridge, Hubert Parry and Charles Villiers Stanford. However, Scott is primarily remembered today for her contribution to musicology. Her early writings were for such publications as *Music and Letters* and *The Musical Times* with her later, more substantial, researches appearing in *Grove's Dictionary of Music and Musicians*. She became a respected authority on the lives of Haydn and Mendelssohn but it is for her pioneering study of Beethoven with which Marion Scott's name will forever be most associated. This was published in 1934 by J. M. Dent & Sons, Ltd. as part of their *Music Masters Series*. It received both critical and public acclaim; testimony to its popularity is that it was republished many times. Through this publication Scott introduced many music lovers, the present writer included, to Beethoven's personal history and the circumstances surrounding the creation of his music. Her thoughtful insights also included reflections on the nature of his music that are still invoked by contemporary writers when discussing the intellectual and musicological perspectives of Beethoven's life and work. The influence of Scott's book may also be found in its subsequent transformations in the

Master Musicians Series of publications, first, was under the authorship of Denis Matthews, and subsequently by Barry Cooper.

The following fragment is typical of Marion Scott's writing about Beethoven:

> 'Nothing rouses a stronger sense of Beethoven's greatness than the nature of the music which he brought with him out of great tribulation. The piano Sonatas in E major, Op. 109 (1820), A flat major, Op. 110 (1821) and C minor, Op. 111 (1822); the stupendous *Missa Solemnis*; the Ninth Symphony, in D minor (1823), in which joy not only shall, but does, "overtake us as a flood" – these were his works, full of blessing and consolation.'

Marion M. Scott, *Beethoven: (The Master Musicians)*. London: Dent, 1940, p. 34.

ROGER SESSIONS

The American composer, educator and writer on music Roger Sessions was blessed with a long life. He died just short of his 100th birthday and during his lifetime became an icon of American contemporary music. His writings also reveal the scholarly musicological erudition that he formed in his formative years at both Harvard and Yale Universities. In 1937 he wrote an essay titled *The New Musical Horizon* in which he commented on the musical ideals of the current generation. He first reflected on the pioneering transformations of the musical horizon as shaped, initially, by such composer as Strauss, Debussy, Ravel, Mahler and Scriabin and, nearer to his own time, those of Schoenberg, Stravinsky,

Hindemith, Berg and Bartók. Sessions, the modernist, took issue with the manner in which music critics wrote about music. By way of illustration, he chastises them for sentimentally alluding to 'the tears that fall on the hero's grave' at the close of the Funeral March in the *Eroica* Symphony and to the evocation of 'frosty northern landscapes' in the music of Sibelius. Such writings he dismissed as 'a mess of verbiage'.

Some of Sessions' vexation is apparent in the following passage that he devotes to Beethoven:

> 'Beethoven's ideas for or against the Revolution were precisely what he shared with millions of his contemporaries. What is great in his work is what he alone was capable of achieving — his music, the sounds, the musical shapes which he conjured up, of which the profoundly human significance transcends his specific preoccupations only somewhat less completely than it does the fundamentally meaningless pomposities of M. Rolland [French writer on music] or Mr. Ernest Newman [English music critic]. The content lies — as Beethoven himself pointed out — in the tones, the lines, accents and contrast, and not in the thousand experiences which, fused together in a single gesture, take composite shape as a musical impulse or idea. It can never be too clearly stated that if musical expression is something unique and untranslatable it does not therefore follow that it is without human significance.'

Edward T. Cone, editor, *Roger Sessions on Music: Collected essays*, Princeton, New Jersey: Princeton University Press, 1979, p. 49.

*

Sessions held the Charles Eliot Norton Professorship for 1968–9 at the University of Harvard (see Leo Schrade). In one of the lectures he gave during his tenureship, he discussed the hard-one freedom of the artist, remarking:

> '[In] the case of artists everyone who has mastered his art feels fully free, simply by virtue of his mastery of his materials, and in strict proportion to his mastery of them. He can do with them anything he choses.'

Sessions then calls to mind his reading about Beethoven:

> 'I remember a book that appeared many years ago, entitled *Beethoven, the Man who Freed Music* [Robert Haven Schauffler, 1929]. The question arose in my mind: "What did he free it from?" From Mozart, perhaps, or Haydn? I do not mean to labour the point; simply to draw attention to the fact that the artist — barring forces quite external to his art — *is* free, in proportion to his mastery of his materials, in every way that has any importance to him. He is free, that is, to make the music which is his own, that which he wants to make. Once he has clearly envisaged what this is, he must follow its demands. In so doing, he is enjoying the most intense musical experience that is open to him, and presumably he finds fulfilment in it.'

Roger Sessions, *Questions about Music*, Cambridge, Massachusetts: Harvard University Press, 1970, pp. 92–3.

*

IGNAZ VON SEYFRIED

The Austrian composer, conductor and pupil of Mozart, Ignaz von Seyfried was on close terms with Beethoven and premiered the original production of his opera *Leonora-Fidelio* (1805). From about this period he left an account of the first performance of the composer's Third Piano Concerto for which Beethoven had not had time to fully write out the piano part. According to Seyfried, such manuscript that was written on the pages was little more than 'scribbled down hieroglyphics'. In effect, Beethoven played the solo part from memory.

Michael Sternberg, *The Concerto: A listener's guide*, Oxford University Press, 1998, pp. 59–63.

After Seyfried's death his handwritten memoirs were published in an appendix to *Beethoven's Studien im Generalbasse* (see below). These include a brief portrait of Beethoven — styled with a measure of obligatory flattery, as by then Beethoven was becoming deified:

> 'Amongst the poets of Germany Goethe was his favourite; he was fond of Walter Scott. Of the rest of the fine arts, and of the sciences, he possessed, without priding himself upon it, more than a superficial knowledge. In the circle of his intimates he spoke out freely upon politics, and with such commanding, well-directed and perspicacious views, as one would scarcely have expected from a recluse living only for and in the interests of his Art.'

Of Beethoven's personal relationships, Seyfried writes:

> 'Rectitude of principle, high morality, propriety of feeling, and pure natural religion were his

distinctions. These virtues reigned within himself and he required them at the hands of others. "As good as his word" was his favourite saying, and nothing angered him more than a broken promise. He was always ready, out of warm benevolence, to help others, and that often at the expense of serious sacrifices in his own person. Whoever turned to him voluntarily, and in perfect confidence, might safely reckon upon him for aid. He new neither avarice nor extravagance, and was but little acquainted with the real value of money, which he used only as a means for procuring the indispensable requirements of life; it was only in the later years that signs of an anxious parsimony became apparent, without however interfering with his natural bias for benevolent actions.'

Ignaz von Seyfried, *Louis van Beethoven's studies in thorough-bass, counterpoint and the art of scientific composition*, Leipzig; New-York: Schuberth and Company, 1853, pp. 22–3.

Seyfried was one of the first writers to describe Beethoven's working method:

'Without a little note book, wherein to jot down his ideas upon the instant, he never appeared in the street. If by chance this was referred to in conversation, he used to parody Joan of Arc's words "*nicht ohne meine Fahne darf ich kommen*" ["I dare not come without my Banner"] and with a tenacity quite surprising did he adhere to this self-imposed law.'

Like other of Beethoven's contemporaries, Seyfried discerned the disorder evident in the composer's domestic affairs:

> '[His] household presented an admirable scene of confusion. Books and music were strewn about in all directions — here the remains of a cold breakfast — there sealed or half-empty bottles — yonder upon the desk the rough sketch of a new quartet, and near it the last new poem or romance. On the piano might be seen the half-finished score of a symphony as yet in embryo — on the table a proof sheet waiting for correction — private and business letters covering the floor — between the windows a respectable stracchino cheese, *ad latus* the fragments of a Verona sausage; yet in spite of this medley, our Composer had the habit, (in manifest contradiction to the fact,) of boasting, at every opportunity, of his accuracy and love of order, with all the eloquence of a Cicero. It was only when something that was wanted had to be hunted for, hours, days, and even weeks, and it remained in obstinate seclusion, that he assumed another tone, and the innocent suffered for the faults of another.'

Ignaz von Seyfried, *ibid*, pp. 15–16.

GEORGE BERNARD SHAW

George Bernard Shaw's fame as a playwright and polemicist has eclipsed his reputation for being a discerning music critic. Eugene Gates, of the Faculty of the Royal Conservatory of Music, Toronto, writes:

> '[Shaw] was ... the most brilliant British music critic to emerge in the late-nineteenth century. His vision of the ideal critic was not a passive reporter of musical events, but rather a vital and initiating force within the music community.'

Journal of Aesthetic Education, Vol. 35, No. 3, 2001.

Shaw was committed to the principle of making music criticism both intelligible and entertaining. To this end he invented the persona of *Corno di Bassetto* (in music, the basset horn) to serve as his spokesperson. Shaw's collected writings on music fill no fewer than three sturdy volumes:

See, Dan H. Laurence, editor: *Shaw's Music: The complete musical criticism in three volumes*, London: Max Reinhardt, the Bodley Head, 1981.

Reflecting on his childhood, Shaw recalls the solace he derived from the music 'that abounded in the house'. He became an accomplished amateur pianist and enjoyed playing piano reductions of Beethoven's symphonies with his sister. His intimate knowledge of the composer's piano sonatas is evident in his many music-review references to them. From Shaw's copious writings, we offer a selection of his estimation of Beethoven, the man and composer.

In the *Saturday Review* of 14 November 1896, Shaw wrote an article concerning the recently published *Beethoven and his Nine Symphonies* by George Grove (London and New York, Novello, Ewer & Co.). Of Beethoven, Shaw remarks:

'Beethoven was the first man who used music with absolute integrity as the expression of his own emotional life. Others had shown how it could be done — had done it themselves as a curiosity of their art in rare, self-indulgent, *unprofessional* moments — but Beethoven made this, and nothing else, his business. Stupendous as the resultant difference was between his music and any other ever heard in the world before his time, the distinction is not clearly apprehended to this day, because there was nothing new in the musical expression of emotion: every progression in Bach is sanctified by emotion; and Mozart's subtlety, delicacy, and exquisite tender touch and noble feeling were the despair of all the musical world. But Bach's theme was not himself, but his religion; and Mozart was always the dramatist and story-teller, making the men and women of his imagination speak, and dramatizing even the instruments in his orchestra, so that you know their very sex the moment their voices reach you. Haydn really came nearer to Beethoven, for he is neither the praiser of God nor the dramatist, but, always within the limits of good manners and of his primary function as a purveyor of formal decorative music, a man of moods. This is how he created the symphony and put it ready-made into Beethoven's hand. The revolutionary giant at once seized it, and, throwing supernatural religion, conventional good manners, dramatic fiction, and all external standards and objects into the lumber room, took his own humanity as the material of his music, and

> expressed it all without compromise, from his roughest jocularity to his holiest aspiration after that purely human reign of intense life.'

George Bernard Shaw, cited in: Percy M. Young, *George Grove, 1820–1900: A biography*, London: Macmillan, 1980, Appendix B.

In Beethoven's Centenary Year, Shaw contributed an article in the *Radio Times* of 18 March 1927. In this he wrote:

> 'Now what Beethoven did, and what made some of his greatest contemporaries give him up as a madman with lucid intervals of clowning and bad taste, was that he used music altogether as a means of expressing moods, and completely threw over pattern-designing as an end in itself. It is true that he used the old patterns all his life with dogged conservatism ... but he imposed on them such an overwhelming charge of human energy and passion, including that highest passion which accompanies thought, and reduces the passion of the physical appetites to mere animalism, that he not only played Old Harry with their symmetry but often made it impossible to notice that there was any pattern at all beneath the storm of emotion.'

Dan H. Laurence, editor, *Shaw's Music: The complete musical criticism in three volumes*, London: Max Reinhardt, the Bodley Head, 1981, Vol. 3, pp. 746–7.

In another article Shaw cites Beethoven, alongside Mozart, as pioneering a new epoch in music — taking the time of

Wagner's birth as a benchmark:

> 'When Wagner was born in 1813, music had newly become the most astonishing, the most fascinating, the most miraculous art in the world. Mozart's *Don Giovanni* had made all musical Europe conscious of the enchantments of the modern orchestra and of the perfect adaptability of music to the subtlest needs of the dramatist. Beethoven had shown how those inarticulate mood-poems, which surge through men who have, like himself, no exceptional command of words, can be written down in music as symphonies. Not that Mozart and Beethoven invented these applications of their art; but they were the first whose works made it clear that the dramatic and subjective powers of sound were enthralling enough to stand by themselves quite apart from the decorative musical structures of which they had hitherto been a mere feature'.

Dan H. Laurence *ibid*, p. 528.

ROBERT SHAW

On 14 February 1955, the American conductor Robert Shaw was invited to address the conference of the Music Teachers' National Association. His text was subsequently published in the Sept.–Oct. issue of the *American Music Teacher*. Shaw defined what music meant to him:

> 'All music is an attempt at communication between human hearts and minds; at the very minimum the creator reaches out to and through

the performer, and both of them reach out to the listener.'

Shaw was passionate that great music was the people's music, stating:

> 'Music is great not because certain self-appointed custodians of Art with a capital A have decreed it so, because it calls out to something deep and persistent in the human thing. Music is great because it carries something so native and true to the human spirit that not even sophisticated intellectuality can deny or destroy its miracle.'

Of Beethoven's contribution to music, Shaw tersely observed:

> 'Beethoven lived in a universe richer than ours, in some ways better than ours, in some ways more terrible. And while he does not communicate his experience to us, he does communicate his attitude towards it. And we recognize his universe; we find it prophetic of our own. It is indeed our universe, but experienced by a consciousness aware of aspects of which we have but dim and transitory glimpses.'

Robert Blocker, *The Robert Shaw Reader*, New Haven; London: Yale University Press, 2004, pp. 350–1.

DMITRI SHOSTAKOVICH

In his student years, the young Shostakovich divided his time between piano studies and composition. A measure of his proficiency at the keyboard is evident from 1919 when, at the age of thirteen, he was allowed to enter the Petrograd Conservatory then headed by Alexander Glazunov. In April 1926, he was accepted on the postgraduate composition course at the Leningrad Conservatoire where he also continued his piano studies. At the preceding Graduate Diploma Examination, it was obligatory to play a work from the classical repertoire. His friend Lydia Zhukova recalled the circumstances:

> 'Two weeks beforehand he still didn't know what he would play. Eventually he chose the *Hammerklavier* Sonata. He said it was inconceivably difficult, and that some of the ninths and tenths were unperformable.'

The evening before the examination, Zhukova called round to hear Shostakovich play though the work. She relates:

> 'He played for me. He was a wonderful pianist, with strong hands and his own precise manner of playing.'

Zhukova, however, felt 'sick at heart', regarding Shostakovich's interpretation as 'only a sketchy performance'. The following day she had cause to revise her opinion, describing her friend and compatriot's playing as 'exhibiting authority and maturity, displaying a symphonic grasp of the whole grandiose work'.

Elizabeth Wilson, *Shostakovich: A life remembered*, Princeton, New Jersey: Princeton University Press, 1994, p. 56.

The following year, Shostakovich gave further evidence

of his abilities as a pianist by securing an 'honorable mention' at the first International Chopin Piano Competition held in Warsaw. Shostakovich's compensation for not being a prizewinner came in the form of a meeting with the conductor Bruno Walter. He was greatly impressed by the composer's First Symphony that he had completed at the age of eighteen as his graduation piece at the Petrograd Conservatory. Its subsequent performance under Walter's direction in Berlin, and the following year in Philadelphia by Leopold Stokowski, did much to establish Shostakovich as a composer.

Although Shostakovich's subsequent life was rendered turbulent, and at times threatening through his conflicts with the government of the Soviet Union, he continued to expresses his views on music. These found an outlet in the form of personal communings, in his diary, and public writings in journals.

From his diary for 1931 we read:

> 'There can be no music without ideology ... The old composers, whether they knew it or not, were upholding a political theory. Most of them, of course, were bolstering the rule of the upper classes. Only Beethoven was a forerunner of the revolutionary movement. If you will read his letters you will see how often he wrote [to] his friends that he wished to give new ideas to the public and rouse it to revolt against its masters.'

Of his own musical agenda he states:

> 'I consider that every artist who isolates himself from the world is doomed. I find it incredible that

> an artist should want to shut himself away from the people, who, in the end, form his audience. I think an artist should serve that greatest possible number of people. I always try to make myself as widely understood as possible, and if I don't succeed, I consider it my own fault.'

In a diary entry for 1938, Shostakovich sought to align himself and his musical compatriots with his own country's musical inheritance that he believed was exemplified in the western musical tradition:

> 'We Soviet musicians must assimilate our Russian and European classical heritage. Only when a composer knows his great predecessors well, and learns from them, can he find his own individual musical idiom, his own creative style. The history of music is full of convincing examples of this. Beethoven felt the beneficial influence of Mozart and Haydn; and even such an original genius as Chopin drew a great deal from Beethoven, especially the musical ideas contained in the adagio of his sonata, Op. 106. Verdi was a composer of exceptionally vivid individuality, and was ill-disposed towards Wagner, yet at various stages his music showed the influence of Wagner. All the greatest composers know the music of the world perfectly. In each case this knowledge was interpreted differently by the individual personality and helped give rise to such inimitable and district styles as those of Bach and Mozart, of Chopin and Beethoven.'

Writing in 1952 in the 18 December issue of *Pravda*,

Shostakovich upheld Beethoven as a humanitarian exemplar:

> 'Beethoven firmly believed that his music should serve the noble cause of justice; he protested angrily against the forces of darkness and violence that reigned at that time; and through his work he rallied mankind to the heroic struggle for a happier future, singing — with his characteristic fiery passion — the joyful hymn of liberated humanity.'

Shostakovich continued:

> '[No] proof is needed of the eminent role which can be played by music in moulding the harmonious personality of the future of man, and in promoting profound and noble emotions in him.'

Shostakovich believed passionately in music's capacity to evoke an emotional response and to act directly on the formation of a person's spiritual world, and thereby to raise his moral standards. With this in mind he once more invoked the spirit of Beethoven:

> 'Listening to Beethoven's immortal works ... evokes kind feelings towards people. And Beethoven himself, addressing his music to millions of listeners, clearly expressed his idea of the main purpose of music: "from heart to heart".'

The Beethovenian will recognise here Shostakovich's quotation as being an adaptation of Beethoven's words 'From the heart, may it again go to the heart', that he wrote above the opening Kyrie in the manuscript of his greatest choral work, the *Missa Solemnis*.

Writing in 1968 in Issue 5 of the Russian language literary magazine *Yunost*, Shostakovich reflected on the future of music:

> 'It is hard to say what will become of music in the future. Probably in the end, a new Bach and a new Beethoven will appear. But so far they have not. Whether music will become simpler or more complex, it is hard to tell in advance; nor can one say with any certainty which of our young composers will in the future be known as twentieth-century classics.'

With the perspective of twentieth century music now established, we can answer Shostakovich's question, at least in part, by acknowledging that he himself is regarded as one of its major composers.

Writing on 15 December 1970 in the Russian daily newspaper *Vechernaya Maska*, Shostakovich once more affirmed his belief in Beethoven's continuing legacy:

> 'Why is Beethoven so dear to us? Chiefly because, though he was born in the eighteenth century, he still today is able to speak to the people, who understand and believe him. Sometimes Beethoven is considered excessively tragic, and tragedy is often equated with pessimism, while it is forgotten that the greatest tragic works in world art are also the most life-asserting. Take, for example, the tragedies of Shakespeare and Goethe ... But can it really be said that the

progressive humanist art of a century ago responds any less acutely to all the sufferings and sorrows of mankind now than it did then? No, and by responding to them, it loudly protests against evil and violence. This is why we consider Beethoven our contemporary. This is why he is loved and understood not only by professional musicians, but by all listeners.'

Dmitry Shostakovich, *Dmitry Shostakovich: About himself and his times*, Moscow: Progress Publishers, 1981, p. 31, p. 75, p. 149, p. 214, p. 287, and pp. 296–7.

JEAN SIBELIUS

Santeri Levas was the personal secretary to Jean Sibelius for twenty years and had many opportunities to observe him at work and to record his personal beliefs. He relates the occasion when Sibelius visited Berlin's State Library, then known as the Royal Library, where he consulted the original score of the Ninth Symphony. Lavas recalls Sibelius remarking:

'It was full of cancellations and alterations' prompting Sibelius to add:

'At first glance one could see that it was a matter of life and death, a contest with God!'

Levas adds:

'His eyes shone as he spoke of Beethoven's gigantic struggle. He was obviously thinking of his own life's work and found satisfaction in the knowledge that he alone did not have to bear the labour-pains of a great musician.'

One day Sibelius gave Levas a copy of F. S. Noli's *Beethoven and the French Revolution* (New York, 1947). This had apparently given the Finnish composer great pleasure and a sense of personal identification with Beethoven. Levas writes:

> 'I had the impression that it gave him some satisfaction to compare himself with that musical giant, the account of whose personal characteristics afforded Sibelius a greater understanding.'

Sibelius, the great tone poet, clearly felt a sense of identification with Beethoven when he remarked:

> 'One could have said of Beethoven — if one absolutely insists — that he wrote programmatic music. For his point of departure was always a specific idea.'

Reflecting on this remark, Levas comments:

> 'In relation to musical history one could perhaps say that Beethoven was the first Romantic and Sibelius the last. But neither was solely a Romantic; both stood on the watershed between two great musical epochs.'

According to Levas, Sibelius most admired in Beethoven 'the inflexible determination to create, and the moral depth of his works'. He once expostulated:

> 'It is inconceivable that they don't appreciate Beethoven's greatness ... Beethoven's works have

many failings, especially from the period of his
deafness. But they live.'

Santeri Levas, *Sibelius: A personal portrait*, London: J. M. Dent, 1972, pp. 60–3.

BEDRICH SMETANA

In his student days, the Czech composer Bedrich Smetana studied violin and piano, thereby discovering the works of Mozart and Beethoven. Concerts given in Prague, under the direction of Hector Berlioz, further enlarged his familiarity with the European classical repertoire. Also at this time he made the acquaintance of Robert and Clara Schuman and, most notably for the progress of his career, Franz Liszt with whom he developed a lasting friendship. Smetana was an accomplished pianist himself and, for a period, occupied the post of Court Pianist to the Austrian Emperor Ferdinand. In 1856, in celebration of the centenary of Mozart's birth, he performed the composer's D minor Piano Concerto – confiding in his journal that he wanted 'to become a Mozart in composition and a Liszt in technique'. In 1847 the ethnomusicologist and biographer of Smetana Frantisek Bartos met the composer. Recalling the event he relates:

> 'He revered Liszt deeply, but for him Beethoven stood out far above everybody else. It was Smetana who taught me to understand the spirit of Beethoven's music and I understood it thanks to Smetana's wonderfully lucid explanations.'

Frantisek Bartos, *Bedrich Smetana: Letters and reminiscences*, Prague: Artia, 1953, pp. 21–3.

It is from Smetana that we gain an insight into the state of contemporary musical appreciation in Sweden. During his stay in Gothenburg in the spring of 1857, Smetana had occasion to write to Liszt. He presents a somewhat bleak view of the state of musical appreciation in the Swedish town:

> 'Honoured Master and Friend; The people here are still solidly fixed in an antediluvian artistic point of view. Mozart is there idol, though he is not really understood, Beethoven is feared, Mendelssohn declared unpalatable, and the moderns are unknown. I performed Schumann's works here for the first time. However, it is fruitless to continue to talk about the conditions prevailing here.'

Sam Morgenstern, editor: *Composers on Music: An anthology of composers' writings*, London: Faber & Faber, 1956, pp. 207–8.

The onset of deafness was a great tribulation to Smetana towards the end of his life, disposing him to compare his misfortune with that of Beethoven's. In 1882 the Austrian composer Wilhelm Kienzl visited Prague and met the elderly Smetana. By then he had lost his hearing and, like Beethoven, resorted in conversation to making use of a notebook. A diary entry of Kienzl's reads:

> 'Smetana was at that time completely deaf ... We understood each other ... mainly by writing [and] with the assistance of gestures ... He could compose only when he felt the urge since at other times the notes lay before him, cold as calculations ... When he was inspired, however, the

whole world seemed to him transfigured. He had
written his greatest works ... under this inspiration
although not a living sound had penetrated to his
dead ear — the fate of Beethoven!'

Originally published in Wilhelm Kienzl, *My life Journey*,
1926 and quoted in Frantisek Bartos, *Bedrich Smetana:
Letters and reminiscences*, Prague: Artia, 1953, pp. 260–1.

MAYNARD SOLOMON

The American musicologist Maynard Solomon has an
established reputation for being an authority on Beethoven.
His work, although not without its critics, is characterised
by a scholarly presentation of the available evidence and the
construction of plausible hypotheses. In his Introduction to
Beethoven, he writes:

> 'The proper study of Beethoven is based on con-
> temporary documents — on letters, diaries, Con-
> versation Books, court and parish records,
> autograph manuscripts and sketches, music pub-
> lications reviews, concert programmes, and
> similar materials. These may be utilized by a biog-
> rapher with relative confidence as to their authen-
> ticity, although even they ... must be approached
> with some caution. A second major source of
> material bearing significantly on Beethoven's life
> and personality consists of the reminiscences of
> his contemporaries. Here more serious questions
> arise as to the validity of anecdotes, reports, and
> memoirs that were written down long after the
> fact by a wide variety of individuals.'

Solomon illustrates the foregoing with reference to Anton Schindler's alleged forgeries:

> '[In] March 1977 [the composer's 150th anniversary] a long-held suspicion was finally confirmed ... Grita Herre and Dagmar Beck, working with handwriting analyses, proved that Anton Schindler had fabricated more than 150 of his own entries in Beethoven's Conversation Books. Until then these entries had been unhesitatingly accepted as authentic by Beethoven scholars — to the extent that some of Schindler's forgeries have formed the basis for biographical and musical interpretations.'

As a consequence, Solomon remarks:

'It is not an easy task to separate [Schindler's] facts from fiction'.

Of the writings of other of Beethoven's contemporaries, Solomon comments:

> 'We have no such extreme problems with regard to other contemporary observers ... Of the leading sources, it is my judgement that the reminisces of Ignaz von Seyfried, Carl Czerny, Gerhard von Breuning ... and Karl Holz are generally trustworthy.'

Solomon also cites the *Biographical Notices* of Franz Wegeler and Ferdinand Ries, but remarks on their occasional 'curious lapses and factual errors' but concludes they are 'in the main unbiased and accurate'.

Solomon concludes that the role of the Beethoven biographer should be 'to construct a safe, clear, well-ordered design' and that such a portrait:

> 'can be purchased only at the price of truth by avoiding the obscurities that riddle the documentary materiel'.

Only thereby, Solomon avers is it possible to chronicle what he describes as 'a series of creative events unique in the history of mankind'.

Maynard Solomon, *Beethoven*, New York: Schirmer, 1977, pp. Xi–xii.

Elsewhere, Solomon writes:

> 'It is common knowledge that Beethoven was a founder of the Romantic movement in music and that his works influenced most of the romantic composers and were models against which nineteenth-century romanticism measures its achievements and failures ... [During] his own lifetime, Beethoven was widely regarded as a radical modernist, whose modernism was seen sharply to distinguished him from the classical standards established, in the main, by Mozart and Haydn. Of course, they too had their share of hostile notices before they were elevated to canonical status; but the classicizing critiques of Beethoven were too intense and pervasive to be regarded as merely the usual, provisional resistance to modifications of cultural traditions. His contemporaries – including many of his advocates – saw him as subverting classical principles and procedures, as radical, iconoclastic, and eccentric. They did not regard him as an eighteenth-century composer.'

*

Maynard Solomon, *Beethoven: Beyond classicism*, in: Robert Winter, and Robert Martin, editors *The Beethoven Quartet Companion*, Berkeley: University of California Press, 1994, p. 59 and pp. 70–1.

OSCAR GEORGE SONNECK

Oscar George Sonneck was an American musicologist who received his higher education in Germany at the universities of Heidelberg and Munich. A few years before his death, in 1928, he conceived the idea of compiling a series of recollections from the writings of those who knew Beethoven or who had visited him at some time or other in his lifetime. The impending Beethoven Death Centenary of 1927 also provided Sonneck with the added incentive to create such a biographical survey. This was duly published in 1926 by G. Schirmer, Inc. under the title *Beethoven: Impressions by his contemporaries.* In his Preface, Sonneck pays tribute to the pioneering efforts of Anton Schindler (*Beethoven Biography*, 1845), Ludwig Nohl (*Beethoven as Depicted by his Contemporaries*, 1877) and Alexander Wheelock Thayer (*Life of Beethoven,* 1921).

Initially, Sonneck studied the works of the hundred and fifty or so recorded reminiscences of contemporaries who visited Beethoven and from these he selected thirty-six for final inclusion in his *Impressions*. Sonneck did not attempt to significantly edit or adapt his chosen writings, but he does provide each of his selected texts with prefatory contextual words that include occasional corrections of fact relating to such matters as the chronology of particular events. Introducing Sonneck's work, the publishers wrote:

> 'Beethoven, being what he was could not very well appear in a different light to every visitor —

and yet, how amazingly at times the impressions of him contradict one another.'

One of the virtues of Sonneck's study is that he presents his selected recollections in a chronological sequence. Thereby, the reader is offered an unfolding picture of Beethoven from his earliest years to his death. The following is a list of those from whom, or to whom, Sonneck makes reference together with the date to which the text in question relates:

Gottfried Fischer (1770 onwards), Christian Gottlob Neefe (1783), Mozart (1787), Carl Ludwig Junker (1791), Johann Schenk (1792), Franz Gerhard Wegeler (1794–96), Frau von Bernhard (1796–1800), Johan Wenzel Tomaschek (1798), Carl Czerny (c. 1800), Countesses Giulietta and Therese Brunswick (c. 1801) Ignaz von Seyfried (1799–1806), Ferdinand Ries (1801–05), Josef August Röckel (1806), Baron de Trémont — Joseph-Girod de Vienney (1809), Bettina von Arnim and Johann von Wolfgang (1810–12), Ignaz Moscheles (1810–14), Louis Spohr (1812–16), Johann Wenzel Tomashek (1814), Cipriani Potter (1818), Anton Schindler (1819), Maurice Schlesinger (1819), Sir John Russell (1821), Gioachino Rossini (1822), Friedrich Johann Rochlitz (1822), Wilhelmine Schröder-Devrient (1822), Louis Schlösser (1822–23), Edward Schulz (1823), Franz Grillparzer (1823), Carl Maria von Weber (1823), Franz Liszt (1823), Anton Schindler (1814–27), Ludwig Rellstab (1825), Sir George Smart (1825), Gerhard von Breuning (1825–27) and Friedrich Wieck (1824–26?).

Oscar George Theodore Sonneck, *Beethoven: Impressions of contemporaries*, London: Oxford University Press, 1927, republished by Dover Publications, Inc., New York, 1967.

Louis Spohr

In his study of Beethoven's contemporaries, Oscar Sonneck describes the German composer, conductor and violinist Louis Spohr in the following terms:

> 'Louis Spohr frankly confessed his inability to comprehend Beethoven's music of the last period. He attributed Beethoven's "aesthetic aberrations" to his deafness, but apparently it never occurred to Spohr that his own ears might have been at fault. Considered in his time either the equal of Paganini as a violinist or second only to him, Louis Spohr laid much greater stress on his importance and fame as a composer. As such, his popularity generations ago certainly was not inferior to that of Beethoven.'

Sonneck was doubtless relying, at least in part, on the views that Spohr himself expressed about Beethoven and his music in his *Autobiography* (1865). From this we learn that in 1808 he played through a rehearsal of Beethoven's Piano Trio in D major, Op. 70, No. 1 – *The Ghost*. Spohr recalls:

> 'It was by no means an enjoyment; for in the first place the pianoforte was woefully out of tune, which however little troubled *Beethoven*, since he could hear nothing of it, and secondly, of the former so-admired excellence of the virtuoso, scarcely anything was left, in consequence of his deafness. In the forte, the poor deaf man hammered in such a way upon the keys, that the entire groups of notes were inaudible, so that one lost all intelligence of the subject unless the eye

followed the score at the same time. I felt moved with the deepest sorrow for anyone so deaf; how then should a musician endure it without despair? *Beethoven's* almost continual melancholy was no longer a riddle to me now.'

As remarked by Sonneck, Spohr found Beethoven's later compositions too modern-sounding and attributed their stridency to the composer's hearing misfortune:

'But as from this time, owing to his constantly increasing deafness, he could no longer hear any music that, of necessity, must have had a prejudicial influence upon his fancy. His constant endeavour to be original and to open new paths, could no longer, as formerly, be preserved from error by the guidance of the ear. Was it then to be wondered at that his works became more and more eccentric, unconnected, and incomprehensible? It is true there are people who imagine they can understand them, and in their pleasure at that, rank them far above his earlier masterpieces. But I am not of the number, and freely confess that I have never been able to relish the last works of Beethoven. Yes I must even reckon the much admired *Ninth Symphony* among them, the three first themes of which, inspite of some solitary flashes of genius, are to me worse than all the eight previous Symphonies, the fourth theme of which is in my opinion so monstrous and tasteless, and in its grasp of *Schiller's Ode* so trivial, that I cannot even now understand how a genius like Beethoven could have written it. I find in it another proof of what I already remarked in

Vienna, that Beethoven was wanting in aesthetical feeling and in a sense of the beautiful.'

Louis Spohr, *Louis Spohr's Autobiography*, London: Longman, Green, Longman, Roberts, & Green, 1865, pp. 188–9. See also: Henry Pleasants, editor and translator, *The Musical Journeys of Louis Spohr*, Norman: University of Oklahoma Press, 1961.

GLEN STANLEY

The music historian Glen Stanley considers Beethoven's achievement in the context of politics, philosophy and culture:

> 'While Beethoven's emotional life, his non-musical intellectual interests, and his musical pursuits are separate aspects of his life and career, they form an ultimate unity in the creative process; music was the medium in which he sought his own answers to the existential and conceptual problems that confronted him ... This music is not abstract but rather personal and subjective, not a declaration of absolute faith in things revealed but the expression of human engagement with metaphysical problems and the (sometimes tortured) existential process of that engagement. In this respect Beethoven's late spirituality — which itself has much earlier roots — differs little from earlier intellectual preoccupations. They all provided strong impulses to compose; equally strong, perhaps stronger still, were the stirrings of his heart and soul — as his emotional life might well have been characterized

in his own time — and his "pure" engagement with music itself, if such a thing is possible. While Beethoven's emotional life, his non-musical intellectual interests, and his musical pursuits are separate aspects of his life and career, they form an ultimate unity in the creative process; music was the medium in which he sought his own answers to the existential and conceptual problems that confronted him.'

Glen Stanley, editor: *The Cambridge Companion to Beethoven,* Cambridge; New York: Cambridge University Press, 2000, p. 31.

ERWIN STEIN

In his essay *Musical Thought: Beethoven and Schoenberg*, the Vienna born, German-Jew musicologist Erwin Stein first discusses Beethoven's powers of invention:

'When we admire the depth of Beethoven's ideas, we owe at least as much admiration to the thinker able to express this depth by dint of an unprecedented wealth of formal relations. That the listener does not generally become aware of the connections and immediately perceives and experiences them as depth of thought, is of the essence of profound art. For depth is the realization of connections which are not obvious. We find that Beethoven's music gives us ever less vent to free play and ever more insists on sense and necessity. His motivic and thematic work, the way in which he arranges his characters, his parts and keys, develops mere musical shape into musical thought. It is, in particular, the astonishing mutability of his motifs which creates an unprecedented wealth of relations.'

Of Beethoven's originality, Stein observes:

'The depth and originality of Beethoven's ideas cannot be adequately described by such words as "intuition" or "inspiration". Beethoven *worked* — not only with his heart, but also with his brain ... Beethoven has taught music to think, an achievement which cannot be undone ... The depth of Beethoven's music consists of its motives and other formal connections. Once we really grasp this fact, we know what music "is about", and where it has to try its luck in the future.'

Of Beethoven's influence upon Schoenberg, Stein comments — with the advent of *Musical Modernism* in mind:

'[Keys] have ceased to have a formative influence, and triads have become sound effects. And yet there's no denying our time's connection with Beethoven. For the strongest creative powers of this age operate in a field which has opened — above all the strongest power, Schoenberg ... The time will come [Stein's essay was written in March 1927] when we shall better understand how Schoenberg's "compositions with twelve notes", too, derives — as a final consequence — from Beethoven.'

Originally published in Beethoven's Death-Centenary Year (1927) and republished in: Erwin Stein, *Orpheus in New Guises*, London: Rockliff, 1953, pp. 90–95.

KARL HEINRICH STOCKHAUSEN

Sometime in the early 1970s, the musicologist Karl Heinrich Wörner interviewed the German composer Karl Heinrich Stockhausen concerning his thoughts on 'the philosophy of music'. Stockhausen — widely acknowledged for his groundbreaking work in the field of recorded and electronic music — recalled how, on 17 December 1970, he was requested to give a lecture to celebrate Beethoven's Birth Centenary. Stockhausen's initial response was to offer his audience an evening 'meditating' on Beethoven's music 'in performance' with a quartet of selected musicians — i.e., musicians sympathetic to Stockhausen's contemporary modernist views and personal style of expression. In the event, Stockhausen required his musicians to play recorded fragments of Beethoven's music so as to, in Stockhausen's word's, 'transform *found* music into *new music*' [Stockhausen's italics]. Stockhausen himself selected and recorded the musical extracts. He justifies his actions on the grounds that Beethoven himself was a tireless searcher for new forms in the creative process:

> 'It is certainly in keeping with the spirit of Beethoven — that timelessly universal spirit — that we should use the whole of his music (and not merely a "theme" from it) as the material for a *development without mediation*, in which not merely sections, but *even the single notes and sounds are spontaneously "developed" the moment they are heard.*' [Stockhausen's italics]

Stockhausen closes:

> 'For this music [Beethoven's music 'transformed' by the performers] is not fenced off and dead,

but is rather a living generative force: an immediate cause and pre-text for the new and unknown.'

Karl Heinrich Wörner, *Stockhausen: Life and work*, London: Faber, 1973, p. 77. This recollection is also published, with some variation in the translation, in: Michael Kurtz, *Stockhausen: A biography*, London: Faber and Faber, 1992, p. 176.

RICHARD STRAUSS

In 1904 the Austrian pianist, conductor and writer on music August Göllerich published a collection of illustrated musical studies, the first volume of which was titled *Beethoven* (Bard, Marquart & Co.). Richard Strauss was invited to contribute an introduction. His opening remarks provide insights into his views on the nature of art, taken in the widest sense of the meaning:

> 'Art is a product of civilisation. It is not its "calling" to lead a self-sufficient, isolated existence in accordance with "laws" which are first arbitrarily formulated or designed to meet the needs of the moment and then proclaimed to be "eternal": its natural calling is to bear witness to the civilisation of an age and of a people.'

Turning his attention to music, Strauss comments:

> 'We observe in the history of music, as in the development of the other arts, an evolution from the representation of indefinite or general and typical concepts to the expression of an orbit of ideas which become increasingly more definite,

individual and intimate.'

In commending Göllerich's study of Beethoven, Strauss expatiates:

> 'A monograph on Beethoven would appear to be best suited to form the first volume of such a collection, because the appreciation of Beethoven's position with regard to our civilisation may well offer today the largest field of agreement between friend and foe. It may be hoped that more-or-less general agreement on this interpretation of Beethoven's life and work will form a sure foundation for agreement on greater and more hotly disputed issues of musical aesthetics.'

Willi Schuh, editor: *Richard Strauss: Recollections and reflections*, London; New York: Boosey & Hawkes, 1953, pp. 10–11.

IGOR STRAVINSKY

As a child Stravinsky showed an aptitude for the piano and by the age of fifteen he had mastered Mendelssohn's Piano Concerto in G minor. In his student days he had lessons in orchestration with Rimsky-Korsakov. He was required to set passages of Beethoven sonatas and Schubert quartets, which the master then criticised and corrected. In his *Autobiography*, Stravinsky pays homage to Beethoven's piano music:

> 'I recognized in him [Beethoven] the indisputable monarch of the instrument. It is the instrument that inspires his thought and determines its

substance. The relations of a composer to his sound-medium may be of two kinds. Some, for example, compose music *for* the piano; others compose *piano music*. Beethoven is clearly in the second category. In all his immense pianistic work, it is the "instrumental" side which is characteristic of him and makes him infinitely precious to me. It is the giant instrumentalist that predominates in him, and it is thanks to that quality that he cannot fail to reach any ear that is open to music.'

Igor Stravinsky, *An Autobiography*, London: Calder and Boyars, 1975, p. 116.

Of Beethoven's Piano Sonata Op. 106, *The Hammerklavier*, Stravinsky remarked:

'This mammoth sonata resembles the later quartet [Op. 130] in the same key in its extraordinary fecundity, huge dimensions, and radical substance. Both works challenge our powers of absorption even now, in fact await full appreciation from a future generation.'

In his discussion of the Op. 106, he further observes:

'Much of the first movement could be included in my category of orchestral sonata.'

Stravinsky considered the third movement to be 'the richest harmonically' of all Beethoven's sonatas, 'insofar as that element can be thought of separately'.

In Stravinsky estimation *The Hammerklavier* is 'contemporary for ever'.

Writing of Beethoven's final trilogy of piano sonatas, Opp. 109. 110 and 111, he comments:

> 'The three final sonatas represent a great ventilation in style — what a more Augustan writer would describe as a rediscovery of the classical spirit ... Beethoven's path of discovery tended, at the end, to lead more and more to contrapuntal means, homophonic thematic developments giving way to thematic transformation in variation and fugue.'

Igor Stravinsky, *Themes and Conclusions*, Faber and Faber, 1972, pp. 272–3.

Reflecting more generally on Beethoven, Stravinsky summed up his feelings in relation to him:

> 'I did not hero-worship Beethoven, nor have I ever done so, and the nature of Beethoven's talent and work are more "human" and more comprehensible to me than are, say the talents and works of more "perfect" composers like Bach and Mozart; I think I know how Beethoven composed. I have little enough Beethoven in me, alas, but some people have found I have some.'

Igor Stravinsky and Robert Craft, *Memories and Commentaries*, London: Faber and Faber, 2002, p. 23, and p. 39.

JOHN WILLIAM NAVIN SULLIVAN

Sullivan was a British born journalist and author whose polymath interests and abilities encompassed a wide range of subjects. These are reflected in his circle of gifted contemporaries who included T. S Eliot, Aldous Huxley, Wyndham Lewis and John Middleton Murray. In addition to being the author of a widely respected study *Beethoven: His spiritual development* (1927) Sullivan published some of the earliest accounts of Einstein's Theory of Relativity, studies on the nature of atoms and the universe, and addressed contemporary questions concerning God and religion. In the Preface to his Beethoven study, Sullivan writes:

> 'I believe that in his greatest music Beethoven was primarily concerned to express his personal vision of life. This vision was, of course, the product of his character and his experience. Beethoven the man and Beethoven the composer are not two unconnected entities, and the known history of the man may be used to throw light upon the character of his music.'

In his formulation of the Beethoven symphonies, Sullivan states:

> 'The transition from the Fourth to the Fifth Symphony is not the transition from one "mood" to another, both equally valid and representative; it is the transition from one level of experience and realization to another; one might say that the transition is vertical, not horizontal. And the Third and Fifth Symphonies are more important than the Fourth in the history of Beethoven because it was the deepest things in him that conditioned his development. The greater importance the world has always

attributed to the Third, Fifth, Seventh and Ninth Symphonies compared with the Fourth, Sixth and Eighth, is not because of any purely musical superiority they possess, but because everyone is more or less clearly aware that greater issues are involved, that something more important for mankind is being expressed.'

J. W. N. Sullivan, *Beethoven: His spiritual development*, 1927, pp. 155–6.

KAROL SZYMANOWSKI

The Polish composer and pianist Karol Szymanowski is regarded as being one of his country's foremost musical personalities of the late nineteenth, early twentieth-century modernist movement. Notwithstanding, his writings reveal a deep respect for the European musical tradition and its inheritance. Of Beethoven, he remarks:

'I believe that Beethoven was the most profoundly eloquent symbol of his time. We know that he was born into the classical tradition, and that this was his starting-point in the quest for a new Ideal. As such he bridged two eras. The colossal burden of historical catastrophes and events of great power and consequence roared like a storm through his consciousness and channelled deep furrows in it. His music became a true likeness reflected on some mystical screen of the immediate historical substance (in the deepest sense of the word) of the fifty years that was his span on earth.'

Placing the composer in the context of his time, Szymanowski continues:

> 'Along with his contemporaries he searched for "that new word which would become flesh", and his seemingly abstract art is clearly marked by the traces of his search and discovery of it. In effect his creative drive depended on the conscious breaking-down of the artistic forms inherited from his ancestors. The psychological source of this apparently destructive, yet in reality *constructive*, work was doubtless a sensitive subconscious state that did not confine itself merely to the sphere of aesthetic matters. In their essence these aesthetic ideas were inherited from his great predecessors; we have eloquent testimony to this in all those works of his first period.'

Turning to Beethoven's later achievements, Szymanowski singles out for special mention the *Choral* Symphony:

> 'The choice of text for the finale of the Ninth Symphony was by no means fortuitous, the result perhaps of purely poetic considerations. The decisive factor was undoubtedly the intellectual and ideological content of Schiller's hymn in which the full gravity and substance of the "word" is positively and specifically expressed. In creating his greatest masterpiece, Beethoven was certainly far removed from purely aesthetic concepts. Instead he was at his closest to the very fountain-head of contemporary life, that internally glowing and uncontrollably coursing Life which is, day in, day out, posing questions

> of untold importance for those of course who
> are capable of understanding their full signifi-
> cance. Without doubt, Beethoven was one of
> those who "understood" and who shouldered
> part of the ideological burden of his era, and
> perhaps his true greatness lies in his ethical
> qualities, rather than in the now slightly faded
> aesthetic qualities of his music.'

Szymanowski affirms the value of Beethoven to him as a composer:

> 'What does Beethoven mean to me? Or rather,
> what did he mean? I need not say anything about
> his objective greatness. It is only a question of
> how I, subjectively, perceive his work. He was a
> profound experience for me in my artistic youth.
> For the first time in the Kingdom of Art I
> understood how one could be consumed by the
> flames of one's own fire.'

Alistair Wightman, editor, *Szymanowski on Music: Selected writings of Karol Szymanowski,* London: Toccata Press, 1999, pp. 166–8.

SAMUEL COLERIDGE-TAYLOR

Samuel Coleridge-Taylor was of mixed European and African descent and is perhaps best remembered today for his cantatas *Hiawatha's Wedding Feast, The Death of Minnehaha* and *Hiawatha's Departure.* In his day, their popularity almost rivaled that of Handel's *Messiah* and Mendelssohn's *Elijah.* His musical accomplishments where however considerable: he was professor of music at the

Crystal Palace School of music; he performed at the Three Choirs Festival with the encouragement of Elgar; and when on tour in the United States he was received by President Theodore Roosevelt at the White House — a rare event for a man of African descent. Writing in the November 1900 issue of *The Crystal Palace Magazine*, Coleridge-Taylor discussed the subject of contemporary music. He attributed the most direct influence on modern composition to Beethoven, of whom he wrote:

> 'Beethoven undoubtedly gave to musical expression that wide view, depth and emotional character which subsequent music has only developed. Beethoven, compared with his predecessors, Bach alone excepted, represents an advance as striking as if one exchanged a spinet for a modern grand piano. Earlier composers were thin, mechanical, and artificial, and had no conception of orchestral use or resource such as Beethoven employed.'

W. C. Berwick Sayers, *Samuel Coleridge-Taylor, Musician: His life and letters*, London; New York: Cassell and Co., 1915, pp. 98–9.

PETER TCHAIKOVSKY

Tchaikovsky studied piano and composition at the nascent Saint Petersburg Conservatory where he received instruction in the formal Western-oriented musical tradition. Later in life he was befriended by the influential patron of the arts Nadezhda von Meck. She was herself a capable pianist, familiar with the classical repertoire and regarded Tchaikovsky as her ideal composer and philosopher-friend. Their extensive correspondence sheds light on many aspects of Tchaikovsky's views on music. In December 1878, Von Meck wrote to her protégée with her thoughts concerning the programmatic nature she considered evident in certain of Beethoven's piano sonatas — unspecified. Her letter prompted the following responses from Tchaikovsky:

> 'In my opinion, any music is programme music. There's no other kind because, for example, symphonies have a programme, overtures even more so, and operas definitely. I know Beethoven sonatas, one of which represents the movement of a wheel [Tchaikovsky is probably thinking here of the *Les Adieux* Piano Sonata, Op. 81a with its associations of a coach taking leave of Beethoven's patron the Archduke Rudolph.] and another a quarrel between husband and wife [Tchaikovsky is probably thinking here of the Piano Sonata, Op. 90 with its alleged associations between Count Moritz Lichnowsky and Josepha (Johanna) Stummer.] ... Programme music was invented by Beethoven, to some extent in the *Eroica* Symphony, but more particularly in the Sixth, the Pastoral ... I think Beethoven was wrong not to give a *programme* for the sonatas you mention. In any case, as I see it, both kinds of music (instrumental and orchestral) have an equal raison d'être, and I don't understand those gentlemen who recognize only one category to the exclusion of the other.'

Tchaikovsky elaborated his views on music giving qualified approval to that of his compatriot Modest Mussorgsky:

'[Even] in his deformity [he] is speaking a new language. Unattractive but fresh.'

Tchaikovsky affirmed to his patron he was a champion of 'great artists who will show art new paths' rather than 'pathetic weakness disguised as serious creation, which you get with Germans like Brahms. They're hopelessly insipid'.

As for the French, Tchaikovsky acknowledged Berlioz had been 'a strong progressive force' but complained how, ten years after his death, his works were only now being performed. He lamented:

'In art, the French are terrible conservatives. They were the last to acknowledge *Beethoven*. Even in the 1840s they thought him nothing more than an impetuous eccentric. The leading French critic, Fétis, complained that Beethoven had made mistakes in harmony and absolutely had to correct those mistakes twenty-five years later.'

Tchaikovsky does, however, close with an enthusiastic outburst:

'Among contemporary French composers my favourites are Bizet and Delibes ... Bizet's *Carmen* I know well. The music does not pretend to be profound, but it is so charming in its simplicity, so vital, so spontaneous and sincere, that I have practically memorized every note of it from beginning to end.'

Edward Garden and Nigel Gottrei, editors, '*To My Best Friend*': *Correspondence between Tchaikovsky and Nadezhda von Meck, 1876–1878,* Oxford: Clarendon

Press, 1993, pp. 122–3. See also: Jay Leyda and Sergi Bertensson, *The Mussorgsky Reader: A life of Modeste Petrovich Musorgsky in letters and documents*, New York: W.W. Norton, 1947, p. 367.

Writing a long letter to von Meck from Florence on 16–18 February 1878 Tchaikovsky enthused on the delights of Florence, telling her that the greatest impression made on him was the Medic Chapel in San Lorenzo. The greatness of Michelangelo prompted Tchaikovsky to find a parallel between him and Beethoven – as others have done:

> 'Here at last I've begun to appreciate Michelangelo's immense genius for the first time. I've begun to recognize a vague kinship with Beethoven. There is the same breadth and strength, the same boldness bordering on uncouthness, and the same sombre mood. Perhaps this idea is not new. Taine perspicaciously compared Raphael with Mozart. Has Michelangelo been compared to Beethoven, I wonder?' [Hippolyte Taine was a French writer and critic.]

The following week, von Meck replied:

> 'I have never come across a comparison between Beethoven and Michelangelo, but what you say is most apposite and true: there is a similarity of character in their works.'

The next month Tchaikovsky raised a subject very dear to him:
    'I don't just like Mozart – I idolize him. For me, *Don Giovanni* is the best opera ... ever written.'

He adds:

> 'It is true that Mozart spread himself too thinly and often wrote not from inspiration but from necessity. But, if you read Otto Jahn's beautifully written biography of him, you will see that he could not help it. Anyway, both Beethoven and Bach have plenty of inferior compositions, unworthy to stand alongside their masterpieces. Such was the force of circumstance that they sometimes had to turn their art into a craft.'

An English edition of Jahn's *Biography of Mozart* was published in 1891. The cited quotation is derived from: Edward Garden, and Nigel Gottrei, editors, *'To My Best Friend': Correspondence between Tchaikovsky and Nadezhda von Meck, 1876–1878*, Oxford: Clarendon Press, 1993, p. 182, p. 195, and p. 219.

In a letter to von Meck written in 1888, Tchaikovsky enthused:

> 'There is no padding in Beethoven. It is astonishing how equal, how significant and forceful this giant among musicians always remains and how well he understands the art of curbing this vast inspiration, never losing sight of balanced, traditional form.'

Ferruccio Bonavia, *Musicians on Music*, London: Routledge & Kegan Paul, 1956, p. 262.

One night, in order to rest from preoccupation with his own music, Tchaikovsky played through Bizet's Carmen from beginning to end. He considered it to be a 'chef d'oeuvre' — a masterpiece. This prompted him to reflect on past and present-day music, his views on which he shared with von Meck in a letter of 30 July 1889:

> 'It seems to me that the era we live in differs from the preceding in one way; our composers are *searching* — and first of all, they *are* searching for pretty and piquant effects — a thing which Mozart and Beethoven and Schubert and Schumann never did.'

Catherine Drinker Bowen, *Beloved Friend: The story of Tchaikovsky and Nadejda von Meck*, London: Hutchinson & Co., 1937, p. 411.

In a diary entry for 1886, headed 'My Taste in Music', Tchaikovsky communed with himself, reflecting that after his death people would probably be interested to know what were his musical predilections — especially since he seldom confided these in general conversation. He resolved 'to speak to the point' and to start with Beethoven, of whom he remarks:

> 'It is usual to praise [Beethoven] unconditionally and whom it is commanded to worship as though he were a god'.

He continued: 'And what is Beethoven to me?'
He responded:

> 'I bow before the greatness of some of his works — but I do not *love* Beethoven. My attitude toward him reminds me of what I experienced in

childhood toward the God Jehovah. I had toward Him (and even now my feelings have not changed) a feeling of wonder, but at the same time also of fear. He created Heaven and earth, He too created me — and still even though I bow before Him, there is no *love*. Christ, on the contrary, inspires truly and exclusively the feeling of *love*. Though He was *God*, He was at the same time man. He suffered like us. We *pity* Him, we love in Him His ideal *human* side. And if Beethoven occupies a place in my heart analogous to the God Jehovah, then Mozart I love as the musical Christ.'

Jacques Barzun, *Pleasures of Music: An anthology of writing about music and musicians*, London: Cassell, 1977, pp. 266–7.

ALEXANDER WHEELOCK THAYER

Alexander Wheelock Thayer is acknowledged — and much admired — for being Beethoven's first scholarly biographer. In the opinion of the present writer, Thayer's biography of Beethoven stands equally against James Boswell's celebrated *Life of Samuel Johnson*. It has been justly described as 'the classic biography of Beethoven' and, notwithstanding its several editorial revisions (see below), Thayer's researches on Beethoven, and his objective manner of writing about him, have set a benchmark that still remains a point of reference for modern-day studies of the composer.

Thayer travelled extensively in Europe to gather materials for his study of the composer. Whenever possible he met with those who had direct contact with him or had reliable first-hand accounts to relate. Thayer's credo was: 'I fight for no theories and cherish no prejudices; my sole point of view is the truth.' In pursuit of this ideal he objectively studied the sources available to him, endeavoring 'to clear away the Romantic fiction' that was then accumulating about Beethoven.

The first edition of the Thayer's biography was published in German in three volumes that appeared between 1866 and 1879. These covered Beethoven's life to the year 1816. Thayer did not live to complete his monumental study. His German colleague Herman Deiters and Hugo Rieman published volume four in 1907 and volume 5 the following year — making use of such of Thayer's original source materials that had survived (regrettably, it is believed some of Thayer's notes were lost). In 1921, the American music critic and musicologist Henry Edward Krehbiel published the first English edition. This was substantially revised and edited by Elliot Forbes (1964 and 1967) to universal acclaim — ' ... a model of objective biography one that is amazingly modern and as valuable today as when it was written ... Thayer's Life remains the definitive biography' — Harold C. Schonberg, *New York Times*. The subsequent studies and reinterpretation of the life and work of Beethoven, by, such luminaries as, Maynard Solomon and Barry Cooper, have further enriched and enlarged our understanding of the enigmatic composer in ways that would assuredly have won the approval of Thayer himself.

VIRGIL THOMSON

In his long life, Virgil Thomson divided his gifts between composition, essay writing and music criticism — in the latter role for many years as music critic to the *New York Herald-Tribune*. We first consider views Thomson expressed about music and musicians in his writings:

From an essay titled *Why composers write*, originally published in 1939 as *The state of music*, Thomson discussed patronage in music. He advanced the proposition that composers, living on subsidies, 'tend to write introspective music of strained harmonic texture and emphatic instrumental style'. He considered such composers 'were not bothered about charm, elegance, sentiment, or comprehensibility'. Rather, he maintained, 'they go for high-flown lyricism and dynamic punch ... they are revolters against convention.' Having set forth his theory Thomson considered the case of Beethoven who was himself the beneficiary of patronage and had received an annuity from his middle years onwards. With this circumstance in mind, Thomson asserts:

> 'Beethoven is their ideal; and they think of themselves as prophets in a wilderness, as martyrs unappreciated, as persecuted men. Appearing to be persecuted is, of course, their way of earning their living. The minute they lose the air of being brave men downed by circumstances, they cease to get free money. Because people with money to give away don't like giving it to serene or successful characters, no matter how poor the latter may be.'

In an essay from 1940, titled *Mozart's Leftism*, Thomson took up the theme of politics in music. He opens with the remarks:

> 'Persons of humanitarian, libertarian, and politically liberal orientation have for a century used Beethoven as their musical standard-bearer.'

Thomson was not, however, personally convinced on the grounds that he maintained (controversially):

> '[It] is hard to find much in Beethoven's life or music — beyond the legend of his having torn up the dedication of his "Heroic" Symphony to Napoleon [Symphony No. 3, the *Eroica*] when the defender of the French Revolution allowed himself to be crowned Emperor — to justify the adoration in which he has always been held by political liberals.'

Later, Thomson reserves further venom for Beethoven:

> 'Mozart was not, like Wagner, a political revolutionary. Nor was he, like Beethoven, an old fraud, who just talked about human rights and dignity but who was really an irascible, intolerant, and scheming careerist, who allowed himself the liberty, when he felt like it, of being unjust toward the poor, lickspittle toward the rich, dishonest in business, unjust and unforgiving toward the members of his own family [!]'

In 1941, Thomson discussed the concept of the masterpiece in music. He first suggested the expression could be taken to mean an artist's 'most accomplished work, the high point of his production'. He adds:

> 'And certain composers (Beethoven was the first of them) are considered to have worked exclusively in this vein.'

Regarding Beethoven's legacy, Thomson continues:

> '[All] the successors of Beethoven who aspired to his authority — Brahms and Bruckner, Wagner

> and Mahler and Tchaikovsky – quite consciously
> imbued their music with the "masterpiece" tone.'

Richard Kostelanetz, editor, *Virgil Thomson: A reader; selected writings, 1924–1984*, New York; London: Routledge, 2002, p. 27, pp. 48–9 and p. 101.

Writing to a Catholic priest on 26 May 1943, Thomson discussed the nature of broadcast music. In the course of this letter, he is more generous to Beethoven than in his earlier pronouncements:

> 'You are quite right. My radio is not a very good instrument, though there are worse on the market. I still think I am right that the narrow range of dynamics which any microphone will carry makes Beethoven one of the least effective composers for broadcasting purposes. This does not mean that I consider Beethoven's music, even in its distorted radio-sound, to be uninteresting. Quite to the contrary. The way it survives processing is to its eternal glory.'

Tim Page, and Vanessa Weeks, editors: *Selected Letters of Virgil Thomson*, New York: Summit Books, 1988, pp. 186–7. See also the entry for Artur Schnabel in which Thomson's views as a music critic are discussed.

MICHAEL TIPPETT

The English composer Sir Michael Tippett studied composition at the Royal College of Music under the guidance of Charles Wood. Tippett relates how he used Bach, Mozart and Beethoven as models to inculcate 'a solid understanding of musical forms and syntax'. Beethoven, in particular, became a central influence on Tippett from his earliest years and remained with him until his last as he himself acknowledged:

> 'When I was a student I submitted entirely to the music of Beethoven. I explored his music so exhaustively that for a long time later on I listened to every other music but his. But as a student I was fascinated by his music and his personality, though I had also a very catholic taste, to which little was foreign. I doubt if in adolescence one can be absorbed by Beethoven and have a real understanding of Mozart. In so far as I have acquired that it has come later.'

Michael Tippett, *Moving into Aquarius*, London: Routledge and Kegan Paul, 1959, p. 101.

Writing of his earliest musical experiences, Tippett remarks on the value he derived from the Henry Wood Promenade Concerts:

'Thus began the springtime of my life, as a human being and as a musician.'

Of the concerts themselves he remarks:

> 'In those days, Henry Wood did all the conducting, except for the last items in the second half of each concert, which were always instrumental solos, vocal ballads etc. plus a final orchestral item conducted by the leader: and on successive Fridays he presented all the Beethoven symphonies, in order from 1 to 9. These I followed with the scores John had lent me. Their impact was

devastating: Beethoven became my musical god
and has remained so ever since.'

John, to whom Tippett makes reference, was his first close friend and the object of his affections. John's proper name was Herbert Sumison. Wood's allocating Friday night exclusively to the music of Beethoven persisted until well into the 1950s, as the present writer recalls with much the same enthusiasm as Tippett, but, alas, with *much less* musical insight!

Composition was the central focus of Tippett's studies at the Royal College of Music. He discovered that Charles Wood admired Beethoven as much as he did, 'especially the string quartets and piano sonatas'. Tippett was not a particularly adept student as he admits:

'At the examinations I was hopelessly at sea, in reality because I could not hear in my head the notes I was writing "by calculation" on the manuscript paper ... The tradition at the RCM was that one never used a piano for such work. I quickly realised that this was impossible for me. Beethoven may have been deaf, but that didn't mean everyone else had to be.'

Michael Tippett, *Those Twentieth Century Blues: An autobiography*, London: Hutchinson, 1991, p. 13.

Tippet discussed music as an independent art form in the context of change and the emergence of the composer in the, sometimes stereotyped, image of the artist as a lone prophet, misunderstood by an increasingly unreceptive society. In this context, in Arnold Whittall's phrase 'Beethoven stood for an attitude to art'. Tippett writes:

'When music as an independent art form flowered at the end of the eighteenth century, the European climate of opinion was already deeply involved in the swift and shattering process by which value was going over from the world of imagination to the world of technics [see below]. And the artistic consequences of the depreciation of value given to the imaginative world, meant that the effort of imaginative creation began to assume, already in Beethoven's time, that superhuman quality, that desperate struggle to restore spiritual order by increasingly transcendent and extraordinary works of art.'

Originally published in: Michael Tippett, *Moving into Aquarius*, London: Routledge and Kegan Paul, 1959, p. 77 and quoted in: Suzanne Robinson, editor: *Michael Tippett: Music and Literature*, Aldershot: Ashgate, 2002, p. 39. See also: Arnold Whittall, *Exploring Twentieth-Century Music: Tradition and innovation*, Cambridge; New York: Cambridge University Press, 2003, pp. 118—9.

In her study of Tippett's writing about music, Suzanne Robinson discusses the composer's 'truth-value' concept in the music of Beethoven. By this, as Robinson remarks, Tippett was alluding to 'that quality of music that reflects the problems of society and attempts to reconcile the world of technics [Tippetts's way of referring to the 'real world' — the world as it is] and the world of imagination [the 'ideal world']. She continues:

'Tippett's deep admiration for Beethoven, for both his music and personality, can be explained in part by the fact that the 'truth-value' of Beethoven's music ... is still relevant [today].'

In substantiating this proposition, Robinson quotes the following from Tippett's reference to Beethoven's music:

'At least ninety-per-cent of all music lovers of *all ages* need the experience which great works of music in this humanistic tradition provide, just as theatre-lovers need Shakespeare. (In my private jargon, I call this the Shakespeare-Beethoven archetype.)'

In pursuing the notion of 'art mirroring society', Robinson cites the utopian message of hope and brotherhood that Beethoven sought to embody in his setting of Schiller's *Ode to Joy* text in the Ninth Symphony. She contrasts this, more to the point, as did Tippett himself with the horrors of Auschwitz as 'the ultimate symbol of our society's utter failure'.

Suzanne Robinson, editor: *Michael Tippett: Music and Literature*, Aldershot: Ashgate, 2002, pp. 50–1.

With the outbreak of war, Tippett's beliefs compelled him to become a Conscientious Objector. Subsequently, for failing to carry out his conditions of exemption he was required to serve a prison sentence in Wormwood Scrubbs, disposing him 'to feel like an outcast'. At the conclusion of hostilities, when the full extent of mankind's suffering became known, Tippett's despair was complete. Later he wrote:

'The climax of my sense of isolation came shortly afterwards when the noble Christian allies decided to put their faith in that masterpiece of technics — the atom bomb. Simultaneously, the concentration camps were opened. I found in these obscenities, as did many others, a most violent and enduring shock of my sense of what humanity might be at all. A denial of any and every affirmation which the poet might make, whether in the name of God or of Mankind.'

Tippett asked the question, 'What price Beethoven now?' Could we any longer, he propositioned, find solace in Beethoven's setting of Schiller's *Ode to Joy*?

Michael Tippett, *Moving into Aquarius*, London: Routledge and Kegan Paul, 1959, p. 153.

ERNST TOCH

The Austrian composer Ernst Toch was a trained pianist of considerable ability and insight — he studied at the Hoch Conservatory in Frankfurt (1909—13). He once described Beethoven's *Pathétique* and *Appassionata* piano sonatas as 'prayers of thanks, by one who has experienced the deity'. In addition, he brought to his own work the power of an intellect that had mastered the study of medicine at the University of Vienna and philosophy at the University of Heidelberg. These experiences may have nurtured within him his deep sense of humanity and the desire to introduce new approaches to music through the medium of his own compositions. Toch's biographer Diane Jezic remarks:

'Beethoven held a unique position in Toch's pantheon of composers, as is clear from his article *Beethoven in the Present, 1927* [Beethoven's death centenary]. Beethoven's work stands beyond approval or rejection, he says, and his appearance belongs more to the history of mankind than to the history of music.'

Jezic adds:

'It is his humanity, Toch believes, that gives Beethoven's works their power of intensity and popularity.'

She suggests:

'With a small rearrangement of his inner makeup, Beethoven could have been a great revolutionary or a philosopher.'

Diane Jezic, *The Musical Migration and Ernst Toch*, Ames: Iowa State University Press, 1989, pp. 134–5.

DONALD FRANCIS TOVEY

The British musicologist, composer, pedagogue and conductor Sir Donald Francis Tovey is best known for his *Essays in Musical Analysis*. They had their origins as programme notes written by him to accompany the concerts given by the Ried Orchestra, Edinburgh — performed largely under Tovey's direction. The *Essays* were published in six volumes with each volume focusing on a particular category of Beethoven's music. Volumes I and II were devoted to the symphonies; Volume III, the concertos; Volume IV, illustrative music, Volume V, vocal music; and Volume VI, supplementary essays. A seventh volume was published posthumously dealing with chamber music. These writings are still respected today for their musicological erudition that Tovey interspersed with passages of wit and mordant humour. His musical analyses seek 'to facilitate the listener's appreciation of [the music's] artistic content and technical merits'. In addition to the *Essays*, Tovey paid tribute to Beethoven and his music in a series of articles that were published in the 1911 edition of the *Encyclopaedia Britannica*.

Writing of Beethoven's artistic development, Tovey observes:

> 'The peculiar interest and difficulty in tracing Beethoven's artistic development are that the changes in the materials and range of his art were as great as those in the form, so that he appears in the light of a pioneer, while the art with which he started was nevertheless already a perfectly mature and highly organized thing.'

Donald Francis Tovey, *Ludwig van Beethoven*, in: Michael Tilmouth, editor: *Donald Francis Tovey: The classics of music: talks, essays, and other writings previously uncollected*, Oxford: Oxford University Press, 2001, p. 333. Tovey's *Beethoven* article originally appeared in the *Encyclopaedia Britannica*, 1914.

Together with his more substantial publications, Tovey contributed to various journals. In one of these (*The Musical Gazette*, July 1902) he makes reference to Beethoven's creative progress:

> 'With Beethoven, progress seems to start out in all directions and all of them lead to truth. The real fact is that in his case the differences between one work and another are evident in outward

> form, and the range covered by each work increased with enormous rapidity throughout his career. But his early works certainly do not stand towards the later as exercises to works of art: they are perfect masterpieces of smaller range. What is right for them would be inadequate for later: what is right for the later would be nonsensical in the earlier.'

Michael Tilmouth, *ibid*, p. 677.

In 1975, the American critic and musicologist Joseph Kerman wrote an essay to commemorate the hundredth anniversary of Tovey's birth, titled *Tovey's Beethoven*. In this, he makes a measured critique of the British musicologist's contribution to Beethoven musicology. He writes:

> 'To Tovey ... and I think many naïve listeners [i.e. not musically trained] ... Beethoven's music more than any other suggested links with life experience. Darkness, mystery, fierceness, ghostliness: Beethoven puts words like these into the critic's mouth in a way that Bach and even Haydn and Brahms do not. Beethoven also suggests psychological states of mind.'

In his summing up of Tovey's achievement, Kerman reflects:

> '[In] some sense [Tovey] ... was ... one of the completest musicians who ever lived. Our latest musical dictionary calls him a "musical historian, pianist, composer and conductor".'

Kerman's reference here is to the entry in *Collins Music Encyclopedia*, London and Glasgow, 1959. Kerman adds 'a list which is obviously half as long as it should be: he was also a legendary teacher, a musical analyst, theorist, music critic, and aesthetician'.

We should also add that Tovey was an accomplished contributor to radio broadcasts, illustrating his remarks at the piano. Kerman concludes:

> 'Beethoven ... brought out the best in [Tovey], and for him richness, consistency, and completeness, *Tovey's Beethoven* stands out as the most impressive achievement, perhaps, yet produced by the art of music criticism.'

Joseph Kerman, *Write All These Down: Essays on music*, Berkeley, California; London: University of California Press, 1994, pp. 155–70.

Edgard Varèse

The French-born composer Edgard Varèse once posed the question:

'What is music but organized noises?'

This outlook disposed him, in his own musical aesthetic, to explore the potential he felt was implicit in timbre, rhythm, 'sound as living matter' and 'musical space as open rather than bounded'. Varèse has been described as the 'Father of electronic music' and 'The stratospheric Colossus of Sound' (Henry Miller). Varèse's pioneering outlook — he was considered by some to be fifty years ahead of his time — disposed his biographer Malcolm MacDonald to find a parallel between Varèse and Beethoven:

'Insofar as the 20th-century had a Beethoven, he is it.'

He finds further similarities with Beethoven:

'He has profoundly altered all our awareness of what music is and can be.'

MacDonald concludes, with further, albeit indirect, homage to Beethoven:

> 'Varèse expressed himself and expressed us. Yes, for we can truly recognize ourselves in his universe. That world is indeed ours. And its tragic force is a spiritual explosion. So that Beethoven and Varèse, across the centuries, are linked by their humanity and their individuality. Both were truly faithful to their natures. Both were men who "believed".'

Malcolm MacDonald, *Varèse: Astronomer in sound*, London: Kahn & Averill, 2003, pp. 72–3 and p. 413.

GIUSEPPE VERDI

The French music critic Camille Bellaigue published a study of musicians under the title *Portraits et silhouettes de musiciens*. He sent Verdi a copy who later expressed his appreciation in a letter of 2 May 1898. In his opening remarks Verdi identifies with Bellaigue's own musical idols:

> '[The book] is very beautiful, deeply thought out, and masterfully expressed. I shall talk to you only about music, simply music, and I join you in applauding the three giants, Palestrina, Bach, Beethoven.'

Verdi's opinions of other composers are worthy of remark. He recognised Gluck's 'powerful dramatic sense' but considered him inferior to Handel. He praised Bellaigue for his 'silhouettes' of Chopin, Schubert and Saint-Saens but it is Rossini who he singled out for special mention:

> 'I cannot help thinking that *Il Barbiere di Siviglia*, with its abundance of musical ideas, its comic verve and its truthful declamation, is the most beautiful *opera buffa* in existence.'

Charles Osborne: editor and translator, *Letters of Giuseppe Verdi*, London: Victor Gollancz, 1971, p. 263.

COSIMA WAGNER

Cosima Wagner was the illegitimate daughter of the Hungarian pianist and composer Franz Liszt and his mistress Marie d'Agoult. Her second marriage to Richard Wagner was an act of sustained veneration for the man and his music. Much of this is preserved in the 2,500 pages of her Diary. From Volume I, we have extracted the following remarks in which she recorded her and Wagner's views concerning Beethoven:

> *22 January 1871*
> 'Richard considers: "Everybody should improvise, every good musician can produce something interesting in his improvisation. But writing it down is quite a different process, then it has to be turned into a sonata, a suite, and so on, and it takes a lot to revitalize a familiar, defined form ... Beethoven was the first to write music which was listened to purely as music, all previous things

were designed to enliven social gatherings or to accompany what was going on in the church or on the stage".' pp. 325–6.

15 February 1871

'I told [Richard] that for me the difference between Beethoven's music and that of the others also seemed to me to lie in the fact that his melodies arise out of the whole tonal fabric, in the way that a flower arises out of the whole plant, whereas other composers think up a theme with more-or-less ease, then append to it their musical work, their fugues, canons, counter-themes, etc. When yesterday we exclaimed, "Ah, that is Beethoven," I asked myself what we meant by that. With other composers Mendelssohn, for example, when we say "That is he," we are defining some routine, an inborn or assumed manner which crops up in unthinking moments; with Beethoven, however, we are recognizing the spirits which he alone can conjure up.' pp. 337–8.

31 May 1871

'At lunch R. sang a theme by Beethoven (the second in the first movement of the F minor Sonata [Op. 57]) and says: "No one before him or after him has ever given us anything like that; it is sublimity when it becomes pleasurable; when it has been caught and one floats in it".'

4 November 1872

From this entry from Cosima Wagner's Diary, we learn of Wagner's views concerning Beethoven's *Hammerklavier* Sonata: '[Richard] tells me he has been going through the first movement of Beethoven's B-flat Sonata and was quite overwhelmed by the beauty and tenderness and richness of its detail, which passes by in such a way that nobody notices all that has been put into it ... He talks about orchestrating this sonata, in order to make it more accessible.' At this point Wagner himself remarked: "As it is, only the greatest of virtuosos can play it, but if it were performed as orchestrated by me, a sort of tradition could be established." Cosima concludes: 'We read though the sonata together with incredible delight, its richness of detail is like flowers hidden in a meadow.' p. 551.

30 October 1874

'In the evening R. studies [Beethoven's] *Les Adieux* Sonata with Herr [Josef] Rubenstein. In his [Wagner's] playing the usual fault of making an emotional work of this kind almost unrecognisable through an unfeeling, unaccented rendition can be discerned again.' A later entry of Cosima's suggests Wagner justified his style of interpretation to Rubinstein: 'R. explains to him that the difficulty of interpreting the works of B.'s middle period lies in the fact that they appear to preserve the old forms, whereas the themes and figurations go far beyond them — they are full of passion and deep emotion.' p. 798.

25 September 1877

From this entry of Cosima Wagner's Diary, we gain an insight into the intellectual nature of her relationship with Wagner and of his estimation of the second movement of Beethoven's C minor Piano Sonata, Op. 111: 'In the evening ... [Richard] reads me ... Voltaire's article on Aristotle in the *Dictionnaire philosophique*. The boldness of its flights of imagination leads to Beethoven, and R. says that were he to try to visualize Beethoven "in all his starry glory", he would surely think of the second movement of Op. 111 (Adagio with variations); he knows nothing more ecstatic, he says, yet at the same time it is never sentimental.' pp. 983–4.

Gregor-Dellin and Dietrich Mack, editors, *Cosima Wagner's Diaries, Vol. 1, 1869-1877*, London: Collins, 1978–80.

RICHARD WAGNER

We learn of Wagner's admiration of Beethoven from his biographer, the composer, teacher and writer on music Ferdinand Praeger. His *Wagner As I Knew Him* appeared in 1892 — the first-full length biography of the composer to be published in English. It earned the endorsement of the Wagner enthusiast George Bernhard Shaw but was later criticized for Praeger's alleged misrepresentations. If we place our trust in the less controversial aspects of Praeger's account, we derive the following impressions:

BEETHOVEN'S YOUTHFUL INFLUENCES ON WAGNER

'Wagner at fifteen was a poet, and the energetic, suggestive music of Beethoven was mentally transformed into living personalities. He has said that he felt as if Beethoven addressed him "personally." Every movement formed itself into a story, glowed with life, and assumed a clear, distinct shape. I do not forget the earlier influence of Weber over him, but then that was more due to emotion than to reason. The novelty of *Der Freischütz*, the freshness of its melodic stream, and the wild imaginative treatment of the romantic story captivated his first affection and enchained it to the last. The whole of his impressions of Beethoven (whom, by the way, Wagner never saw) were embodied by him in a sketch written for a periodical and entitled, "A Pilgrimage to Beethoven." Although the incidents painted there are not to be taken as having happened to the pilgrim, Wagner, yet the story is clear on one point — the unbounded spell Beethoven exercised over him.'

Ferdinand Praeger, *Wagner as I knew him*, London; New York: Longmans, Green, 1892, p. 37.

Praeger continues:

'Beethoven was his daily study. He was carefully storing all the grand thoughts of the great master, but his fiery enthusiasm had not yet come to that burning-point when it should ignite his own latent powers. His acquaintance with the scores of Beethoven has never been equalled. It was extraordinary. He had them so much by heart that he could play on the piano, with his own awkward fingering, whole movements.'

Ferdinand Praeger, *Ibid*, p.40.

*

Wagner outlined his own debt to Beethoven in his Autobiography *My Life* from which we cite the following passages:

WAGNER'S RESPONSE TO LEARNING OF THE DEATH OF BEETHOVEN:

'Another work also exercised a great fascination over me, namely, the overture to *Fidelio* in E major, the introduction to which affected me deeply. I asked my sisters about Beethoven, and learned that the news of his death had just arrived. Obsessed as I still was by the terrible grief caused by Weber's death, this fresh loss, due to the decease of this great master of melody, who had only just entered my life, filled me with strange anguish, a feeling nearly akin to my childish dread of the ghostly fifths on the violin. It was now Beethoven's music that I longed to know more thoroughly; I came to Leipzig, and found his music to *Egmont* on the piano at my sister Louisa's. After that I tried to get hold of his sonatas. At last, at a concert at the Gewandhaus, I heard one of the master's symphonies for the first time; it was the Symphony in A major. The effect on me was indescribable. To this must be added the impression produced on me by Beethoven's features, which I saw in the lithographs that were circulated everywhere at that time, and by the fact that he was deaf, and lived a quiet secluded life. I soon conceived an image of him in my mind as a sublime and unique supernatural being, with whom none could compare. This image was associated in my brain with that of Shakespeare; in ecstatic dreams I met both of them, saw and spoke to them, and on awakening found myself bathed in tears.'

*

Richard Wagner, *My Life*, London: Constable and Company Ltd., 1911, pp. 35–6.

Wagner's prose works extend to eight substantial volumes, English editions of which appeared in translation over the period 1895–1907 from the hand of William Ashton Ellis. In Volume I, Wagner reveals facets of his respect for Beethoven:

ON BEETHOVEN'S POWERS OF INVENTION

'Assuredly there had never been an artist who pondered less upon his art. The brusque impetuosity of his nature shows he felt as an actual personal injury, almost as direct as every other shackle of convention, the ban imposed on his genius by these forms. Yet his rebellion consisted in nothing but the exuberant unfolding of his inner genius, unrestrained by those outward forms themselves. He never did radically alter an existing form of instrumental music; in his last sonatas, quartets, symphonies and so forth, we may demonstrate beyond dispute a structure such as of the first. But compare these works with one another; compare for example the Eighth Symphony in F with the Second in D, and marvel at the wholly new world that fronts us in well nigh the identical form.'

My Life, p. 83.

BEETHOVEN COMPARED WITH COLUMBUS

'Did Columbus teach us to take ship across the ocean, and thus to bind in one each continent of Earth; did his world-historical discovery convert the narrow-seeing national-man into a universal and all-seeing *Man*: so, by the hero who explored the broad and seeming shoreless sea of absolute Music unto its very bounds, are won the new and never dreamt-of coasts which this sea no longer now divorces from the old and primal continent of man, but *binds together* with it for the new-born, happy art-life of the Manhood of the Future. And this hero is none other than — Beethoven.

My Life, p. 115.

ON BEETHOVEN'S INSTRUMENTAL MUSIC

'It was *Beethoven* who opened up the boundless faculty of Instrumental Music for expressing elemental storm and stress. His power it was, that took the basic essence of the Christian's Harmony, that bottomless sea of unhedged fullness and unceasing motion, and clove in twain the fetters of its freedom. *Harmonic Melody* — for so must we designate this melody divorced from speech, in distinction from the Rhythmic Melody of dance — was capable, though merely borne by instruments, of the most limitless expression together with the most unfettered treatment. In long, connected tracts of sound, as in larger, smaller, or even smallest fragments, it turned beneath the Master's poet hand to vowels, syllables, and words and phrases of a speech in which a message hitherto unheard, and never spoken yet, could promulgate itself. Each letter of this speech was an infinitely soul-full element; and the measure of the joinery of these elements was utmost free commensuration, such as could be exercised by none but a tone-poet who longed for the unmeasured utterance of this unfathomed yearning.'

My Life, p. 121.

ON THE FIFTH SYMPHONY

'What inimitable art did Beethoven employ in his "C-minor Symphony," in order to steer his ship from the ocean of infinite yearning to the haven of fulfilment! He was able to raise the utterance of his music *almost* to a moral resolve, but not to speak aloud that final word; and after every onset of the Will, without a moral handhold, we feel tormented by the equal possibility of falling back again to suffering, as of being led to lasting victory. Nay, this falling-back must almost seem to us more "necessary" than the morally ungrounded triumph, which therefore — not being a necessary consummation, but a mere arbitrary gift of grace — has not the power to lift us up and yield to us that *ethical* satisfaction which we demand as outcome of the yearning of the heart.'

My Life, p. 123.

*

ON THE SEVENTH SYMPHONY

'This symphony is the *Apotheosis of Dance* herself: it is Dance in her highest aspect, as it were the loftiest Deed of bodily motion incorporated in an ideal mould of tone. Melody and Harmony unite around the sturdy bones of Rhythm to firm and fleshy human shapes, which now with giant limbs' agility, and now with soft, elastic pliance, *almost before our very eyes*, close up the supple, teeming ranks; the while now gently, now with daring, now serious, now wanton, now pensive, and again exulting, the deathless strain sounds forth and forth; until, in the last whirl of delight, a kiss of triumph seals the last embrace.'

My Life, pp. 124–5.

ON THE NINTH SYMPHONY

'The Last Symphony of Beethoven is the redemption of Music from out her own peculiar element into the realm of *universal Art*. It is the human Evangel of the art of the Future. Beyond it no forward step is possible; for upon it the perfect Art-work of the Future alone can follow, the *universal Drama* to which Beethoven has forged for us the key ... "*Freude!*" ("*Rejoice!*") ... *With this word he cries to men: "Breast to breast, ye mortal millions! This one kiss to all the world!"* — And *this Word* will be the language of the *Art-work of the Future.*'

William Ashton Ellis, *Richard Wagner's Prose Works: Vol. 1, The art-work of the future*, edited and translated by William

Ashton Ellis, London: Kegan Paul, Trench, Trübner, 1895, p. 126.

In 1870, Wagner published his study *Beethoven* to correspond with the centenary celebrations then arising in connection with the composer's birth. An English translation appeared in 1893 by Edward Dannreuther. Wagner's stated aim, as he outlined in his *Preface*, was 'to deliver an oration ... in honour of the great musician ... at a greater length than would have been possible had he actually addressed an audience'. We cite the following passages, some of which overlap with the texts from which we have previously quoted:

> BEETHOVEN AND SONATA-FORM
> 'It may be said that Beethoven was and remained a composer of sonatas, for in far the greater number and the best of his instrumental compositions, the outline of the sonata-form was the veil-like tissue through which he gazed into the veil-like realm of sounds; or, through which, emerging from that realm, he made himself intelligible; whilst other forms, particularly the mixed ones of vocal music, despite the most extraordinary achievements in them, he only touched upon in passing, as if by way of experiment.'

Beethoven, p. 36.

> BEETHOVEN'S DEBT
> TO HIS PREDECESSORS
> 'Beethoven's earlier works are not incorrectly held to have sprung from Haydn's model; and a closer relationship to Haydn than Mozart may be traced even in the later development of his genius

'... Beethoven would not recognise Haydn as his teacher, though the latter was generally taken for such, and he even suffered injurious expressions of youthful arrogance to escape him about Haydn. It seems as though he felt himself related to Haydn like one born a man to a childish elder. As regards form he agreed with his teacher, but the unruly demon of his inner music, fettered by that form, impelled him to a disclosure of his power, which, like everything else in the doings of gigantic musicians, could only appear incomprehensibly rough.'

Beethoven, pp. 37–8.

BEETHOVEN'S YOUTHFUL INDEPENDENCE OF MIND

'We see young Beethoven ... facing the world at once with that defiant temperament which, throughout his life, kept him in almost savage independence: his enormous self-confidence, supported by haughtiest courage, at all times prompted him to defend himself from the frivolous demands made upon music by a pleasure-seeking world. He had to guard a treasure of immeasurable richness against the importunities of effeminate taste. He was the soothsayer of the innermost world of tones, and he had to act as such in the very forms in which music was displaying itself as a merely diverting art.'

Beethoven, p. 39.

*

BEETHOVEN'S CAPACITY TO ENRICH TRADITIONAL MUSICAL FORMS

'He never altered any of the extant forms of instrumental music on principle; the same structure can be traced in his last sonatas, quartets, symphonies, etc., as unmistakably as in his first. But compare these works with one another; place the Eighth Symphony in F major beside the Second in D, and wonder at the entirely new world, almost in precisely the same form!'

Beethoven, p. 42.

BEETHOVEN'S POWERS OF INVENTION

'[The] feature in Beethoven's musical productions which is so particularly momentous for the history of art is this; that in every technical detail, by means of which for clearness' sake the artist places himself in a conventional relation to the external world, is raised to the highest significance of a spontaneous effusion.'

Beethoven, p. 45.

BEETHOVEN'S RESPONSE TO NATURE

'He cast his glance upon phenomena that answered in wondrous reflex, illuminated by his inner light. The essential nature of things now again speaks to him, and he sees things displayed in the calm light of beauty. Again he understands the forest, the brook, the meadow, the blue sky, the song of birds, the flight of clouds, the roar of storms, the beatitude of blissfully moving repose. All he perceives and constructs is permeated with that wondrous serenity which music has gained through him ... Who does not hear the Redeemer's word when listening to the *Pastoral* Symphony?'

Beethoven, pp. 54–5.

ON THE STRING QUARTET IN C-SHARP MINOR, OP. 131

'[Whilst] listening to the work, we are bound to eschew any definite comparisons, being solely conscious of an immediate revelation from another world ... The longer introductory *Adagio*, than which probably nothing more melancholy has been expressed in tones, I would designate as the awakening on the morn of a day that throughout its tardy course shall fulfil not a single desire ... Nonetheless, it is a penitential prayer, a conference with God in the faith of the eternally good ... And now, in the short transitional *Allegro Moderato*, it is as though the Master, conscious of his strength, puts himself in position to work his spells; with renewed power he now practises his magic (*Andante*) in banning a lovely figure the witness of pure heavenly innocence, so that he may incessantly enrapture himself by its new and unheard-of transformations, induced by the refraction of the rays of light he casts upon it. We may now (*Presto*) fancy him, profoundly happy from within, casting an inexpressibly serene glance upon the outer world; and again, it stands before him as in the *Pastoral* Symphony. Everything is luminous, reflecting his inner happiness ... He contemplates Life itself (*Adagio*) – a short but troubled meditation — as though he were diving into the deep dream of his soul. He has again caught sight of the inner world; he awakens, and strikes the strings for a dance, such as the world has never heard (*Allegro* Finale). It is the World's own dance: wild delight, cries of anguish, love's ecstasy, highest rapture, misery, rage; voluptuous now, and sorrowful; lightning's quiver, storm's roll; and compelling all things, proudly and firmly wielding them from whirl to whirlpool, to the abyss.'

Beethoven, pp. 61–3.

ON BEETHOVEN'S SETTING OF SCHILLER'S ODE TO JOY

'It is quite evident that Schiller's words have only been made to fit the main melody as best they could; for that melody is at first fully developed, and emitted by instruments alone, when it inspires us with inexpressible emotions of joy at the "paradise regained". The most consummate art has never produced anything artistically more simple than that melody, the childlike innocence of which, when it is first heard in the most equable whisper of the bass stringed-instruments, in unison, breathes upon us with a saintly breath ... there is nothing like the sweet fervour to which every newly-added voice further animates this prototype of purest innocence, until every embellishment, every glory of elevated feeling, unites in it and around it, like the breathing world round a finally revealed dogma of purest love.'

Beethoven, pp. 70–1.

BEETHOVEN COMPARED WITH SHAKESPEARE

'Shakespeare ... remained wholly incomparable, until German genius produced in Beethoven a being that can only be analogically explained by comparison with him.'

Beethoven, p. 79.

WAGNER'S CONCLUDING CELEBRATORY TRIBUTE TO BEETHOVEN

'[Nothing] can more inspiringly stand beside the triumphs of [the] bravery [of the German people] in this wonderful year of 1870 than the memory of our great *Beethoven*, who just a hundred years ago was born to the German people ... Let us then celebrate the great path-finder in the wilderness of degenerate paradise! But let us celebrate him worthily — not less worthily than the victories of German bravery: for the world's benefactor takes precedence of the world's conqueror!'

Richard Wagner, *Beethoven: With [a] supplement from the philosophical works of A. Schopenhauer*, translated by E. Dannreuther, London: Reeves, 1893, pp. 112–3.

BRUNO WALTER

The German-born conductor Bruno Walter was destined to become a concert pianist. At the age of nine he appeared in that capacity, with the Berlin Philharmonic Orchestra, playing a concerto movement and the following year he performed a full concerto. However, it was hearing the

Berlin Philharmonic under the direction of Hans von Bülow that resolved Walter to follow the career of an orchestral conductor. Although subsequently achieving a reputation as a leading conductor of opera, Walter is also remembered for his performances and recordings of the works of Beethoven to which 'he gave insight into his priorities and in a warm and non-tyrannical manner — as contrasted with some of his [conductor] colleagues'.

In his *Autobiography*, Walter reflects on the nature of youthful response to music:

> 'It is my belief that young people at that age of life are more easily impressed by what is heroic and grandiose; that they more easily understand works of art in which passionate feelings are violently uttered in raised accents, and that the lighter sounds of cheerfulness are less impressive to them.'

Following this generalization, Walter writes:

> 'Thus, Beethoven was my god, and I considered Mozart merely pretty. Schumann's stormy romanticism spoke to me more eloquently than Schubert's blissful melodies.'

Describing his own youthful spiritual development, Walter remarks that his walks and wanderings were as important to him as his formal studies:

> 'Studying is the absorption and digestion of knowledge; reading, as Schopenhauer correctly says, is "thinking with other people's thoughts". During those summers, in addition to a wealth of

> impressions from outside, thoughts of my own
> came pouring forth.'

He continues:
> 'There began a direct relation between me and towards
> the world.'

This personal awakening disposed Walter to reflect, romantically, on the nature of the workings of creativity in the mind of the wanderer:

> 'It seems to me that the Muses ... prefer to bestow
> their feminine favour upon wanderers and
> roamers ...'.

Not surprisingly, Walter's conclusion led him to think of Beethoven:

> 'Would anybody venture to assert that Beethoven
> could have written his symphonies or Goethe his
> poems without the inspiration that came to them
> on their wanderings?'

Bruno Walter, *Theme and Variations: An autobiography*, London: H. Hamilton, 1948, p. 32 and p. 38.

ANTON WEBERN

In a notebook entry from 1905, Webern gave expression to his deepest thoughts that reveal his maturing aesthetic and his engagement with ideas of purity, truth and his reverence for Beethoven:

> 'The genius of Beethoven reveals itself more and
> more clearly to me. It gives me a higher power,

knowledge, knowledge in the end when one veil after another is torn away, and his genius shines for me ever more radiantly — and one day the moment will come when I am directly imbued, in brightest purity, with his divinity. He is the comfort of my soul, which searches and cries after truth.'

In the 1920s, Webern assisted Arnold Schoenberg with the production of his concerts in association with *The Society for Private Musical Performances*, some of which were held at the Schwarzwald School, founded by Eugenie Schwarzwald — a long-time supporter of Schoenberg. The repertoire had a focus on Beethoven and on the anniversary of his birthday, Webern reportedly told his students:

'Beethoven's birthday should be observed by all humanity as the most important of holidays'.

In point of fact, there is no authentic record of the date of Beethoven's birth; however, the registry of his baptism, on 17 December 1770, survives in the records of the Parish of St. Regius, Bonn. Presumably, this is the date that Webern had in mind.

There are echoes of Webern's sentiments to his students that he expressed in a letter of 21 December 1911 to his friend, and fellow-composer, Alban Berg:

'There are few such marvellous events as Christmas. One must consider, after almost 2,000 years, the nights when a great man was born is still celebrated by almost all the people on earth as a moment during which everybody says only kind things and wishes to do good to all. This is truly wonderful. Should not Beethoven's birthday be celebrated the same way?'

*

Kathryn Bailey, *The Life of Webern*, Cambridge: Cambridge University Press, 1998, p. 44 and pp. 125–6.

On 3 February 1905, Anton Webern attended a concert at which Gustav Mahler was also present. Afterwards, Mahler expounded his views on music that affected Webern deeply. He recalls:

> 'These happy hours in his presence will always remain in my memory as exceedingly happy ones, since it was the first time that I received the immediate impression of a truly great personality. Almost all his words that I could hear are embedded in my memory, and so I want to note them down in this book [Webern's Diary] that is so dear to me.'

Webern's recollection of Mahler's words are:

> "Nature is for us the model in this realm. Just as in nature the entire universe has developed from the primeval cell, from plants, animals, and man beyond to God, the Supreme Being, so also in music should a larger structure develop from a single motive in which is contained the germ of everything that is yet to be."

Webern adds:

> 'With Beethoven ... one almost always finds a new motive in the development. The entire development should, however, be carried out from a single motive; in that sense Beethoven

was simply not to be considered a great contrapuntalist.'

From Webern we learn Mahler was of the opinion:

'Variation is the most important factor in a musical work ... A theme should have to be really especially beautiful, as some by Schubert are, in order to make its unaltered return refreshing.'

Hans Moldenhauer, *Anton von Webern: A chronicle of his life and work,* London: Victor Gollancz, 1978, p. 75.
Several of Webern's pupils have left accounts of Webern as their teacher of piano. The following is a selection relating to Beethoven:

Donna Zincover was a gifted girl who came from a wealthy family in Warsaw. She tragically lost her sight in an accident — a circumstance that affected her teacher Webern deeply. Notwithstanding her misfortune, she continued her studies of Beethoven's sonatas with him. She describes Webern's method of instruction:

'He did not actually teach piano playing, that is, as an instrument with its own technical requirements, but was concerned only with how a particular piece should sound. I would say he taught a Beethoven sonata as he would conduct a symphony ... Webern could bring out the musical aspects admirably, but he was not exactly interested in technical training. He gave the pupils the right things to play according to their state of technical advancement. He held: "It does not matter so much what they play but that they play well." ... He thought that sighted and blind people alike must learn to find their way about on a piano mainly by practising, and the will to express oneself musically acts as the stimulus and wellspring for determination and perseverance.'

K. H. Lehrigstein, a junior teaching-colleague of Webern's, recalls his contribution to the 1934–35 Beethoven course at the *Israelite Institute for the Blind*:

'Webern played the examples from Beethoven's piano sonatas himself. Because his analysis was so detailed, he never had to play as much as the exposition of a single movement. When he came to a technically more difficult bit, he was not perturbed. I remember one instance when he was confronted with a rapid passage leading into something he wanted to show. He simply gave a rough outline of the demanding passage and humorously commented: "You know, some people can do it," saying it with such mock admiration that he made us all laugh.'

Kurt Manschinger studied with Webern for a full six years. He recalls this period in his memoirs:

'When analysing a Beethoven sonata or a Brahms symphony, he found so many hidden connections which eluded others, and of which perhaps even the composer themselves might not always have been conscious ... His patience was limitless, and he was very generous with the time allotted to me. A lesson supposed to last one hour usually lasted two. Beethoven, of course, was his god, then came Brahms and Mahler, finally Schoenberg.'

Hans Moldenhauer, *Anton von Webern: A chronicle of his life and work*, London: Victor Gollancz, 1978, p. 288, p. 420 and p. 505.

KURT WEILL

In April 1918, Kurt Weill enrolled as a music student at the Berlin Hochscule für Musik. Soon after his arrival he wrote to his brother Hans:

> 'If only I could fall madly in love and forget everything else. I am sure that would do me good. There is only one force which has an effect on me equal to what I imagine love to be like — and that is Beethoven.'

Ronald Taylor, *Kurt Weill: Composer in a divided world*, London: Simon & Schuster, 1991. p. 22.

Later in the year, Weill enrolled at the Humboldt University summer music school. He commenced his studies with Englebert Humperdinck who, however, was unwell and was not always able to give full attention to his students — he died soon after. Weill became somewhat disillusioned as he expressed in another letter to Hans on 9 August:

> 'I am completely incapacitated by the utter desolation of this place [he is referring to life at the summer school] ... It's as difficult for me to get anything done in this environment as it was easy for me to work in Berlin. You see how dependent I am on inspiration from my teacher, from my fellow students, and from the opera and

concerts in Berlin. Will I ever be able to create
true art if I don't continue to be exposed to these
influences? Sure, we both know I'll never be
another Schubert or Beethoven; I think many
others have suffered from the "sickness" of
thinking they would be.'

Lys Symonette and Kim H. Kowalke, editors and translators: *Speak Low (when you speak love): The letters of Kurt Weill and Lotte Lenya*, London: Hamish Hamilton, 1996, p. 27.

FELIX WEINGARTNER

The Austrian conductor, composer and pianist Felix Weingartner is today primarily remembered for his interpretations of Beethoven's symphonies — he was the first conductor to make commercial recordings of all nine symphonies. Whilst they are still recognized for being pioneering, many consider his interpretations to be subjective by today's performance-standards on the basis, for example, of tempo fluctuations that are inconsistent with the printed score.

When on holiday as a young boy, Weingartner recalls his first awakening interest in Beethoven that was to set the course of his future destiny as a major interpreter of the composer's works:

'While in Baden, I had for the first time heard
the name of Beethoven; my grandfather had
related that he had once, in his youth, sat at the
same table as the master. It happened at an inn
and my grandfather, without knowing who the
other was, had been struck by his strange appearance, his air of living apart from the world, his

loud tones when he spoke, and the large ear-trumpet he held at his ear when anybody addressed him. On inquiry my grandfather had been told who his fellow guest had been. This tale made such a deep impression on me that I remembered the name of Beethoven and connected it with something vast, like St. Stephen's Tower and the Danube, so that now I readily comprehend why, when my mother – or another member of my family – suddenly said: "Beethoven lived here", I was strangely thrilled.'

Felix Weingartner, *Buffets and Rewards: A musician's reminiscences.* London: Hutchinson & Co., 1937, p. 18.

RALPH VAUGHAN WILLIAMS

On 1 July 1956, Vaughan Williams wrote to his biographer Michael Kennedy in response to his request to provide him with answers to various questions. Writing of Beethoven he remarked:

'[I] could see no point in Beethoven when I was a boy – and I am still temperamentally allergic to him. But I am beginning to find out that he is nevertheless a very great man. I used to enjoy Schumann's sentimental songs very much when I was young, but I can't bear them now. Schubert has also gone off the boil as far as I am concerned. But Bach remains!'

Michael Kennedy, *The Works of Ralph Vaughan Williams*, London: Oxford University Press, 1964, p. 386.

*

HUGO WOLF

The Austrian composer Hugo Wolf was regarded as a child prodigy, commencing study of the piano and violin at the age of four. He eventually enrolled at the Vienna Conservatory where, his friend Peter Miller recalls, he applied himself diligently to the study of Beethoven's piano sonatas:

> 'He spent day after day in the big Vienna library, absorbed in music of every kind, chiefly that of Beethoven and of Bach, dissecting it, committing it to memory.'

Years later Miller called upon Wolf and happened to see in his room a dilapidated copy of Beethoven's sonatas. Turning the leaves over, he noticed many indications on them of careful study, and remarked upon them to Wolf.

> 'Yes', said Wolf very seriously, 'those were bad days. I lived in a garret, and had no piano; so I used to take out the sonatas separately, and study them in the Prater.'

Ernest Newman, *Hugo Wolf*, New York: Dover Publications, 1966, p. 14.

In February 1883, Richard Wagner died — a circumstance that affected Wolf deeply. The following year, *The Vienna Academic Wagner Society* sponsored an anniversary concert — "In Memory of Richard Wagner". The celebrated virtuoso pianist Anton Rubinstein was invited to play a selection of Beethoven's piano sonatas. Wolf was in the audience and wrote a review of the recital — in characteristically trenchant terms — that give an insight into Rubinstein's style of performance:

'Rubinstein moves among our ivory crushers like Gulliver among the Lilliputians ... As for Beethoven's sonatas, he must bow to Bülow [Hans von Bülow], who, three years ago, played the last six sonatas for us, and so perfectly as to persuade us immediately that Beethoven should be played in this way and in no other. The dreadfully hurried tempi, the unexampled interpretive liberties, the nonchalance with which Rubinstein treats particularly prominent passages such as the recitative phrase in the first movement of the Sonata in D minor, etc., all these [are] dark blemishes on the luminous glory of his heroic deeds. Perhaps it was simply not Anton Rubinstein's night for Beethoven?'

In April 1884, Wolf reflected on the music season and gave expression to his views on music. He singled out for praise Schubert's Symphony in B minor that he described as 'a faithful mirror of its creator's artistic individuality'. He lamented, as so many others have also done, that it is 'but a fragment ... [whose] form resembles the composer's own mortal life, cut off by death in the bloom of life, at the summit of his creative power.'

Wolf closed with further remarks about Schubert in the context of Beethoven, the composer whom he so revered. His moving words make a fitting close to our Anthology:

'As if by agreement between muses and fates, the fruitful isle of song was Schubert's birthright from the former, to be transformed by the bubbling spring of his melodies, in the short span of his mortal existence, into a fabulous magic garden whose freshness and fragrance will never, never fade. From this enchanted island he now beheld the giant Beethoven crossing the ocean in the storm, defying the elements in his furious passage. Then was the islander's heart seized by a mighty urge. To follow Beethoven in his desolate and dangerous course was now Schubert's only thought. But that was hard, for that Titan loved to sail among rocks, sandbanks, reefs and whirlpools and surf. And if he made for the open sea, he surged ahead on the wings of the storm, calling down thunder and lightning, a god annihilating with a mere glance whomever he encountered.'

Henry Pleasants, editor and translator, *The Music Criticism of Hugo Wolf*, New York: Holmes & Meier Publishers, 1978

BIBLIOGRAPHY

The author has individually consulted all the publications listed in this bibliography and can confirm that each makes reference, in some way or other, to Beethoven and his works. It will be evident from their titles which of these are publications devoted exclusively to the composer. Others that make only passing reference to Beethoven and his compositions, nevertheless unfailingly bear testimony to his genius and humanity. The diversity of the titles listed testifies to the centrality of Beethoven to western culture and beyond; the mere survey of these should be of itself a rewarding experience for a lover of so-called classical music. The entries are confined to book publications, reflecting the scope of the author's researches. The cut-off date for this was 2007; no works after this date are listed, notwithstanding the author is mindful that Beethoven musicology, and related publication, continue to be a major field of endeavour.

Abraham, Gerald. *Beethoven's second-period quartets*. London: Oxford University Press: Humphrey Milford, 1944.

Abraham, Gerald. *Essays on Russian and East European music*. Oxford: Clarendon Press: New York: Oxford University Press, 1985.

Abraham, Gerald, Editor. *The age of Beethoven, 1790-1830*. London: Oxford University Press, 1982.

Abraham, Gerald. *The tradition of Western music*. London: Oxford University Press, 1974.

Abse, Dannie and Joan. *The Music lover's literary companion*. London: Robson Books, 1988.

Adorno, Theodor W., Translator. *Alban Berg: master of the smallest link*. Cambridge: Cambridge University Press, 1991.

Adorno, Theodor W. *Beethoven: the philosophy of music; fragments and texts*. Cambridge: Polity Press, 1998.

Albrecht, Daniel, Editor. *Modernism and music: an anthology of sources*. Chicago; London: University of Chicago Press, 2004.

Albrecht, Theodore, Translator and Editor. *Letters to Beethoven and other correspondence*. Lincoln, New England: University of Nebraska Press, 3 vols., 1996.

Allsobrook, David Ian. *Liszt: my travelling circus life*. London: Macmillan, 1991.

Anderson, Christopher, Editor and Translator. *Selected writings of Max Reger*. New York; London: Routledge, 2006.

Anderson, Emily, Editor and Translator. *The letters of Beethoven*. London: Macmillan, 3 vols.,1961.

Anderson, Martin, Editor. *Klemperer on music: shavings from a musician's workbench*. London: Toccata Press, 1986.

Antheil, George. *Bad boy of music*. London; New York: Hurst & Blackett Ltd., 1945.

Appleby, David P. *Heitor Villa-Lobos: a bio-bibliography*. New York: Greenwood Press, 1988.

Aprahamian, Felix, Editor. *Essays on music: an anthology from The Listener*. London, Cassell, 1967.

Armero, Gonzalo and Jorge de Persia. *Manuel de Falla : his life & works*. London: Omnibus Press, 1999.

Arnold, Ben, Editor. *The Liszt companion*. Westport, Connecticut; London: Greenwood Press, 2002.

Arnold, Denis and Nigel Fortune, Editors. *The Beethoven companion*. London: Faber and Faber, 1973.

Ashbrook, William. *Donizetti*. London: Cassell, 1965.

Auner, Joseph Henry. *A Schoenberg reader: documents of a life*. New Haven Connecticut; London: Yale University Press, 2003.

Avins, Styra, Editor. *Johannes Brahms: life and letters*. Oxford: Oxford University Press, 1997.

Azoury, Pierre H. *Chopin through his contemporaries: friends, lovers, and rivals*. Westport, Connecticut: Greenwood Press, 1999.

Badura-Skoda, Paul. *Carl Czerny: On the Proper Performance of all Beethoven's Works for the Piano*. Universal Edition: A. G. Wien, 1970.

Bailey, Cyril. *Hugh Percy Allen*. London: Oxford University

Press, 1948.

Bailey, Kathryn. *The life of Webern*. Cambridge: Cambridge University Press, 1998.

Barenboim, Daniel. *A life in music*. London: Weidenfeld & Nicolson, 1991.

Barlow, Michael. *Whom the gods love: the life and music of George Butterworth*. London: Toccata Press, 1997.

Barrett-Ayres, Reginald. *Joseph Haydn and the string quartet*. New York: Schirmer Books, 1974.

Bartos, Frantisek. *Bedrich Smetana: Letters and reminiscences*. Prague: Artia, 1953.

Barzun, Jacques. *Pleasures of music: an anthology of writing about music and musicians*. London: Cassell, 1977.

Bauer-Lechner, Natalie. *Recollections of Gustav Mahler*. London: Faber Music, 1980.

Bazhanov, N. Nikolai. *Rakhmaninov*. Moscow: Raduga, 1983.

Beaumont, Antony, Editor. *Ferruccio Busoni: Selected letters*. London: Faber and Faber, 1987.

Beaumont, Antony, Editor. *Gustav Mahler, letters to his wife*. London: Faber and Faber, 2004.

Beecham, Thomas. *A mingled chime: an autobiography*. New York: Da Capo Press, 1976.

Bekker, Paul. *Beethoven*. London: J. M. Dent & Sons, 1925.

Bellasis, Edward. *Cherubini: memorials illustrative of his life*. London: Burns and Oates, 1874.

Bennett, James R. Sterndale. *The life of William Sterndale Bennett*. Cambridge: University Press, 1907.

Benser, Caroline Cepin. *Egon Wellesz (1885–1974): chronicle of twentieth-century musician*. New York: P. Lang, 1985.

Berlioz, Hector. *Evenings in the orchestra*. Harmondsworth: Penguin Books, 1963.

Berlioz, Hector. *The musical madhouse (Les grotesques de la musique)*. Rochester, New York: University of Rochester Press, 2003.

Bernard, Jonathan W., Editor. *Elliott Carter: collected essays and lectures, 1937-1995*. Rochester, New York; Woodbridge: University of Rochester Press, 1998.

Bernstein, Leonard. *The joy of music*. New York: Simon and Schuster, 1959.

Bertensson, Sergei. *Sergei Rachmaninoff: a lifetime in music*. London: G. Allen & Unwin, 1965.

Biancolli, Louis. *The Flagstad manuscript*. New York: Putnam, 1952.

Bickley, Nora, Editor. *Letters from and to Joseph Joachim*. London: Macmillan, 1914.

Bie, Oskar. *A history of the pianoforte and pianoforte players*. New York: Da Capo Press, 1966.

Blaukopf, Herta. *Mahler's unknown letters*. London: Gollancz, 1986.

Blaukopf, Kurt and Herta. *Mahler: his life, work and world*. London: Thames and Hudson, 1991.

Bliss, Arthur. *As I remember*. London: Thames Publishing, 1989.

Block, Adrienne Fried. *Amy Beach, passionate Victorian: the life and work of an American composer, 1867–1944*. New York: Oxford University Press, 1998.

Bloch, Ernst. *Essays on the philoso-

phy of music. Cambridge: Cambridge University Press, 1985.

Blocker, Robert. *The Robert Shaw reader*. New Haven; London: Yale University Press, 2004.

Blom, Eric. *A musical postbag*. London: J. M. Dent, 1945.

Blom, Eric. *Beethoven's pianoforte sonatas discussed*. London: J. M. Dent, 1938.

Blom, Eric. *Classics major and minor: with some other musical ruminations*. London: J. M. Dent, 1958.

Blum, David. *The art of quartet playing: the Guarneri Quartet in conversation with David Blum*. London: Gollancz, 1986.

Blume, Friedrich. *Classic and Romantic music: a comprehensive survey*. London: Faber and Faber, 1972.

Boden, Anthony. *The Parrys of the Golden Vale: background to genius*. London: Thames Publishing, 1998.

Bonavia, Ferruccio. *Musicians on music*. London: Routledge & Kegan Paul, 1956.

Bonds, Mark Evan *After Beethoven: imperatives of originality in the symphony*. Cambridge, Massachusetts; London: Harvard University Press, 1996.

Bonis, Ferenc, Editor. *The selected writings of Zoltán Kodály*. London; New York: Boosey & Hawkes, 1974.

Bookspan, Martin. *André Previn: a biography*. London: Hamilton, 1981.

Boros, James and Richard Toop, Editors. *Brian Ferneyhough: Collected writings*. Amsterdam: Harwood Academic, 1995.

Boulez, Pierre. *Stocktakings from an apprenticeship*. Oxford: Clarendon Press, 1991.

Boult, Adrian. *Boult on music: words from a lifetime's communication*. London: Toccata Press, 1983.

Boult, Adrian. *My own trumpet*. London, Hamish Hamilton, 1973.

Boult, Adrian with Jerrold Northrop Moore. *Music and friends: seven decades of letters to Adrian Boult from Elgar, Vaughan Williams, Holst, Bruno Walter, Yehudi Menuhin and other friends*. London: Hamish Hamilton, 1979.

Bovet, Marie Anne de. *Charles Gounod: his life and his works*. London: S. Low, Marston, Searle & Rivington, Ltd., 1891.

Bowen, Catherine Drinker. *Beloved friend: the story of Tchaikowsky and Nadejda von Meck*. London: Hutchinson & Co., 1937.

Bowen, Meiron, Editor. *Gerhard on music: selected writings*. Brookfield, Vermont: Ashgate, 2000.

Bowen, Meirion. *Michael Tippett*. London: Robson Books, 1982.

Bowen, Meiron, Editor. *Music of the angels: essays and sketchbooks of Michael Tippett*. London: Eulenburg, 1980.

Bowen, Meiron, Editor. *Tippett on music*. Oxford: Clarendon Press, 1995.

Bowers, Faubion. *Scriabin: a biography*. Mineola: Dover; London: Constable, 1996.

Boyden, Matthew. *Richard Strauss*. London: Weidenfeld & Nicolson, 1999.

Bozarth, George S., Editor. *Brahms studies: analytical and historical perspectives; papers delivered at the International Brahms Conference, Washington, DC, 5-8 May 1983.* Oxford: Clarendon Press, 1990.

Brand, Juliane, Christopher Hailey and Donald Harris, Editors. *The Berg-Schoenberg correspondence: selected letters.* Basingstoke: Macmillan, 1987.

Brandenbugh, Sieghard, Editor. *Haydn, Mozart, & Beethoven: studies in the music of the classical period: essays in honor of Alan Tyson.* Oxford: Clarendon Press, 1998.

Braunstein, Joseph. *Musica Æterna, program notes for 1961–1971.* New York: Musica Æterna, 1972.

Braunstein, Joseph. *Musica Æterna, program notes for 1971–1976.* New York: Musica Æterna, 1978.

Brendel, Alfred. *Alfred Brendel on music: collected essays.* Chicago, Iliinois: A Cappella Books, 2001.

Brendel, Alfred. *The veil of order: Alfred Brendel in conversation with Martin Meyer.* London: Faber and Faber, 2002.

Breuning, Gerhard von. *Memories of Beethoven: from the house of the black-robed Spaniards.* Cambridge: Cambridge University Press, 1992.

Briscoe, James R., Editor. (Brief Description): *Debussy in performance.* New Haven: Yale University Press, 1999.

Brott, Alexander Betty Nygaard King. *Alexander Brott: my lives in music.* Oakville, Ontario; Niagara Falls, New York: Mosaic Press, 2005.

Brown, Alfred Peter. *The symphonic repertoire. Vol. 2, The first golden age of the Viennese symphony: Haydn, Mozart, Beethoven, and Schubert.* Bloomington, Indiana: Indiana University Press, 2002.

Brown, Maurice John Edwin. *Schubert: a critical biography.* London: Macmillan; New York: St. Martin's Press, 1958.

Broyles, Michael. *Beethoven: the emergence and evolution of Beethoven's heroic style.* New York: Excelsior Music Publishing Co., 1987.

Brubaker, Bruce and Jane Gottlieb, Editors. *Pianist, scholar, connoisseur: essays in honor of Jacob Lateiner.* Stuyvesant, N.Y., Pendragon Press, 2000.

Buch, Esteban. *Beethoven's Ninth: a political history.* Chicago; London: University of Chicago Press, 2003.

Burk, John N., Editor. *Letters of Richard Wagner: the Burrell collection.* London: Gollancz, 1951.

Burnham, Scott G. *Beethoven hero.* Princeton, New Jersey: Princeton University Press, 1995.

Burnham, Scott G and Michael P. Steinberg, Editors. *Beethoven and his world.* Princeton, New Jersey; Oxford: Princeton University Press, 2000.

Burton, William Westbrook, Editor. *Conversations about Bernstein.* New York; Oxford: Oxford University Press, 1995.

Busch, Fritz. *Pages from a musician's life.* London: Hogarth Press, 1953.

Busch, Hans, Editor. *Verdi's Aida: the history of an opera in letters and documents.* Minneapolis:

University of Minnesota Press, 1978.

Busch, Hans, Editor. *Verdi's Falstaff in letters and contemporary reviews.* Bloomington: Indiana University Press, 1997.

Busch, Marie, Translator. *Memoirs of Eugenie Schumann.* London: W. Heinemann, 1927.

Bush, Alan Dudley. *In my eighth decade and other essays.* London: Kahn & Averill, 1980.

Busoni, Ferruccio. *Letters to his wife.* Translated by Rosamond Ley. New York: Da Capo Press, 1975.

Byron, Reginald. *Music, culture, & experience: selected papers of John Blacking.* Chicago: University of Chicago Press, 1995.

Cairns, David. *Responses: musical essays and reviews.* New York: Da Capo Press, 1980.

Cardus, Neville. *Talking of music.* London: Collins, 1957.

Carley, Lionel. *Delius: a life in letters.* London: Scolar Press in association with the Delius Trust, 1988.

Carley, Lionel. *Grieg and Delius: a chronicle of their friendship in letters.* London: Marion Boyars, 1993.

Carner, Mosco. *Major and minor.* London: Duckworth, 1980

Carner, Mosco. *Puccini: a critical biography.* London: Duckworth, 1958.

Carroll, Brendan G. *The last prodigy: a biography of Erich Wolfgang Korngold.* Portland, Oregon: Amadeus Press, 1997.

Carse, Adam von Ahn. *The life of Jullien: adventurer, showman-conductor and establisher of the Promenade Concerts in England, together with a history of those concerts up to 1895.* Cambridge England: Heffer, 1951.

Carse, Adam von Ahn. *The orchestra from Beethoven to Berlioz: a history of the orchestra in the first half of the 19th century, and of the development of orchestral baton-conducting.* Cambridge: W. Heffer, 1948.

Casals, Pablo. *Joys and sorrows: reflections by Pablo Casals as told to Albert E. Kahn.* London: Macdonald, 1970.

Casals, Pablo. *The memoirs of Pablo Casals as told to Thomas Dozier.* London: Life en Español, 1959.

Chappell, Paul. *Dr. S. S. Wesley, 1810–1876: portrait of a Victorian musician.* Great Wakering: Mayhew-McCrimmon, 1977.

Chasins, Abram. *Leopold Stokowski, a profile.* New York: Hawthorn Books, 1979.

Charlton, Davi, Editor and Martyn Clarke Translator. *E.T.A. Hoffmann's musical writings: Kreisleriana, The Poet and the Composer.* Cambridge: Cambridge University Press, 1989.

Chávez, Carlos. *Musical thought.* Cambridge: Harvard University Press, 1961.

Chesterman, Robert, Editor. *Conversations with conductors: Bruno Walter, Sir Adrian Boult, Leonard Bernstein, Ernest Ansermet, Otto Klemperer, Leopold Stokowski.* Totowa, New Jersey: Rowman and Littlefield, 1976.

Chissell, Joan. *Clara Schumann: a dedicated spirit; a study of her life and work.* London: Hamilton, 1983.

Chua, Daniel K. L. *The "Galitzin" quartets of Beethoven: Opp.127, 132, 130.* Princeton: Princeton

University Press, 1995.

Citron, Marcia, Editor. *The letters of Fanny Hensel to Felix Mendelssohn*. Stuyvesant, New York: Pendragon Press, 1987.

Clark, Walter Aaron. *Enrique Granados: poet of the piano*. Oxford, England; New York, N.Y.: Oxford University Press, 2006.

Clark, Walter Aaron. *Isaac Albéniz: portrait of a romantic*. Oxford; New York: Oxford University Press, 1999.

Clive, Peter. *Beethoven and his world*. Oxford University Press, 2001.

Closson, Ernest. *History of the piano*. Translated by Delano Ames and edited by Robin Golding. London: Paul Elek, 1947.

Cockshoot, John V. *The fugue in Beethoven's piano music*. London: Routledge & Kegan Paul, 1959.

Coe, Richard N, Translator. *Life of Rossini by Stendhal*. London: Calder & Boyars, 1970.

Coleman, Alexander, Editor. *Diversions & animadversions: essays from The new criterion*. New Brunswick, New Jersey; London: Transaction Publishers, 2005.

Colerick, George. *From the Italian girl to Cabaret: musical humour, parody and burlesque*. London: Juventus, 1998.

Coleridige, A. D. *Life of Moscheles, with selections from his diaries and correspondence by his wife*. London: Hurst & Blackett, 1873.

Colles, Henry Cope. *Essays and lectures*. London: Humphrey Milford, Oxford University Press, 1945.

Cone, Edward T., Editor. *Roger Sessions on music: collected essays*. Princeton, New Jersey: Princeton University Press, 1979.

Cone, Edward T. *The composer's voice*. Berkeley; London: University of California Press, 1974.

Cook, Susan and Judy S. Tsou, Editors. *Cecilia reclaimed: feminist perspectives on gender and music*. Urbana: University of Illinois Press, 1994.

Cooper, Barry. *Beethoven: The master musicians series*. Oxford: Oxford University Press, 2000.

Cooper, Barry. *Beethoven and the creative process*. Oxford: Clarendon Press, 1990.

Cooper, Barry. *Beethoven's folksong settings: chronology, sources, style*. Cambridge: Cambridge University Press, 1991.

Cooper, Barry. *The Beethoven compendium: a guide to Beethoven's life and music*. London: Thames and Hudson, 1991.

Cooper, Martin. *Beethoven: the last decade, 1817–1827*. London: Oxford University Press, 1970.

Cooper, Martin. *Judgements of value: selected writings on music*. Oxford; New York: Oxford University Press, 1988.

Cooper, Martin. *Ideas and music*. London: Barrie and Rockliff, 1965.

Cooper, Victoria L. *The house of Novello: the practice and policy of a Victorian music publisher, 1829–1866*. Aldershot, Hants: Ashgate, 2003.

Coover, James. *Music at auction: Puttick and Simpson (of London), 1794–1971: being an annotated, chronological list of sales of musical materials*. Warren, Michigan: Harmonie Park Press, 1988.

Copland, Aaron. *Copland on music*. London: Deutsch, 1961.

Corredor, J. Ma. *Conversations with Casals*. London: Hutchinson, 1956.

Cott, Jonathan. *Stockhausen: conversations with the composer*. London: Picador, 1974.

Cottrell, Stephen. *Professional music making in London: ethnography and experience*. Aldershot: Ashgate, 2004.

Cowell, Henry. *Charles Ives and his music*. New York: Oxford University Press, 1955.

Cowling, Elizabeth. *The cello*. London: Batsford, 1983.

Crabbe, John. *Beethoven's empire of the mind*. Newbury: Lovell Baines, 1982.

Craft, Robert. *An improbable life: memoirs*. Nashville: Vanderbilt University Press, 2002.

Craft, Robert, Editor. *Stravinsky: selected correspondence*. London: Faber and Faber, 3 Vols. 1982–1985.

Craw, Howard Allen. *A biography and thematic catalog of the works of J. L. Dussek: 1760–1812*. Ann Arbor: Michigan, 1965.

Crawford, Richard, R. Allen Lott and Carol J. Oja, Editors. *A Celebration of American music: words and music in honor of H. Wiley Hitchcock*. Ann Arbor: University of Michigan Press, 1990.

Craxton, Harold and Tovey, Donald Francis. *Beethoven: Sonatas for Pianoforte*. London: The Associated Board, [1931].

Crichton, Ronald: Editor. *The memoirs of Ethel Smyth*. New York: Viking, 1987.

Crist, Stephen A. and Roberta M. Marvin, Editors. *Historical musicology: sources, methods, interpretations*. Rochester, New York: University of Rochester Press, 2004.

Crofton, Ian and Donald Fraser, Editors. *A dictionary of musical quotations*. London: Croom Helm, 1985.

Crompton, Louis, Editor. *Shaw, Bernard: The great composers: reviews and bombardments*. Berkeley; London: University of California Press, 1978.

Csicserry-Ronay, Elizabeth, Translator and Editor. *Hector Berlioz: The art of music and other essays: (A travers chants)*. Bloomington: Indiana University Press, 1994.

Curtiss, Mina Kirstein. *Bizet and his world*. London: Secker & Warburg, 1959.

Cuyler, Louise Elvira. *The symphony*. New York: Harcourt Brace Jovanovich, 1973.

Dahlhaus, Carl. *Ludwig van Beethoven: approaches to his music*. Oxford: Clarendon Press, 1991.

Dahlhaus, Carl. *Nineteenth-century music*. Translated by J. Bradford Robinson. Berkeley; London: University of California Press, 1989.

Daniels, Robin. *Conversations with Cardus*. London: Gollancz, 1976.

Daniels, Robin. Conversations with Menuhin. London: Macdonald General Books, 1979.

Day, James. *Vaughan Williams*. London: Dent, 1961.

Davies, Peter Maxwell. *Studies from two decades*. Selected and introduced by Stephen Pruslin.

London: Boosey & Hawkes, 1979.

Dean, Winton. *Georges Bizet: his life and work*. London: J.M. Dent, 1965.

Deas, Stewart. *In defence of Hanslick*. London: Williams and Norgate, 1940.

Debussy, Claude. *Debussy on music*. London: Secker & Warburg, 1977.

Delbanco, Nicholas. *The Beaux Arts Trio*. London: Gollancz, 1985.

Demény, Janos, Editor. *Béla Bartók: letters*. London: Faber and Faber, 1971.

Dent, Edward Joseph. *Selected essays*. Edited by Hugh Taylor. Cambridge; New York: Cambridge University Press, 1979.

Deutsch, Otto Erich. *Mozart: a documentary biography*. London: Adam & Charles Black, 1965.

Deutsch, Otto Erich. *Schubert: a documentary biography*. London: J.M. Dent, 1946

Deutsch, Otto Erich. *Schubert: memoirs by his friends*. London: Adam & Charles Black, 1958.

Dibble, Jeremy. *C. Hubert H. Parry: his life and music*. Oxford: Clarendon Press, 1992.

Dibble, Jeremy. *Charles Villiers Stanford: man and musician*. Oxford: Oxford University Press, 2002.

Donakowski, Conrad L. *A muse for the masses: ritual and music in an age of democratic revolution, 1770–1870*. Chicago: University of Chicago Press, 1977.

Dower, Catherine. *Alfred Einstein on music: selected music criticisms*. New York: Greenwood Press, 1991.

Downs, Philip G. *Classical music: the era of Haydn, Mozart, and Beethoven*. New York: W.W. Norton, 1992.

Drabkin, William. *Beethoven: Missa Solemnis*. Cambridge: Cambridge University Press, 1991.

Dreyfus, Kay. *The farthest north of humanness: letters of Percy Grainger, 1901–1914*. South Melbourne; Basingstoke: Macmillan, 1985.

Dubal, David, Editor. *Remembering Horowitz: 125 pianists recall a legend*. New York: Schirmer Books, 1993.

Dubal, David. *The world of the concert pianist*. London: Victor Gollancz, 1985.

Dvořák, Otakar. *Antonín Dvořák, my father*. Spillville, Iowa: Czech Historical Research Center, 1993.

Dyson, George. *The progress of music*. London: Oxford University Press, Humphrey Milford, 1932.

Eastaugh, Kenneth. *Havergal Brian: the making of a composer*. London: Harrap, 1976.

Edwards, Allen. *Flawed words and stubborn sounds: a conversation with Elliott Carter*. New York: Norton & Company, 1971.

Edwards, Frederick George. *Musical haunts in London*. London: J. Curwen & Sons, 1895.

Ehrlich, Cyril. *First philharmonic: a history of the Royal Philharmonic Society*. Oxford: Clarendon Press, 1995.

Einstein, Alfred. *A short history of music*. London: Cassell and Company Ltd., 1948.

Einstein, Alfred. *Essays on music*. London: Faber and Faber, 1958.

Einstein, Alfred. *Mozart: his character, his work*. London: Cassell and Company Ltd., 1946.

Einstein, Alfred. *Music in the Romantic era*. London: J.M. Dent Ltd., 1947.

Ekman, Karl. *Jean Sibelius, his life and personality*. New York: Tudor Publishing. Co., 1945.

Elgar, Edward. *A future for English music: and other lectures*, Edited by Percy M. Young. London: Dobson, 1968.

Elkin, Robert. *Queen's Hall, 1893–1941*. London: Rider, 1944.

Ella, John. *Musical sketches, abroad and at home: with original music by Mozart, Czerny, Graun, etc., vocal cadenzas and other musical illustrations*. London: Ridgway, Vol. 1., 1869.

Ellis, William Ashton. *The family letters of Richard Wagner*. Edited and translated by William Ashton Ellis and enlarged with introduction and notes by John Deathridge. Basingstoke: Macmillan, 1991.

Ellis, William Ashton. *Richard Wagner's prose works: Vol. 1, The art-work of the future*. Edited and translated by William Ashton Ellis. London: Kegan Paul, Trench, Trübner, 1895.

Ellis, William Ashton. *Richard Wagner's prose works: Vol. 2, Opera and drama*. Edited and translated by William Ashton Ellis. London: Kegan Paul, Trench, Trübner, 1900.

Ellis, William Ashton. *Richard Wagner's prose works: Vol. 3, The theatre*. Edited and translated by William Ashton Ellis. London: Kegan Paul, Trench, Trübner, 1907.

Ellis, William Ashton. *Richard Wagner's prose works: Vol. 4, Art and. politics*. Edited and translated by William Ashton Ellis. London: Kegan Paul, Trench, Trübner, 1895.

Ellis, William Ashton. *Richard Wagner's prose works: Vol. 5, Actors and singers*. Edited and translated by William Ashton Ellis. London: Kegan Paul, Trench, Trübner, 1896.

Ellis, William Ashton. *Richard Wagner's prose works: Vol. 6, Religion and art*. Edited and translated by William Ashton Ellis. London: Kegan Paul, Trench, Trübner, 1897.

Ellis, William Ashton. *Richard Wagner's prose works: Vol. 7, In Paris and Dresden*. Edited and translated by William Ashton Ellis. London: Kegan Paul, Trench, Trübner, 1898.

Ellis, William Ashton. *Richard Wagner's prose works: Vol. 8, Posthumous*. Edited and translated by William Ashton Ellis. London: Kegan Paul, Trench, Trübner, 1899.

Elterlein, Ernst von. *Beethoven's pianoforte sonatas: explained for the lovers of the musical art*. London: W. Reeves, 1898.

Engel, Carl. *Musical myths and facts*. London: Novello, Ewer & Co.; New York: J.L. Peters, 1876.

Eosze, László. *Zoltán Kodály: his life and work*. London: Collet's, 1962.

Etter, Brian K. *From classicism to modernism: Western musical culture and the metaphysics of order*. Aldershot: Ashgate, 2001.

Ewen, David. *From Bach to Stravinsky: the history of music by its foremost critics*. New York, Greenwood Press, 1968.

Ewen, David. *Romain Rolland's Essays on music.* New York: Dover Publications, 1959.

Fay, Amy. *Music-study in Germany: from the home correspondence of Amy Fay.* New York: Dover Publications, 1965.

Fenby, Eric. *Delius as I knew him.* London: Quality Press, 1936.

Ferguson, Donald Nivison. *Masterworks of the orchestral repertoire: a guide for listeners.* Minneapolis: University of Minnesota Press, 1954.

Fétis, François-Joseph. *Curiosités historiques de la musique: complément nécessaire de la Musique mise à la portée de tout le monde.* Paris: Janet et Cotelle, 1830.

Fifield, Christopher. *Max Bruch: his life and works.* London: Gollancz, 1988.

Fifield, Christopher. *True artist and true friend: a biography of Hans Richter.* Oxford: Clarendon Press, 1993.

Finson, Jon and R. Larry Todd, Editors. *Mendelssohn and Schumann: essays on their music and its context.* Durham, N.C.: Duke University Press, 1984.

Fischer, Edwin. *Beethoven's pianoforte sonatas: a guide for students & amateurs.* London: Faber and Faber, 1959.

Fischer, Edwin. *Reflections on music.* London: Williams and Norgate, 1951.

Fischer, Hans Conrad and Erich Kock. *Ludwig van Beethoven: a study in text and pictures.* London: Macmillan; New York, St. Martin's Press, 1972.

Fischmann, Zdenka E. Janáček-Newmarch correspondence. 1st limited and numbered edition. Rockville, MD: Kabel Publishers, 1986.

Fitzlyon, April. *Maria Malibran: diva of the romantic age.* London: Souvenir Press, 1987.

FitzLyon, April. *The price of genius: a life of Pauline Viardot.* London: John Calder, 1964.

Forbes, Elliot, Editor. *Thayer's life of Beethoven.* Princeton, New Jersey: Princeton University Press, 1967.

Foreman, Lewis. *Bax: a composer and his times.* London: Scolar Press, 1983.

Foreman, Lewis, Editor. *Farewell, my youth, and other writings by Arnold Bax.* Aldershot: Scolar Press, 1992.

Foster, Myles Birket. *History of the Philharmonic Society of London, 1813–1912: a record of a hundred years' work in the cause of music.* London: Bodley Head, 1912.

Foulds, John. *Music today: its heritage from the past, and legacy to the future.* London: I. Nicholson and Watson, limited, 1934.

Frank, Mortimer H. *Arturo Toscanini: the NBC years.* Portland, Oregon: Amadeus Press, 2002.

Fraser, Andrew Alastair. *Essays on music.* London: Oxford University Press, H. Milford, 1930.

Frohlich, Martha. *Beethoven's Appassionata' sonata.* Oxford: Clarendon Press, 1991.

Gal, Hans. *The golden age of Vienna.* London: Max Parrish & Co. Limited, 1948.

Gal, Hans. *The musician's world: great composers in their letters.* London: Thames and Hudson,

1965.

Galatopoulos, Stelios. *Bellini: life, times, music*. London: Sanctuary, 2002.

Garden, Edward and Nigel Gottrei, Editors. *'To my best friend': correspondence between Tchaikovsky and Nadezhda von Meck, 1876–1878*. Oxford: Clarendon Press, 1993.

Geck, Martin. Beethoven. London: Haus, 2003.

Gerig, Reginald. *Famous pianists & their technique*. Washington: R. B. Luce, 1974.

Gilliam, Bryan. *The life of Richard Strauss*. Cambridge: Cambridge University Press, 1999.

Gilliam, Bryan, Editor. *Richard Strauss and his world*. Princeton, New Jersey: Princeton University Press, 1992.

Gillies, Malcolm and Bruce Clunies Ross, Editors. *Grainger on music*. Oxford; New York: Oxford University Press, 1999.

Gillies, Malcolm and David Pear, Editors. *The all-round man: selected letters of Percy Grainger, 1914–1961*. Oxford: Clarendon Press, 1994.

Gillies, Malcolm, Editor. *The Bartók companion*. London: Faber and Faber, 1993.

Gillmor, Alan M. *Erik Satie*. Basingstoke: Macmillan Press, 1988.

Glehn, M. E. *Goethe and Mendelssohn : (1821–1831)*. London: Macmillan, 1874.

Glowacki, John, Editor. *Paul A. Pisk: Essays in his honor*. Austin, Texas: University of Texas, 1966

Gollancz, Victor. *Journey towards music: a memoir*. London: Victor Gollancz Ltd., 1964.

Good, Edwin Marshall. *Giraffes, black dragons, and other pianos: a technological history from Cristofori to the modern concert grand*. Stanford, California: Stanford University Press, 1982.

Gordon, David. *Musical visitors to Britain*. London: Routledge, 2005.

Gordon, Stewart. *A history of keyboard literature: music for the piano and its forerunners*. Schirmer Books: New York: London : Prentice Hall International, 1996.

Gorrell, Lorraine. *The nineteenth-century German lied*. Portland, Oregon: Amadeus Press, 1993.

Goss, Glenda D. *Jean Sibelius: the Hämeenlinna letters: scenes from a musical life, 1875–1895*. Esbo, Finland: Schildts, 1997.

Goss, Madeleine. *Bolero: the life of Maurice Ravel*. New York: Tudor, 1945.

Gotch, Rosamund Brunel, Editor. *Mendelssohn and his friends in Kensington: letters from Fanny and Sophy Horsley, written 1833–36*. London: Oxford University Press, 1938.

Gounod, Charles. *Charles Gounod; autobiographical reminiscences: with family letters and notes on music; from the French*. London: William Heinemann, 1896.

Grabs, Manfred, Editor. *Hanns Eisler: a rebel in music; selected writings*. Berlin: Seven Seas Publishers, 1978.

Grace, Harvey. *A musician at large*. London: Oxford University Press, H. Milford, 1928.

(La) Grange, Henry-Louis de. *Gustav Mahler*. Oxford: Oxford University Press, 1995.

Graves, Charles L. *Hubert Parry: his life and works.* London: Macmillan, 1926.

Graves, Charles L. *Post-Victorian music: with other studies and sketches.* London: Macmillan and Co., limited, 1911.

Graves, Charles L. *The life & letters of Sir George Grove, Hon. D.C.L. (Durham), Hon. LL.D. (Glasgow), formerly director of the Royal college of music.* London: Macmillan and Co., Ltd.; New York: The Macmillan Co., 1903.

Gray, Cecil. *Musical chairs, or, between two stools: being the life and memoirs of Cecil Gray.* London: Home & Van Thal, 1948.

Gregor-Dellin and Dietrich Mack, Editors. *Cosima Wagner's diaries.: Vol. 1, 1869 - 1877.* London: Collins, 1978-1980.

Griffiths, Paul. *Modern music: the avant-garde since 1945.* London: J. M. Dent & Sons Ltd., 1981.

Griffiths, Paul. *Olivier Messiaen and the music of time.* London: Faber and Faber, 1985.

Griffiths, Paul. *Peter Maxwell Davies.* London: Robson Books, 1988.

Griffiths, Paul. *The sea on fire: Jean Barraqué.* Rochester, New York: Woodbridge: University of Rochester Press, 2003.

Griffiths, Paul. *The string quartet.* London: Thames and Hudson, 1983.

Grout, Donald Jay and Claude V. Palisca, Editors. *A history of Western music.* London: J. M. Dent, 1988.

Grove, George. *Beethoven and his nine symphonies.* London: Novello, Ewer, 1896.

Grover, Ralph Scott. *Ernest Chausson: the man and his music.* London: The Athlone Press, 1980.

Grover, Ralph Scott. *The music of Edmund Rubbra.* Aldershot: Scolar Press, 1993.

Grun, Bernard. *Alban Berg: letters to his wife.* Edited and translated by Bernard Grun. London: Faber and Faber, 1971.

Gutman, David. *Prokofiev.* London: Omnibus Press, 1990.

Hadow, William Henry. *Collected essays.* London: H. Milford at the Oxford University Press, 1928.

Hadow, William Henry. *Beethoven's Op. 18 Quartets.* London: H. Milford at the Oxford University Press, 1926.

Haggin, Bernard H. *Music observed.* New York: Oxford University Press, 1964.

Hailey, Christopher. *Franz Schreker, 1878–1934: a cultural biography.* Cambridge: Cambridge University Press, 1993.

Hall, Michael. *Leaving home: a conducted tour of twentieth-century music with Simon Rattle.* London: Faber and Faber, 1996.

Hall, Patricia and Friedemann Sallis, Editors. (Brief Description): *A handbook to twentieth-century musical sketches.* Cambridge: Cambridge University Press, 2004.

Hallé, C. E. *Life and letters of Sir Charles Hallé: being an autobiography (1819–1860) with correspondence and diaries.* London: Smith, Elder & Co., 1896.

Halstead, Jill. *The woman composer: creativity and the gendered poli-*

tics of musical composition. Aldershot: Ashgate, 1997.

Hamburger, Michael, Editor and Translator. *Beethoven letters, journals, and conversations.* New York: Thames and Hudson, 1951.

Hammelmann, Hanns A. and Ewald Osers. *The correspondence between Richard Strauss and Hugo von Hofmannsthal.* London: Collins, 1961.

Hanson, Lawrence and Elisabeth Hanson. *Tchaikovsky: the man behind the music.* New York: Dodd, Mead & Co, 1967.

Harding, James. *Massenet.* London: J. M. Dent & Sons Ltd., 1970.

Harding, James. *Saint-Saëns and his circle.* London: Chapman & Hall, 1965.

Harding, Rosamond E. M. *Origins of musical time and expression.* London: Oxford University Press, 1938.

Harman, Alec with Anthony Milner and Wilfrid Mellers. *Man and his music: the story of musical experience in the West.* London: Barrie & Jenkins, 1988.

Harper, Nancy Lee. *Manuel de Falla: his life and music.* Lanham, Maryland; London: The Scarecrow Press, 2005.

Hartmann, Arthur. *'Claude Debussy as I knew him' and other writings of Arthur Hartmann.* Edited by Samuel Hsu, Sidney Grolnic, and Mark Peters. Rochester, New York; Woodbridge: University of Rochester Press, 2003.

Haugen, Einar and Camilla Cai. *Ole Bull: Norway's romantic musician and cosmopolitan patriot.* Madison: The University of Wisconsin Press, 1993.

Headington, Christopher. *The Bodley Head history of Western music.* London: The Bodley Head, 1974.

Heartz, Daniel. *Music in European capitals: the galant style, 1720–1780.* New York; London: W. W. Norton, 2003.

Hedley, Arthur, Editor. *Selected correspondence of Fryderyk Chopin: abridged from Fryderyk Chopin's correspondence.* London: Heinemann, 1962.

Heiles, Anne Mischakoff. *Mischa Mischakoff: journeys of a concertmaster.* Sterling Heights, Michigan: Harmonie Park Press, 2006.

Henderson, Sanya Shoilevska. *Alex North, film composer: a biography, with musical analyses of a Streetcar named desire, Spartacus, The misfits, Under the volcano, and Prizzi's honor.* Jefferson, N.C.; London: McFarland, 2003.

Henschel, George. *Personal recollections of Johannes Brahms: some of his letters to and pages from a journal kept by George Henschel.* Boston: R G. Badger, 1907.

Henze, Hans Werner. *Bohemian fifths: an autobiography.* London: Faber and Faber, 1998.

Henze, Hans Werner. *Music and politics: collected writings 1953–81.* London: Faber and Faber, 1982.

Herbert, May, Translator. *Early letters of Robert Schumann.* London: George Bell and Sons, 1888.

Heyman, Barbara B. *Samuel Barber: the composer and his music.* New York: Oxford University

Press, 1992.
Heyworth, Peter. *Otto Klemperer, his life and times.* Cambridge: Cambridge University Press, 2 Vols. 1983–1996.
Hildebrandt, Dieter. *Pianoforte: a social history of the piano.* London: Hutchinson, 1988.
Hill, Peter. *The Messiaen companion.* London: Faber and Faber, 1995.
Hill, Peter and Nigel Simeone. *Messiaen.* New Haven Connecticut; London: Yale University Press, 2005.
Hiller, Ferdinand. *Mendelssohn: Letters and recollections.* New York: Vienna House, 1972.
Hines, Robert Stephan. *The orchestral composer's point of view: essays on twentieth-century music by those who wrote it.* Norman: University of Oklahoma Press, 1970.
Ho, Allan B. *Shostakovich reconsidered.* London: Toccata Press, 1998.
Hodeir, André. *Since Debussy: a view of contemporary music.* New York: Da Capo Press, 1975.
Holmes, Edward. *The life of Mozart: including his correspondence.* London: Chapman and Hall, 1845.
Holmes, John L. *Composers on composers.* New York: Greenwood Press, 1990.
Hopkins, Antony. *The concertgoer's companion.* London: J.M. Dent & Sons Ltd., 1984.
Hopkins, Antony. *The seven concertos of Beethoven.* Aldershot: Scolar Press, 1996.
Holt, Richard. *Nicolas Medtner (1879–1951): a tribute to his art and personality.* London: D. Dobson, 1955.
Honegger, Arthur. *I am a composer.* London: Faber and Faber, 1966.
Hoover, Kathleen and John Cage. *Virgil Thomson: his life and music.* New York; London: T. Yoseloff, 1959.
Horgan, Paul. *Encounters with Stravinsky: a personal record.* London: The Bodley Head, 1972.
Horowitz, Joseph. *Conversations with Arrau.* London: Collins, 1982.
Horowitz, Joseph. Understanding Toscanini. London: Faber and Faber, 1987.
Horwood, Wally. *Adolphe Sax, 1814–1894: his life and legacy.* Bramley: Bramley Books, 1980.
Howie, Crawford. *Anton Bruckner: a documentary biography.* Lewiston, N.Y.; Lampeter: Edwin Mellen Press, 2002.
Hueffer, Francis. *Correspondence of Wagner and Liszt.* New York: Greenwood Press, 2 Vols.1969.
Hughes, Spike. *The Toscanini legacy: a critical study of Arturo Toscanini's performances of Beethoven, Verdi, and other composers.* London: Putnam, 1959.
Hullah, Annette. *Theodor Leschetizky.* London and New York: J. Land & Co., 1906.
Le Huray, Peter and James Day, Editors. *Music and aesthetics in the eighteenth and early-nineteenth centuries.* Cambridge: Cambridge University Press, 1988.
D'Indy, Vincent. *César Franck.* New York: Dover Publications, 1965.
Jacobs, Arthur. *Arthur Sullivan: A Victorian musician.* Aldershot: Scolar Press, 1992.

Jahn, Otto. *Life of Mozart.* London: Novello, Ewer & Co., 1882.

Jefferson, Alan. *Sir Thomas Beecham: a centenary tribute.* London: World Records Ltd., 1979.

Jezic, Diane. *The musical migration and Ernst Toch.* Ames: Iowa State University Press, 1989.

Johnson, Douglas Porter, Editor. *The Beethoven sketchbooks: history, reconstruction, inventory.* Oxford: Clarendon, 1985.

Johnson, Stephen. *Bruckner remembered.* London: Faber and Faber, 1998.

Jones, David, Wyn. *Beethoven: Pastoral symphony.* Cambridge: Cambridge University Press, 1995.

Jones, David Wyn. *The life of Beethoven.* Cambridge: Cambridge University Press, 1998.

Jones, David Wyn. *The symphony in Beethoven's Vienna.* Cambridge: Cambridge University Press, 2006.

Jones, J. Barrie, Editor. *Gabriel Fauré: a life in letters.* London: Batsford, 1989.

Jones, Peter Ward, Editor and Translator. *The Mendelssohns on honeymoon: the 1837 diary of Felix and Cécile Mendelssohn Bartholdy, together with letters to their families.* Oxford: Clarendon Press, 1997.

Jones, Timothy. *Beethoven, the Moonlight and other sonatas, Op. 27 and Op. 31.* Cambridge; New York, N.Y.: Cambridge University Press, 1999.

Kalischer, A. C., Editor. *Beethoven's letters: a critical edition.* London: J. M. Dent, 1909.

Kárpáti, János. *Bartók's chamber music.* Stuyvesant, New York: Pendragon Press, 1994.

Keefe, Simon P. *The Cambridge companion to the concerto.* Cambridge, New York, N.Y.: Cambridge University Press, 2005.

Keller, Hans. *The great Haydn quartets: their interpretation.* London: J. M. Dent, 1986.

Keller, Hans, Editor. *The memoirs of Carl Flesch.* New York: Macmillan, 1958.

Keller, Hans, and Christopher Wintle. *Beethoven's string quartets in F minor, Op. 95 and C minor, Op. 131: two studies.* Nottingham: Department of Music, University of Nottingham, 1995.

Kelly, Thomas Forrest. *First nights at the opera: five musical premiers.* New Haven: Yale University Press, 2004.

Kennedy, Michael. *Adrian Boult.* London: Hamish Hamilton, 1987.

Kennedy, Michael. *Barbirolli, conductor laureate: the authorised biography.* London: Hart-Davis, MacGibbon, 1973.

Kennedy, Michael, Editor. *The autobiography of Charles Hallé; with correspondence and diaries.* London: Paul Elek, 1972.

Kennedy, Michael. *Hallé tradition: a century of music.* Manchester: Manchester University Press, 1960.

Kennedy, Michael. *The works of Ralph Vaughan Williams.* London: Oxford University Press, 1964.

Kemp, Ian. *Tippett: the composer and his music.* London; New York: Eulenburg Books, 1984.

Kerman, Joseph. *The Beethoven quartets.* London: Oxford University Press, 1967, c1966.

Kerman, Joseph. *Write all these down: essays on music.* Berkeley, California; London: University of California Press, 1994.

Kildea, Paul, Editor. *Britten on music.* Oxford: Oxford University Press, 2003.

Kinderman, William. *Beethoven.* Oxford: Oxford University Press, 1997.

Kinderman, William. *Beethoven's Diabelli variations.* Oxford: Clarendon Press; New York: Oxford University Press, 1987.

Kinderman, William, Editor. *The string quartets of Beethoven.* Urbana, Ilinois: University of Illinois Press, 2005.

King, Alec Hyatt. *Musical pursuits: selected essays.* London: British Library, 1987.

Kirby, F. E. *Music for piano: a short history.* Amadeus Press: Portland, 1995.

Kirkpatrick, John, Editor. *Charles E. Ives: Memos.* New York: W.W. Norton, 1972.

Knapp, Raymond. *Brahms and the challenge of the symphony.* Stuyvesant, N.Y.: Pendragon Press, c.1997.

Knight, Frida. *Cambridge music: from the Middle Ages to modern times.* Cambridge, England.: New York: Oleander Press, 1980.

Knight, Max, Translator. *A confidential matter: the letters of Richard Strauss and Stefan Zweig, 1931–1935.* Berkeley; London: University of California Press, 1977.

Kok, Alexander. *A voice in the dark: the philharmonia years.* Ampleforth: Emerson Edition, 2002.

Kopelson, Kevin. *Beethoven's kiss: pianism, perversion, and the mastery of desire.* Stanford, California: Stanford University Press, 1996.

Kostelanetz, Richard, Editor. *Aaron Copland: a reader; selected writings 1923–1972.* New York; London: Routledge, 2003.

Kostelanetz, Richard. *Conversing with Cage.* New York; London: Routledge, 2003.

Kostelanetz, Richard. *On innovative musicians.* New York: Limelight Editions, 1989.

Kostelanetz, Richard, Editor. *Virgil Thomson: a reader ; selected writings, 1924–1984.* New York; London: Routledge, 2002.

Kowalke, Kim H. *Kurt Weill in Europe.* Ann Arbor, Michigan: UMI Research Press, 1979.

Krehbiel, Henry Edward. *The pianoforte and its music.* New York: Cooper Square Publishers, 1971.

Kruseman, Philip, Editor. *Beethoven's own words.* London: Hinrichsen Edition, 1948.

Kurtz, Michael. *Stockhausen: a biography.* London: Faber and Faber, 1992.

Lam, Basil. *Beethoven string quartets.* Seattle: University of Washington Press, 1975.

Lambert, Constant. *Music ho!: a study of music in decline.* London: Faber and Faber, Ltd. 1934.

Landon, H. C. Robbins. *Beethoven: a documentary study.* London: Thames and Hudson, 1970.

Landon, H. C. Robbins. *Beethoven: his life, work and world.* London: Thames and Hudson,

1992.

Landon, H. C. Robbins. *Essays on the Viennese classical style: Gluck, Haydn, Mozart, Beethoven.* London: Barrie & Rockliff The Cresset Press, 1970.

Landon, H. C. Robbins. *Haydn: chronicle and works/Haydn, the late years, 1801–1809.* Bloomington: Indiana University Press, 1977.

Landon, H. C. Robbins. *Haydn: his life and music.* London: Thames and Hudson, 1988.

Landon, H. C. Robbins. *Haydn in England, 1791–1795.* London: Thames and Hudson, 1976.

Landon, H. C. Robbins. *Haydn: the years of 'The creation', 1796–800.* London: Thames and Hudson, 1977.

Landon, H. C. Robbins. *Mozart: the golden years, 1781–1791.* New York: Schirmer Books, 1989.

Landon, H. C. Robbins. *1791, Mozart's last year.* London: Thames and Hudson, 1988.

Landon, H. C. Robbins *The collected correspondence and London notebooks of Joseph Haydn.* London: Barrie and Rockliff, 1959.

Landon, H. C. Robbins: Editor. *The Mozart companion.* London: Faber, 1956.

Landowska, Wanda. *Music of the past.* London: Geoffrey Bles, 1926.

Lang, Paul Henry. *Musicology and performance.* New Haven: Yale University Press, 1997.

Lang, Paul Henry. *The creative world of Beethoven.* New York: W. W. Norton 1971.

Laurence, Dan H., Editor. *Shaw's music: the complete musical criticism in three volumes.* London: Max Reinhardt, the Bodley Head, 1981.

Lawford-Hinrichsen, Irene. *Music publishing and patronage: C. F. Peters, 1800 to the Holocaust.* Kenton: Edition Press, 2000.

Layton, Robert, Editor. *A guide to the concerto.* Oxford: Oxford University Press, 1996.

Layton, Robert, Editor. *A guide to the symphony.* Oxford: Oxford University Press, 1995.

Lebrecht, Norman. *The maestro myth: great conductors in pursuit of power.* London: Simon & Schuster, 1991.

Lee, Ernest Markham. *The story of the symphony.* London: Scott Publishing Co., 1916.

Leibowitz, Herbert A., Editor. *Musical impressions: selections from Paul Rosenfeld's criticism.* London: G. Allen & Unwin, 1970.

Lenrow, Elbert, Editor and Translator. *The letters of Richard Wagner to Anton Pusinelli.* New York: Vienna House, 1972.

Leonard, Maurice. *Kathleen: the life of Kathleen Ferrier: 1912–1953.* London: Hutchinson, 1988.

Lesure, François and Roger Nichols, Editors. *Debussy, letters.* London: Faber and Faber, 1987.

Letellier, Robert Ignatius, Editor and Translator. *The diaries of Giacomo Meyerbeer.* Madison: Fairleigh Dickinson University Press; London: Associated University Presses, 4 Vols., 1999–2004.

Levas, Santeri. *Sibelius: a personal portrait.* London: J. M. Dent, 1972.

Levy, Alan Howard. *Edward Mac-

Dowell, an American master. Lanham, Md. & London: Scarecrow Press, 1998.

Levy, David Benjamin. *Beethoven: the Ninth Symphony.* New Haven, Connecticut; London: Yale University Press, 2003.

Leyda, Jay and Sergi Bertensson. *The Musorgsky reader: a life of Modeste Petrovich Musorgsky in letters and documents.* New York: W.W. Norton, 1947.

Lewis, Thomas P., Editor. *Raymond Leppard on music: an anthology of critical and personal writings.* White Plains, N.Y.: Pro/Am Music Resources, 1993.

Liébert, Georges. *Nietzsche and music.* Chicago: University of Chicago Press, 2004.

Liszt, Franz. *An artist's journey: lettres d'un bachelier ès musique, 1835–1841.* Chicago: University of Chicago Press, 1989.

Litzmann, Berthold, Editor. *Clara Schumann: an artist's life, based on material found in diaries and letters.* London: Macmillan; Leipzig: Breitkopf & Härtel, 2 Vols. 1913.

Litzmann, Berthold, Editor. *Letters of Clara Schumann and Johannes Brahms, 1853–1896.* New York, Vienna House. 2 Vols. 1971.

Lloyd, Stephen. *William Walton: muse of fire.* Woodbridge, Suffolk: The Boydell Press, 2001.

Locke, Ralph P. and Cyrilla Barr, Editors. *Cultivating music in America: women patrons and activists since 1860.* Berkeley: University of California Press, 1997.

Lockspeiser, Edward. *Debussy: his life and mind.* London: Cassell. 2 Vols. 1962–1965.

Lockspeiser, Edward. *The literary clef: an anthology of letters and writings by French composers.* London: J. Calder. 1958.

Lockwood, Lewis, Editor. *Beethoven essays: studies in honor of Elliot Forbes.* Cambridge, Massachusetts: Harvard University Department of Music: Distributed by Harvard University Press, 1984.

Lockwood, Lewis and Mark Kroll, Editors. *The Beethoven violin sonatas: history, criticism, performance.* Urbana: University of Illinois Press, 2004.

Loft, Abram. *Violin and keyboard: the duo repertoire.* New York: Grossman Publishers. 2 Vols. 1973.

Longyear, Rey Morgan. *Nineteenth-century romanticism in music.* Englewood Cliffs: Prentice-Hall, 1969.

Lowe, C. Egerton. *Beethoven's pianoforte sonatas: hints on their rendering, form, etc., with appendices on definition of sonata, music forms, ornaments, pianoforte pedals, and how to discover keys.* London: Novello, 1929.

Macdonald, Hugh, Editor. *Berlioz: Selected letters.* London: Faber and Faber, 1995.

Macdonald, Malcolm, Editor. *Havergal Brian on music: selections from his journalism: Volume One, British music.* London: Toccata Press, 1986.

MacDonald, Malcolm. *Varèse: astronomer in sound.* London: Kahn & Averill, 2003.

MacDowell, Edward. *Critical and historical essays: lectures deliv-*

ered at Columbia University. Edited by W. J. Baltzell. London: Elkin; Boston: A.P. Schmidt, 1912.

MacFarren, Walter. Memories: an autobiography. London: Walter Scott Publishing Co.,1905.

Mackenzie, Alexander Campbell. *A musician's narrative.* London: Cassell and company, Ltd, 1927.

McCarthy, Margaret William, Editor. *More letters of Amy Fay: the American years, 1879–1916.* Detroit: Information Coordinators, 1986.

McClary, Susan. *Feminine endings: music, gender, and sexuality.* Minneapolis: University of Minnesota Press, 1991.

McClatchie, Stephen, Editor and Translator. *The Mahler family letters.* Oxford: Oxford University Press, 2006.

McVeigh, Simon. *Concert life in London from Mozart to Haydn.* Cambridge: Cambridge University Press, 1993.

Mahler, Alma. *Gustav Mahler: memories and letters.* Enlarged edition revised and edited and with and introduction by Donald Mitchell. London: John Murray, 1968.

Mai, François Martin. *Diagnosing genius: the life and death of Beethoven.* Montreal; London: McGill-Queen's University Press, 2007.

Del Mar, Norman. *Orchestral variations: confusion and error in the orchestral repertoire.* London: Eulenburg, 1981.

Del Mar, Norman. *Richard Strauss: a critical commentary on his life and works.* London: Barrie & Jenkins. 3 Vols. 1978.

(La) Mara [pseudonym]. *Letters of Franz Liszt.* London: H. Grevel & Co., 2 Vols. 1894.

Marek, George Richard. *Puccini.* London: Cassell & Co., 1952.

Marek, George Richard. *Toscanini.* London: Vision, 1976.

(De) Marliave, Joseph. *Beethoven's quartets.* New York: Dover Publications (reprint), 1961.

Martin, George Whitney. *Verdi: his music, life and times.* London: Macmillan, 1965.

Martner, Knud, Editor. *Selected letters of Gustav Mahler.* London; Boston: Faber and Faber, 1979.

Martyn, Barrie. *Nicolas Medtner: his life and music.* Aldershot: Scolar Press, 1995.

Martyn, Barrie. *Rachmaninoff: composer, pianist, conductor.* Aldershot: Scolar, 1990.

Massenet, Jules. *My recollections.* Westport, Connecticut: Greenwood Press.1970.

Matheopoulos, Helena. *Maestro: encounters with conductors of today.* London: Hutchinson, 1982.

Matthews, Denis. *Beethoven.* London: J. M. Dent, 1985.

Matthews, Denis. *Beethoven piano sonatas.* London: British Broadcasting Corporation, 1967.

Matthews, Denis. *In pursuit of music.* London: Victor Gollancz Ltd., 1968.

Matthews, Denis. *Keyboard music.* Newton Abbot: London David & Charles, 1972.

Mellers, Wilfrid Howard. *Caliban reborn: renewal in twentieth-century music.* London: Victor Gollancz, 1967.

Mellers, Wilfrid Howard. *The sonata

principle (from c. 1750). London: Rockliff, 1957.

Mendelssohn Bartholdy. *Letters from Italy and Switzerland.* London: Longman, Green, Longman, and Roberts, 1862.

Mendelssohn Bartholdy, Paul. *Letters of Felix Mendelssohn Bartholdy, from 1833 to 1847.* London: Longman, Green, Longman, Roberts, & Green, 1864.

Menuhin, Yehudi and Curtis W. Davis. *The music of man.* London: Macdonald and Jane's, 1979.

Menuhin, Yehudi. *Theme and variations.* London: Heinemann Educational Books Ltd., 1972.

Menuhin, Yehudi. *Unfinished journey.* London: Macdonald and Jane's, 1977.

Messian, Olivier. *Music and color: conversations with Claude Samuel.* Portland, Oregon: Amadeus, 1994.

Miall, Antony. *Musical bumps.* London: J.M. Dent & Sons Ltd, 1981.

Michotte, Edmond. *Richard Wagner's visit to Rossini (Paris 1860): and, An evening at Rossini's in Beau-Sejour (Passy), 1858.* Chicago; London: University of Chicago Press, 1982.

Mies, Paul. *Beethoven's sketches: an analysis of his style based on a study of his sketchbooks.*
New York: Johnson Reprint, 1969.

Milhaud, Darius. *My happy life.* London: Boyars, 1995.

Miller, Mina. *The Nielsen companion.* London: Faber and Faber, 1994.

Milsom, David. *Theory and practice in late nineteenth-century violin performance: an examination of style in performance, 1850–1900.* Aldershot: Ashgate, 2003.

Mitchell, Donald, Editor. *Letters from a life: the selected letters and diaries of Benjamin Britten 1913–1976.* London: Faber and Faber. 3 Vols., 1991.

Mitchell, Donald and Hans Keller, Editors. *Music survey: new series 1949–1952.* London: Faber Music in association with Faber & Faber, 1981.

Mitchell, Jon C. *A comprehensive biography of composer Gustav Holst, with correspondence and diary excerpts: including his American years.* Lewiston, New York: Edwin Mellen Press, 2001.

Moldenhauer, Hans. *Anton von Webern: a chronicle of his life and work.* London: Victor Gollancz, 1978.

Monrad-Johansen. Edvard Grieg. New York: Tudor Publishing Co., 1945.

Moore, Gerald. *Am I too loud?: memoirs of an accompanist.* London: Hamish Hamilton, 1962.

Moore, Gerald. *Farewell recital: further memoirs.* Harmondsworth: Penguin Books, 1979.

Moore, Gerald. *Furthermoore: interludes in an accompanist's life.* London: Hamish Hamilton, 1983.

Moore, Jerrold Northrop. *Edward Elgar: a creative life.* Oxford: Oxford University Press, 1984.

Moore, Jerrold Northrop. *Elgar, Edward. The windflower letters: correspondence with Alice Caroline Stuart Wortley and her family.* Oxford: Clarendon Press; New York: Oxford University Press, 1989.

Moore, Jerrold Northrop. *Elgar, Edward. Edward Elgar: letters of a lifetime*. Oxford: Clarendon Press; New York: Oxford University Press, 1990.

Moore, Jerrold Northrop. *Elgar, Edward. Elgar and his publishers: letters of a creative life*. Oxford: Clarendon, 1987.

Moreux, Serge. *Béla Bartók*. London: Harvill Press, 1953.

Morgan, Kenneth. *Fritz Reiner, maestro and martinet*. Urbana: University of Illinois Press, 2005.

Cone, Edward T., Editor. *Music, a view from Delft: selected essays*. Chicago: University of Chicago Press, 1989.

Morgan, Robert P. *Twentieth-century music: a history of musical style in modern Europe and America*. New York: Norton, 1991.

Morgenstern, Sam., Editor. *Composers on music: an anthology of composers' writings*. London: Faber & Faber, 1956.

Morrow, Mary Sue. *Concert life in Haydn's Vienna: aspects of a developing musical and social institution*. Stuyvesant, New York: Pendragon Press, 1989.

Moscheles, Felix, Editor and Translator. *Letters from Felix Mendelssohn-Bartholdy to Ignaz and Charlotte Moscheles*. London: Trübner and Co., 1888.

Mudge, Richard B., Translator. *Glinka, Mikhail Ivanovich: Memoirs*. Norman: University of Oklahoma Press, 1963.

Munch, Charles. *I am a conductor*. New York: Oxford University Press, 1955.

Mundy, Simon. *Bernard Haitink: a working life*. London: Robson Books, 1987.

Musgrave, Michael. *The musical life of the Crystal Palace*. Cambridge: Cambridge University Press, 1995.

Music & Letters. *Beethoven: special number*. London: Music & Letters, 1927.

Musical Times. *Special Issue*. John A. Fuller-Maitland London: Vol. VIII, No. 2, 1927.

Myers, Rollo H., Editor. *Twentieth-century music*. London: Calder and Boyars, 1960.

National Gallery (Great Britain). *Music performed at the National Gallery concerts, 10th October 1939 to 10th April 1946*. London: Privately printed, 1948.

Nattiez, Jean-Jacques, Editor. *Orientations: collected writings — Pierre Boulez*. London: Faber and Faber, 1986.

Nauhaus, Gerd, Editor. *The marriage diaries of Robert & Clara Schumann*. London: Robson Books, 1994.

Nectoux, Jean Michel. *Gabriel Fauré: a musical life*. Translated by Roger Nichols. Cambridge: Cambridge University Press, 1991.

Nettl, Paul. *Beethoven handbook*. Westport, Connecticut: Greenwood Press, 1975.

Neumayr, Anton. *Music and medicine*. Bloomington, Illinois: Medi-Ed Press, 1994–1997

Newbould, Brian. *Schubert and the symphony: a new perspective*. Surbiton: Toccata Press, 1992.

Newlin, Dika. *Schoenberg remembered: diaries and recollections (1938–76)*. New York: Pendragon Press, 1980.

Newman, Ernest. *From the world of*

music: essays from 'The Sunday Times'. London: J. Calder, 1956.

Newman, Ernest. *Hugo Wolf.* New York: Dover Publications, 1966.

Newman, Ernest, Annotated and Translated. *Memoirs of Hector Berlioz from 1803 to 1865, comprising his travels in Germany, Italy, Russia, and England.* New York: Knopf, 1932.

Newman, Ernest. *More essays from the world of music: essays from the 'Sunday Times'*. London: John Calder, 1958.

Newman, Ernest. *Musical studies.* London; New York: John Lane, 1910.

Newman, Ernest. *Testament of music: essays and papers.* London: Putnam, 1962.

Newman, Richard. *Alma Rosé: Vienna to Auschwitz.* Portland, Oregon: Amadeus Press, 2000.

Newman, William S. *The sonata in the classic era.* Chapel Hill: University of North Carolina Press 1963.

Newman, William S. *The sonata in the Classic era.* New York; London: W.W. Norton, 1983.

Newmarch, Rosa Harriet. *Henry J. Wood.* London & New York: John Lane, 1904.

Nicholas, Jeremy. *Godowsky: the pianists' pianist; a biography of Leopold Godowsky.* Hexham: Appian Publications & Recordings, 1989.

Nichols, Roger. *Debussy remembered.* London: Faber and Faber, 1992.

Nichols, Roger. *Mendelssohn remembered.* London: Faber and Faber, 1997.

Nichols, Roger. *Ravel remembered.* London: Faber and Faber, 1987.

Niecks, Frederick. *Robert Schumann.* London: J. M. Dent, 1925.

Nielsen, Carl. *Living music.* Copenhagen, Wilhelm Hansen, 1968.

Nielsen, Carl. *My childhood.* Copenhagen, Wilhelm Hansen, 1972.

Nikolska, Irina. *Conversations with Witold Lutoslawski, (1987–92).* Stockholm: Melos, 1994.

Nohl, Ludwig. *Beethoven depicted by his contemporaries.* London: Reeves, 1880.

De Nora, Tia. *Beethoven and the construction of genius: musical politics in Vienna, 1792–1803.* Berkeley: University of California Press, 1997.

Norton, Spencer, Editor and Translator. *Music in my time: the memoirs of Alfredo Casella.* Norman: University of Oklahoma Press, 1955.

Nottebohm, Gustav. *Two Beethoven sketchbooks: a description with musical extracts.* London: Gollancz, 1979.

Oakeley, Edward Murray. *The life of Sir Herbert Stanley Oakeley.* London: George Allen, 1904.

Lucas, Brenda and Michael Kerr. *Virtuoso: the story of John Ogdon.* London: H. Hamilton, 1981.

Oliver, Michael, Editor. *Settling the score: a journey through the music of the twentieth century.* London: Faber and Faber, 1999.

Olleson, Philip. *Samuel Wesley: the man and his music.* Woodbridge: Boydell Press, 2003.

Olleson, Philip, Editor. *The letters of Samuel Wesley: professional and social correspondence, 1797–1837.* Oxford; New York: Oxford University Press, 2001.

Olmstead, Andrea. *Conversations with Roger Sessions*. Boston: Northeastern University Press, 1987.

Orenstein, Arbie, Editor. *A Ravel reader: correspondence, articles, interviews*. New York: Columbia University Press, 1990.

Orenstein, Arbie. *Ravel: man and musician*. New York: Columbia University Press, 1975.

Orledge, Robert. *Charles Koechlin (1867–1950): his life and works*. New York: Harwood Academic Publishers, 1989.

Orledge, Robert. *Gabriel Fauré*. London: Eulenburg Books, 1979.

Orledge, Robert. *Satie remembered*. London: Faber and Faber, 1995.

Orledge, Robert. *Satie the composer*. Cambridge: Cambridge University Press, 1990.

Orlova, Alexandra. *Glinka's life in music: a chronicle*. Ann Arbor: UMI Research Press, 1988.

Orlova, Alexandra. *Musorgsky's days and works: a biography in documents*. Ann Arbor: UMI Research Press, 1983.

Orlova, Alexandra. *Tchaikovsky: a self-portrait*. Oxford: Oxford University Press, 1990.

Osborne, Charles, Editor and Translator. *Letters of Giuseppe Verdi*. London: Victor Gollancz, 1971.

Osmond-Smith David, Editor and Translator. *Luciano Berio: Two interviews with Rossana Dalmonte and Bálint András Varga*. New York; London: Boyars, 1985.

Ouellette, Fernand. *Edgard Varèse*. London: Calder & Boyars, 1973.

Paderewski, Ignacy Jan and Mary Lawton. *The Paderewski memoirs*. London: Collins, 1939.

Page, Tim: Editor. *The Glenn Gould reader*. London: Faber and Faber, 1987.

Page, Tim. *Music from the road: views and reviews, 1978–1992*. New York; Oxford: Oxford University Press, 1992.

Page, Tim and Vanessa Weeks, Editors. *Selected letters of Virgil Thomson*. New York: Summit Books, 1988.

Page, Tim. *Tim Page on music: views and reviews*. Portland, Oregon: Amadeus Press, 2002.

Palmer, Christopher. *Herbert Howells, (1892–1983): a celebration*. London: Thames, 1996.

Palmer, Christopher, Editor. *Sergei Prokofiev: Soviet diary 1927 and other writings*. London: Faber and Faber, 1991.

Palmer, Fiona M. *Domenico Dragonetti in England (1794–1846): the career of a double bass virtuoso*. Oxford: Clarendon, 1997.

Palmieri, Robert, Editor. *Encyclopedia of the piano*. New York: Garland, 1996.

Panufnik, Andrzej. *Composing myself*. London: Methuen, 1987.

Parsons, James, Editor. *The Cambridge companion to the Lied*. Cambridge: Cambridge University Press, 2004.

Paynter, John, Editor. *Between old worlds and new: occasional writings on music by Wilfrid Mellers*. London: Cygnus Arts, 1997.

Pestelli, Giorgio. *The age of Mozart and Beethoven*. Cambridge: Cambridge University Press, 1984.

Peyser, Joan. *Bernstein: a biography: revised & updated*. New York: Billboard Books, 1998.

Phillips-Matz, Mary Jane. *Verdi: a biography.* Oxford: Oxford University Press, 1993.

Piggott, Patrick. *The life and music of John Field, 1782–1837: creator of the nocturne.* London: Faber and Faber, 1973.

Plantinga, Leon. *Beethoven's concertos: history, style, performance.* New York: Norton, 1999.

Plantinga, Leon. *Clementi: his life and music.* London: Oxford University Press, 1977.

Plantinga, Leon. *Romantic music: a history of musical style in nineteenth-century Europe.* New York; London: Norton, 1984.

Plaskin, Glenn. *Horowitz: a biography of Vladimir Horowitz.* London: Macdonald, 1983.

Pleasants, Henry, Editor and Translator. *Hanslick, Eduard: Music criticisms, 1846–99.* Baltimore: Penguin Books, 1963.

Pleasants, Henry, Editor and Translator. *Hanslick's music criticisms.* New York: Dover Publications, 1988.

Pleasants, Henry, Editor and Translator. *The music criticism of Hugo Wolf.* New York: Holmes & Meier Publishers, 1978.

Pleasants, Henry, Editor and Translator. *The musical journeys of Louis Spohr.* Norman: University of Oklahoma Press, 1961.

Pollack, Howard. *Aaron Copland: the life and work of an uncommon man.* New York: Henry Holt, 1999.

Poulenc, Francis. *My friends and myself.* London: Dennis Dobson, 1978.

Powell, Richard, Mrs. *Edward Elgar: memories of a variation.* Aldershot, Hants, England: Scolar Press; Brookfield, Vermont, USA: Ashgate Publishing. Co., 1994.

Poznansky, Alexander, Editor. *Tchaikovsky through others' eyes.* Bloomington: Indiana University Press, 1999.

Praeger, Ferdinand. *Wagner as I knew him.* London; New York: Longmans, Green, 1892.

Previn, Andre. *Antony Hopkins. Music face to face.* London, Hamish Hamilton, 1971.

Prieberg, Fred K. *Trial of strength: Wilhelm Furtwängler and the Third Reich.* London: Quartet, 1991.

Procter-Gregg, Humphrey. *Beecham remembered.* London: Duckworth, 1976.

Prokofiev, Sergey. *Prokofiev by Prokofiev: a composer's memoir.* London: Macdonald and Jane's, 1979.

Rachmaninoff, Sergei. *Rachmaninoff's recollections told to Oskar von Riesemann.* London: George Allen & Unwin, 1934.

Radcliffe, Philip. *Beethoven's string quartets.* Cambridge: Cambridge University Press, 1978.

Radcliffe, Philip. *Piano Music in: The Age of Beethoven, The New Oxford History of Music, Vol. VIII.* Gerald Abraham, (Editor), 1988, p. 340.

Ratner, Leonard G. *Romantic music: sound and syntax.* New York: Schirmer Books, 1992.

Raynor, Henry. *A social history of music: from the middle ages to Beethoven.* London: Barrie & Jenkins, 1972.

Rees, Brian. *Camille Saint-Saëns: a life.* London: Chatto & Windus, 1999.

Reich, Willi, Editor. *Anton Webern: The path to the new music.* London; Bryn Mawr: Theodore Presser in association with Universal Edition, 1963.

Reid, Charles. *John Barbirolli: a biography.* London, Hamish Hamilton, 1971.

Reid, Charles. *Malcolm Sargent: a biography.* London: Hamilton, 1968.

Rennert, Jonathan. *William Crotch (1775–1847): composer, artist, teacher.* Lavenham: Terence Dalton, 1975.

Rice, John A. *Antonio Salieri and Viennese Opera.* Chicago, Illinois: University of Chicago Press, 1998.

Rice, John A. *Empress Marie Therese and music at the Viennese court, 1792–1807.* Cambridge: Cambridge University Press, 2003.

Richards, Fiona. *The Music of John Ireland.* Aldershot: Ashgate, 2000.

Rigby, Charles. *Sir Charles Hallé: a portrait for today.* Manchester: Dolphin Press, 1952.

Ringer, Alexander, Editor. *The early Romantic era: between Revolutions; 1789 and 1848.* Basingstoke: Macmillan, 1990.

Roberts, John P.L. and Ghyslaine Guertin, Editors. *Glenn Gould: Selected letters.* Toronto; Oxford: Oxford University Press, 1992.

Robertson, Alec. *More than music.* London: Collins, 1961.

Robinson, Harlow, Editor and Translator. *Selected letters of Sergei Prokofiev.* Boston: Northeastern University Press, 1998.

Robinson, Harlow. *Sergei Prokofiev: a biography.* London: Hale, 1987.

Robinson, Paul A. *Ludwig van Beethoven, Fidelio.* Cambridge: Cambridge University Press, 1996.

Robinson, Suzanne, Editor. *Michael Tippett: music and literature.* Aldershot: Ashgate, 2002.

Rochberg, George. *The aesthetics of survival: a composer's view of twentieth-century music.* Ann Arbor, Michigan: University of Michigan Press, 2004.

Rodmell, Paul. *Charles Villiers Stanford.* Aldershot: Ashgate, 2002.

Roeder, Michael Thomas. *A history of the concerto.* Portland, Oregon: Amadeus Press, 1994.

Rohr, Deborah Adams. *The careers of British musicians, 1750–1850: a profession of artisans.* Cambridge: Cambridge University Press, 2001.

Rolland, Romain. *Goethe and Beethoven.* New York; London: Blom, 1968.

Rolland, Romain. *Beethoven and Handel.* London: Waverley Book Co., 1917.

Rolland, Romain. *Beethoven the creator.* Garden City, New York: Garden City Pub., 1937.

Roscow, Gregory, Editor. *Bliss on music: selected writings of Arthur Bliss, 1920–1975.* Oxford: Oxford University Press, 1991.

Rosen, Charles. *Beethoven's piano sonatas: a short companion.* New Haven, Connecticut: London: Yale University Press, 2002.

Rosen, Charles. *Critical entertainments: music old and new.* Cambridge, Massachusetts; London: Harvard University Press, 2000.

Rosen, Charles. *The classical style: Haydn, Mozart, Beethoven.* London: Faber and Faber, 1976.

Rosen, Charles. *The romantic generation.* Cambridge, Massachusetts: Harvard University Press, 1995.

Rosenthal, Albi. *Obiter scripta: essays, lectures, articles, interviews and reviews on music, and other subjects.* Oxford: Offox Press; Lanham: Scarecrow Press, 2000.

Rostal, Max. *Beethoven: the sonatas for piano and violin; thoughts on their interpretation.* London: Toccata Press, 1985.

Rostropovich, Mstislav and Galina Vishnevskaya. *Russia, music, and liberty.* Portland, Oregan: Amadeus Press, 1995.

Rubinstein, Arthur. *My many years.* London: Jonathan Cape, 1980.

Rubinstein, Arthur. *My young years.* London: Jonathan Cape, 1973.

Rumph, Stephen C. *Beethoven after Napoleon: political romanticism in the late works.* Berkeley; London: University of California Press, 2004.

Rye, Matthew Rye. *Notes to the BBC Radio Three Beethoven Experience, Friday 10 June 2005,* www.bbc.co.uk/radio3/Beethoven.

Sachs, Harvey. *Toscanini.* London: Weidenfeld and Nicholson, 1978.

Sachs, Joel. *Kapellmeister Hummel in England and France.* Detroit: Information Coordinators, 1977.

Saffle, Michael, Editor. *Liszt and his world: proceedings of the International Liszt Conference held at Virginia Polytechnic Institute and State University, 20–23 May 1993.* Stuyvesant, New York: Pendragon Press, 1998.

Safránek, Milos. *Bohuslav Martinu, his life and works.* London: Allan Wingate, 1962.

Saint-Saëns, Camille. *Outspoken essays on music.* Westport, Connecticut: Greenwood Press, 1970.

Saussine, Renée de. *Paganini.* Westport, Connecticut: Greenwood Press, 1976.

Sayers, W. C. Berwick. *Samuel Coleridge-Taylor, musician: his life and letters.* London; New York: Cassell and Co., 1915.

Schaarwächter, Jürgen. *HB: aspects of Havergal Brian.* Aldershot: Ashgate, 1997.

Schafer, R. Murray. *E.T.A. Hoffmann and music.* Toronto: University of Toronto Press, 1975.

Schafer, R. Murray, Editor. *Ezra Pound and music: the complete criticism.* London: Faber and Faber, 1978.

Schat, Peter. *The tone clock.* Chur, Switzerland; Langhorne, Pa.: Harwood Academic Publishers, 1993.

Schenk, Erich. *Mozart and his times.* Edited and Translated by Richard and Clara Winstin. London: Secker & Warburg, 1960.

Schindler, Anton Felix. *Beethoven as I knew him.* Edited by Donald W. MacArdle and Translated by Constance S. Jolly from the German edition of 1860 London: Faber and Faber, 1966.

Schlosser, Johann. *Beethoven: the first biography, 1827.* Edited by Barry Cooper. Portland, Oregon: Amadeus Press, 1996.

Schnabel, Artur. *My life and music.*

London: Longmans, 1961.

Schnittke, Alfred. *A Schnittke reader.* Bloomington: Indiana University Press, 2002.

Scholes, Percy Alfred. *Crotchets: a few short musical notes.* London: John Lane, 1924.

Schonberg, Harold C. *The great pianists.* London: Victor Gollancz, 1964.

Schrade, Leo. *Beethoven in France: the growth of an idea.* New Haven; London: Yale University Press, H. Milford, Oxford University Press, 1942.

Schrade, Leo. *Tragedy in the art of music.* Cambridge, Massachusetts: Harvard University Press, 1964.

Schuh, Willi. *Richard Strauss: a chronicle of the early years 1864–1898.* Cambridge: Cambridge University Press, 1982.

Schuh, Willi, Editor. *Richard Strauss: Recollections and reflections.* London; New York: Boosey & Hawkes, 1953.

Schuller, Gunther. *Musings: the musical worlds of Gunther Schuller.* New York: Oxford University Press, 1986.

Schumann, Robert. *Music and musicians: essays and criticisms.* London: William Reeves, 1877.

Schuttenhelm, Editor. *Selected letters of Michael Tippett.* London: Faber and Faber, 2005.

Schwartz, Elliott. *Music since 1945: issues, materials, and literature.* New York: Schirmer Books, 1993.

Scott, Marion M. *Beethoven: (The master musicians).* London: Dent, 1940.

Scott-Sutherland, Colin. *Arnold Bax.* London: J. M. Dent, 1973.

Searle, Muriel V. *John Ireland: the man and his music.* Tunbridge Wells: Midas Books, 1979.

Secrest, Meryle. *Leonard Bernstein: a life.* London: Bloomsbury, 1995.

Seeger, Charles. *Studies in musicology II, 1929–1979.* Edited by Anne M. Pescatello. Berkeley; London: University of California Press, 1994.

Selden-Goth, Gisela, Editor. *Felix Mendelssohn: letters.* London: Paul Elek Publishers Ltd, 1946.

Senner, Wayne M., Robin Wallace and William Meredith, Editors. *The critical reception of Beethoven's compositions by his German contemporaries.* Lincoln: University of Nebraska Press, in association with the American Beethoven Society and the Ira F. Brilliant Center for Beethoven Studies, San José State University, 1999.

Seroff, Victor I. *Rachmaninoff.* London: Cassell & Company, 1951.

Sessions, Roger. *Questions about music.* Cambridge, Massachusetts: Harvard University Press, 1970.

Sessions, Roger. *The musical experience of composer, performer, listener.* New York: Atheneum, 1966, 1950.

Seyfried, Ignaz von. *Louis van Beethoven's Studies in thorough-bass, counterpoint and the art of scientific composition.* Leipzig; New-York: Schuberth and Company, 1853.

Sharma, Bhesham R. *Music and culture in the age of mechanical reproduction.* New York: Peter Lang, 2000.

Shaw, Bernard. *How to become a musical critic.* London: R. Hart Davis, 1960.

Shaw, Bernard. *London music in 1888–89 as heard by Corno di Bassetto (later known as Bernard Shaw): with some further autobiographical particulars.* London: Constable and Company, 1937.

Shaw, Bernard. *Music in London, 1890–1894.* London: Constable and Company Limited, 3 Vols., 1932.

Shedlock, John South. *Beethoven's pianoforte sonatas: the origin and respective values of various readings.* London: Augener Ltd., 1918.

Shedlock, John South. *The pianoforte sonata: its origin and development.* London: Methuen, 1895.

Shepherd, Arthur. *The string quartets of Ludwig van Beethoven.* Cleveland: H. Carr, The Printing Press, 1935.

Sheppard, Leslie and Herbert R. Axelrod. *Paganini: containing a portfolio of drawings by Vido Polikarpus.* Neptune City, New Jersey: Paganiniana Publications, 1979.

Short, Michael. *Gustav Holst: the man and his music.* Oxford: Oxford University Press, 1990.

Shostakovich, Dmitry. *Dmitry Shostakovich: about himself and his times.* Moscow: Progress Publishers, 1981.

Simpson, John Palgrave. *Carl Maria von Weber: the life of an artist, from the German of his son Baron, Max Maria von Weber.* London: Chapman and Hall, 1865.

Simpson, Robert. *Beethoven symphonies.* London: British Broadcasting Corporation, 1970.

Sipe, Thomas. *Beethoven: Eroica symphony.* Cambridge: Cambridge University Press, 1998.

Sitwell, Sacheverell. *Mozart.* Edinburgh: Peter Davies Limited, 1932.

Skelton, Geoffrey. *Paul Hindemith: the man behind the music; a biography.* London: Victor Gollancz, 1975.

Smallman, Basil. *The piano trio: its history, technique, and repertoire.* Oxford: Clarendon Press; Oxford; New York: Oxford University Press, 1990.

Smidak, Emil. *Isaak-Ignaz Moscheles: the life of the composer and his encounters with Beethoven, Liszt, Chopin, and Mendelssohn.* Aldershot, Hampshire, England: Scolar Press; Brookfield, Vermont, USA: Gower Publishing Co., 1989.

Smith, Barry. *Peter Warlock: the life of Philip Heseltine.* Oxford: Oxford University Press, 1994.

Smith, Joan Allen. *Schoenberg and his circle: a Viennese portrait.* New York: Schirmer Books, London: Collier Macmillan, 1986.

Smith, Richard Langham, Editor. *Debussy on music: the critical writings of the great French composer Claude Debussy.* London: Secker & Warburg, 1977.

Smith, Ronald. *Alkan.* London: Kahn and Averill, 1976.

Snowman, Daniel. *The Amadeus Quartet: the men and the music.* London: Robson Books, 1981.

Solomon, Maynard. *Beethoven.* New York: Schirmer, 1977.

Solomon, Maynard. *Beethoven*

essays. Cambridge, Massachusetts; London: Harvard University Press, 1988.

Solomon, Maynard. *Late Beethoven: music, thought, imagination*. Berkeley; London: University of California Press, 2003.

Solomon, Maynard. *Mozart: a life*. London: Hutchinson, 1995.

Sonneck, Oscar George Theodore. *Beethoven: impressions of contemporaries*. London: Oxford University Press, 1927.

Spalding, Albert. *Rise to follow: an autobiography*. London: Frederick Muller Ltd., 1946.

Spohr, Louis. *Louis Spohr's autobiography*. London: Longman, Green, Longman, Roberts, & Green, 1865.

Stafford, William. *Mozart myths: a critical reassessment*. Stanford, California: Stanford University Press, 1991.

Stanford, Charles Villiers. *Interludes: records and reflections*. London: John Murray, 1922.

Stanley, Glen, Editor. *The Cambridge companion to Beethoven*. Cambridge; New York: Cambridge University Press, 2000

Stedman, Preston. *The symphony*. Englewood Cliffs, New Jersey; London: Prentice-Hall, 1979.

Stedron, Bohumír, Editor and Translator. *Leos Janácek: letters and reminiscences*. Prague: Artia, 1955.

Stein, Erwin, Editor. *Arnold Schoenberg: letters*. London: Faber and Faber, 1964.

Stein, Erwin. *Orpheus in new guises*. London: Rockliff, 1953.

Stein, Jack Madison. *Poem and music in the German lied from Gluck to Hugo Wolf*. Cambridge, Massachusetts: Harvard University Press, 1971.

Stein, Leonard, Editor. *Style and idea: selected writings of Arnold Schoenberg*. London: Faber and Faber, 1975.

Steinberg, Michael P. *Listening to reason: culture, subjectivity, and nineteenth-century music*. Princeton, New Jersey: Princeton University Press, 2004.

Steinberg, Michael. *The concerto: a listener's guide*. New York: Oxford University Press, 1998.

Steinberg, Michael. *The symphony: a listener's guide*. Oxford; New York: Oxford University Press, 1995.

Sternfeld, Frederick William. *Goethe and music: a list of parodies and Goethe's relationship to music; a list of references*. New York: Da Capo Press, 1979.

Stivender, David. *Mascagni: an autobiography compiled, edited and translated from original sources*. New York: Pro/Am Music Resources; London: Kahn & Averill, 1988.

Stone, Else and Kurt Stone, Editors. *The writings of Elliott Carter: an American composer looks at modern music*. Bloomington: Indiana University Press, 1977.

Stowell, Robin. *Beethoven: violin concerto*. Cambridge: Cambridge University Press, 1998.

Stowell, Robin: Editor. *The Cambridge companion to the cello*. Cambridge: Cambridge University Press, 1999.

Stowell, Robin: Editor. *The Cambridge companion to the string quartet*. Cambridge: Cambridge University Press, 2003.

Stratton, Stephen Samuel. *Men-

delssohn. London: J.M. Dent & Co.; New York: E.P. Dutton & Co., 1901.

Straus, Joseph N. *Remaking the past: musical modernism and the influence of the tonal tradition.* Cambridge, Massachusetts: Harvard University Press, 1990.

Stravinsky, Igor. *An autobiography.* London: Calder and Boyars, 1975.

Stravinsky, Igor. *Themes and conclusions.* London: Faber and Faber, 1972.

Stravinsky, Igor and Robert Craft. *Conversations with Igor Stravinsky.* London: Faber and Faber, 1959.

Stravinsky, Igor and Robert Craft. *Dialogues and a diary.* London: Faber and Faber 1968.

Stravinsky, Igor and Robert Craft. *Memories and commentaries.* London: Faber and Faber, 2002.

Strunk, Oliver. *Source readings in music history, 4: The Classic era.* London: Faber and Faber 1981.

Sullivan, Blair, Editor. *The echo of music: essays in honor of Marie Louise Göllner.* Warren, Michigan: Harmonie Park Press, 2004.

Sullivan, Jack, Editor. *Words on music: from Addison to Barzun.* Athens: Ohio University Press, 1990.

Symonette, Lys and Kim H. Kowalke, Editors and Translators. *Speak low (when you speak love): the letters of Kurt Weill and Lotte Lenya.* London: Hamish Hamilton, 1996.

Swalin, Benjamin F. *The violin concerto: a study in German romanticism.* New York, Da Capo Press, 1973.

Szigeti, Joseph. *With strings attached: reminiscences and reflections.* London: Cassell & Co. Ltd, 1949.

Tanner, Michael, Editor. *Notebooks, 1924–1954: Wilhelm Furtwängler.* London: Quartet Books, 1989.

Taylor, Robert, Editor. *Furtwängler on music: essays and addresses.* Aldershot: Scolar, 1991.

Taylor, Ronald. *Kurt Weill: composer in a divided world.* London: Simon & Schuster, 1991.

Tchaikovsky, Peter Ilich. *Letters to his family: an autobiography.* Translated by Galina von Meck. London: Dennis Dobson, 1981.

Tertis, Lionel. *My viola and I: a complete autobiography; with, 'Beauty of tone in string playing', and other essays.* London: Paul Elek, 1974.

Thayer, Alexander Wheelock. *Salieri: rival of Mozart.* Edited by Theodore Albrecht. Kansas City, Missouri: Philharmonia of Greater Kansas City, 1989.

Thomas, Michael Tilson. *Viva voce: conversations with Edward Seckerson.* London: Faber and Faber 1994.

Thomson, Andrew. *Vincent d'Indy and his world.* Oxford: Clarendon Press, 1996.

Thomson, Virgil. *The musical scene.* New York: Greenwood Press, 1968.

Thomson, Virgil. *Virgil Thomson.* London: Weidenfeld & Nicolson, 1967.

Tillard, Françoise. *Fanny Mendelssohn.* Amadeus Press: Portland, 1996.

Tilmouth, Michael, Editor. *Donald Francis Tovey: The classics of* music: talks, essays, and other writings previously uncollected. Oxford: Oxford University Press, 2001

Tippett, Michael. *Moving into Aquarius*. London: Routledge and Kegan Paul, 1959.

Tippett, Michael. *Those twentieth century blues: an autobiography.* London: Hutchinson, 1991.

Todd, R. Larry, Editor. *Nineteenth-century piano music.* New York; London: Routledge, 2004.

Todd, R. Larry, Editor. *Schumann and his world.* Princeton: Princeton University Press, 1994.

Tommasini, Anthony. *Virgil Thomson: composer on the aisle.* New York: W.W. Norton, 1997.

Tortelier, Paul. *A self-portrait: in conversation with David Blum.* London: Heinemann, 1984.

Tovey, Donald Francis. *A Companion to Beethoven's Pianoforte Sonatas.* Revised by Barry Cooper. London: The Associated Board, [1931], 1998.

Tovey, Donald Francis. *Beethoven.* London: Oxford University Press, 1944.

Tovey, Donald Francis. *Essays and lectures on music.* London: Oxford University Press, 1949.

Tovey, Donald Francis. *Essays in musical analysis.* London: Oxford University Press, H. Milford, 7 Vols., 1935–41.

Tovey, Donald Francis. *The forms of music: musical articles from The Encyclopaedia Britannica.* London: Oxford University Press, 1944.

Toye, Francis. *Giuseppe Verdi: his life and works.* London: William Heinemann Ltd., 1931.

Truscott, Harold. *Beethoven's late string quartets.* London: Dobson, 1968.

Tyler, William R. *The letters of Franz Liszt to Olga von Meyendorff, 1871–1886, in the Mildred Bliss Collection at Dumbarton Oaks.* Translated by William R. Tyler. Washington: Dumbarton Oaks, Trustees for Harvard University; Cambridge, Massachusetts: distributed by Harvard University Press, 1979.

Tyrrell, John. *Janácek: years of a life. Vol. 1, (1854–1914) The lonely blackbird.* London: Faber and Faber, 2006.

Tyrrell, John, Editor and Translator. *My life with Janácek: the memoirs of Zdenka Janácková.* London: Faber and Faber, 1998.

Tyson, Alan, Editor. *Beethoven studies 2.* Cambridge: Cambridge University Press, 1977.

Tyson, Alan, Editor. *Beethoven studies 3.* Cambridge: Cambridge University Press, 1982.

Tyson, Alan. *Mozart: studies of the autograph scores.* Cambridge, Massachusetts; London: Harvard University Press, 1987.

Tyson, Alan. *The authentic English editions of Beethoven.* London: Faber and Faber, 1963.

Underwood, J. A., Editor. *Gabriel Fauré: his life through his letters.* London: Marion Boyars, 1984.

Vechten, Carl van, Editor. *Nikolay, Rimsky-Korsakov: My musical life.* London: Martin Secker & Warburg Ltd., 1942.

Vinton, John. *Essays after a dictionary: music and culture at the close of Western civilization.* Lewisburg: Bucknell University Press, 1977.

Volkov, Solomon, Editor. *Testi-

Volta, Ornella, Editor. *A mammal's notebook: collected writings of Erik Satie*. London: Atlas Press, 1996.

Wagner, Richard. *Beethoven: With [a] supplement from the philosophical works of A. Schopenhauer*. Translated by E. Dannreuther. London: Reeves, 1893.

Wagner, Richard. *My life*. London: Constable and Company Ltd., 1911.

Walden, Valerie. *One hundred years of violoncello: a history of technique and performance practice, 1740–1840*. Cambridge: Cambridge University Press, 1998.

Walker, Alan. *Franz Liszt. Volume 1, The virtuoso years: 1811–1847*. New York: Alfred A. Knopf, 1983.

Walker, Alan. *Franz Liszt. Volume 2, The Weimar years: 1848–1861*. London: Faber and Faber, 1989.

Walker, Alan. *Franz Liszt. Volume 3, The final years, 1861–1886*. London: Faber and Faber, 1997.

Walker, Bettina. *My musical experiences*. London: Richard Bentley and Son, 1890.

Walker, Ernest. *Free thought and the musician, and other essays*. London; New York: Oxford University Press, 1946.

Walker, Frank. *Hugo Wolf: a biography*. London: J. M. Dent, 1951.

Walker, Frank. *The man Verdi*. London: Dent, 1962.

Wallace, Grace, [Lady Wallace]. *Beethoven's letters (1790–1826): from the collection of Dr. Ludwig Nohl. Also his letters to the Archduke Rudolph, Cardinal-Archbishop of Olmutz, K. W., from the collection of Dr. Ludwig Ritter Von Kŏchel*. London: Longmans, Green, 2 Vols., 1866.

Wallace, Robin. *Beethoven's critics: aesthetic dilemmas and resolutions during the composer's lifetime*. Cambridge; New York: Cambridge University Press, 1986.

Walter, Bruno. *Theme and variations: an autobiography*. London: H. Hamilton, 1948.

Warrack, John Hamilton. *Writings on music*. Cambridge: Cambridge University Press, 1981.

Wasielewski, Wilhelm Joseph von. *Life of Robert Schumann: with letters, 1833–1852*. London: William Reeves, 1878.

Watkins, Glenn. *Proof through the night: music and the Great War*. Berkeley: University of California Press, 2003.

Watkins, Glenn. *Pyramids at the Louvre: music, culture, and collage from Stravinsky to the postmodernists*. Cambridge, Massachusetts; London: Belknap Press of Harvard University Press, 1994.

Watkins, Glenn. *Soundings: music in the twentieth century*. New York: Schirmer Books London: Collier Macmillan, 1988.

Watson, Derek. *Liszt*. London: J. M. Dent, 1989.

Weaver, William, Editor. *The Verdi-Boito correspondence*. Chicago; London: University of Chicago Press, 1994.

Wegeler, Franz. *Remembering Beethoven: the biographical*

notes of Franz Wegeler and Ferdinand Ries. London: Andre Deutsch, 1988.

Weingartner, Felix. *Buffets and rewards: a musician's reminiscences.* London: Hutchinson & Co., 1937.

Weinstock, Herbert. *Rossini: a biography.* New York: Limelight, 1987.

Weiss, Piero and Richard Taruskin. *Music in the Western World: a history in documents.* New York: Schirmer; London: Collier Macmillan, 1984.

Weissweiler, Eva *The complete correspondence of Clara and Robert Schumann.* New York: Peter Lang, 2 Vols., 1994.

Whittaker, William Gillies. *Collected essays.* London: Oxford University Press, 1940.

Whittall, Arnold. *Exploring twentieth-century music: tradition and innovation.* Cambridge; New York: Cambridge University Press, 2003.

Whittall, Arnold. *Music since the First World War.* London: J. M. Dent, 1977.

Whitton, Kenneth S. *Lieder: an introduction to German song.* London: Julia MacRae, 1984.

Wightman, Alistair, Editor. *Szymanowski on music: selected writings of Karol Szymanowski.* London: Toccata Press, 1999.

Wilhelm, Kurt. *Richard Strauss: an intimate portrait.* London: Thames and Hudson, 1999.

Will, Richard James. *The characteristic symphony in the age of Haydn and Beethoven.* Cambridge: Cambridge University Press, 2002.

Willetts, Pamela J. *Beethoven and England: an account of sources in the British Museum.* London: British Museum, 1970.

Williams, Adrian, Editor and Translator. *Liszt, Franz: Selected letters.* Oxford: Clarendon Press, 1998.

Williams, Adrian. *Portrait of Liszt: by himself and his contemporaries.* Oxford: Clarendon Press, 1990.

Williams, Ralph Vaughan. *Heirs and rebels: letters written to each other and occasional writings on music.* London; New York: Oxford University Press, 1959.

Williams, Ralph Vaughan. *Some thoughts on Beethoven's Choral symphony: with writings on other musical subjects.* London; Oxford University Press, 1953.

Williams, Ralph Vaughan. *The making of music.* Ithaca, New York: Cornell University Press, 1955.

Williams, Ursula Vaughan. *R.V.W.: a biography of Ralph Vaughan Williams.* London: Oxford University Press, 1964.

Wilson, Conrad. *Notes on Beethoven: 20 crucial works.* Edinburgh: Saint Andrew Press, 2003.

Wilson, Elizabeth. *Shostakovich: a life remembered.* Princeton, New Jersey: Princeton University Press, 1994.

Winter, Robert, Editor. *Beethoven, performers, and critics: the International Beethoven Congress, Detroit, 1977.* Detroit: Wayne State University Press, 1980.

Winter, Robert. *Compositional origins of Beethoven's opus 131.* Ann Arbor, Michigan: UMI Research Press, 1982.

Winter, Robert and Robert Martin,

Editors. *The Beethoven quartet companion*. Berkeley: University of California Press, 1994.

Wolf, Eugene K. and Edward H. Roesner, Editors. *Studies in musical sources and style: essays in honor of Jan LaRue*. Madison, Wisconsin: A-R Editions, 1990.

Wolff, Christoph and Robert Riggs. *The string quartets of Haydn, Mozart and Beethoven: studies of the autograph manuscripts: a conference at Isham Memorial Library, March 15–17, 1979*. Cambridge, Massachusetts: Department of Music, Harvard University, 1980.

Wolff, Konrad. *Masters of the keyboard: individual style elements in the piano music of Bach, Haydn, Mozart, Beethoven, Schubert, Chopin, and Brahms*. Bloomington: Indiana University Press, 1990.

Wörner, Karl Heinrich. *Stockhausen: life and work*. London: Faber, 1973.

Wright, Donald, Editor. *Cardus on music: a centenary collection*. London: Hamish Hamilton, 1988.

Wyndham, Henry Saxe. *August Manns and the Saturday concerts: a memoir and a retrospect*. London and Felling-on-Tyne, New York, The Walter Scott Publishing Co., Ltd., 1909.

Yastrebtsev, V.V. Edited and Translated by Florence Jonas. *Reminiscences of Rimsky-Korsakov*. New York: Columbia University Press, 1985.

Yates, Peter. *Twentieth century music: its evolution from the end of the harmonic era into the present era of sound*. London: Allen & Unwin Ltd., 1968.

Young, Percy M. *Beethoven: a Victorian tribute based on the papers of Sir George Smart*. London: D. Dobson, 1976.

Young, Percy M. *George Grove, 1820–1900: a biography*. London: Macmillan, 1980.

Young, Percy M. *Letters of Edward Elgar and other writings*. London: Geoffrey Bles, 1956.

Young, Percy M., Editor. *Letters to Nimrod: Edward Elgar to August Jaeger, 1897–1908*. London: Dennis Dobson, 1965.

Young, Percy M. *The concert tradition: from the middle ages to the twentieth century*. London: Routledge and Kegan Paul, 1965.

Young, Rob, Editor. *(Brief Description): Undercurrents: the hidden wiring of modern music*. London; New York, N.Y.: Continuum, 2002.

Yourke, Electra Slonimsky, Editor. *Nicolas Slonimsky: writings on music*. New York, N.Y.; London: Routledge, 4 Vols. 2003-2005.

Slonimsky, Nicolas. *The great composers and their works*. Edited by Electra Slonimsky Yourke. New York: Schirmer Books, 2 Vols. 2000.

Ysaÿe, Antoine. *Ysaÿe: his life, work and influence*. London: W. Heinemann, 1947.

Zamoyski, Adam. *Paderewski*. London: Collins, 1982.

Zegers, Mirjam, Editor. *Louis Andriessen: The art of stealing time*. Todmorden: Arc Music, 2002.

Zemanova, Mirka, Editor. *Janácek's uncollected essays on music*. London: Marion Boyars, 1989.

INDEX

Abraham, Gerald 1-3, 372, 395
Adorno, Theodor W. 3, 5, 40, 41, 104, 252, 372
Allgemeine musikalische Zeitung (AmZ) X, 5-8, 57, 149
Arnold, Matthew 9
Arrau, Claudio 10-12, 90-91, 152, 385
Arrigo, Boito 12-13
Ashkenazy, Vladimir 13-14

Balakirev, Mily 16, 155
Barenboim, Daniel 17-19, 113, 152, 373
Barford, Philip 19-22
Bartók, Béla 17, 22-23, 218, 284, 379, 382, 392
Bax, Arnold 23-24, 381, 398
Beecham, Thomas 24-25, 77, 373, 386, 395
Bekker, Paul 25-27
Berg, Alban 27, 284
Berlioz, Hector 28-32, 79, 143, 163, 171, 301, 324, 373, 376, 378, 389, 393
Bernstein, Leonard 31-33, 373, 375, 376, 394, 398
Bizet, Georges 34-35, 324, 378, 379
Blacking, John 36, 376
Bliss, Arthur 36-40, 373, 396, 402
Bloch, Ernst 40, 42, 43, 104, 373
Boulez, Pierre 17, 43-44, 374, 392
Brahms, Johannes 10, 45-46, 54, 63, 96, 146, 148, 161, 259, 275, 324, 331, 340, 364, 372, 374, 375, 384, 387, 389, 405
Brendel, Alfred 46-48, 113, 228, 270, 375
Breuning, Gerhard von 49-51, 125, 304, 307, 375
Britten, Benjamin 52-54, 387, 391
Broadwood & Sons 55-60
Broyles, Michael 60-63, 375
Bruckner, Anton 63-65, 117, 331, 385, 386
Bülow, Hans von 65-66, 166, 246,

359, 369
Burnham, Scott 66-68, 102, 150-151, 375
Bush, Alan 68-70, 376
Busoni, Ferruccio 70-74, 122, 276-277, 373, 376

Cage, John 75, 385, 387
Cardus, Neville 24-25, 75-78, 227, 376, 378, 405
Carter, Elliot 78-80, 373, 379, 400
Cooper, Barry 80-81, 329
Cooper, Elliot 80, 256, 260, 262, 264, 283, 329, 377, 397, 402
Cooper, Martin VI, 82-84, 269-270, 377
Copland, Aaron 84-86, 378, 387, 395
Crabbe, John 86-88, 378

Dahlhaus, Carl 88-90, 378
Davis, Collin 90-91, 202
Debussy, Claude 22, 23, 44, 79, 91-96, 122, 145, 218, 283, 375, 379, 384, 385, 388, 389, 393, 399
Delius, Frederick 23, 96-97, 376, 381
Dennis, David B. 97-105
Dukas, Paul 107
Dvořák, Antonín 108, 379
Dyson, Sir George 108-109, 379

Eisler, Hanns 109-110, 382
Elterlein, Ernst von 110-111, 380

Falla, Manuel de 111-112, 372, 384
Fay, Amy 112-113, 173, 381, 390
Fischer, Edwin 113-114, 172, 381
Frogley, Alain 114-115, 170
Furtwängler, Wilhelm 116-117, 196, 395, 401

Gal, Hans 118-120, 139, 148, 194, 381
Gould, Glen 120-121, 394, 396
Grainger, Percy 122-123, 379, 382
Gray, Cecil 123-124, 383

Grillparzer, Franz VIII 51, 99, 124-125, 211, 307
Grout, Donald J. 126, 383
Grove, Sir George 9, 126-130, 213, 289, 291, 383, 405
Gurney, Ivor 131-132

Hadow, Sir William Henry 132-133, 383
Hallé, Sir Charles 133-136, 383, 386, 396
The Harmonicon 137-138
Headington, Christopher 138-139, 384
Holst, Gustav 139, 213, 374, 391, 399
Honegger, Arthur 140-141, 385
Hugo, Victor 29, 101, 141

d'Indy, Vincent 142-143, 401
Ives, Charles 143-144, 378, 387

Jahn, Otto 145, 386
Leoš Janácek 145-146
Joachim, Joseph 146-148, 152, 373

Kahlert, Karl August 149-150
Kant, Emanuel 26, 150
Kinderman, William 151-152, 387
Klemperer, Otto 152-153, 372, 376, 385
Kodály, Zoltán 153-155, 374, 380
Korsakov, Nikolai Rimsky 16, 155-156, 315, 402, 405
Kossak, Ernst Ludwig 156-157

Lang, Paul Henry 157-160, 260, 373, 388
Leppard, Raymond 160-162, 389
Liszt, Franz 10, 59, 112, 115, 133, 147, 148, 162-174, 176, 246, 247, 255, 301-302, 307, 343, 372, 385, 389, 390, 397, 399, 402-404

MacDowell, Edward 176-177, 389

Mahler, Gustav 66, 146, 152, 179-182, 283, 332, 362-364, 373, 382, 390
Mai, François Martin 183, 390
Matthews, Denis 183-187, 283, 390
McEwan, Sir John B. 177-179
Mellers, Wilfred 187-190, 260-261, 384, 390, 394
Mendelssohn, Felix 13, 146, 156, 157, 161, 190-196, 242, 282, 302, 344, 377, 381-382, 385, 386, 391-393, 398, 399, 401
Menuhin, Yehudi 196-202, 374, 378, 391
Messiaen, Oliver 17, 202-203, 383, 385
Milhaud, Darius 203-204, 391

Neumayr, Anton 204-205, 392
Newman, Ernest 32, 205-209, 284, 368, 392-393
Nielsen, Carl 209-210, 391, 393
Nohl, Ludwig 210-211, 306, 393, 403
Nora, Tia de 212-213, 393

Palisca, Claude V. 126, 383
Parry, Sir Hubert 213-215, 282, 379, 383
Pestelli, Giorgio 215-216, 394
Pizzetti, Ildebrando 216
Previn, Andre 217-218, 374, 395
Prokofiev, Sergei 156, 218-222, 383, 394-396

Radcliffe, Philip 222-224, 395
Ravel, Maurice 85, 122, 216, 224-227, 283, 382, 393-394
Richter, Hans 227, 381
Ries, Ferdinand 49, 56, 227-232, 304, 307, 404
Rimsky-Korsakov, Nikolai 16, 155-156, 315, 402, 405
Rolland, Romain 101, 232-235, 396
Ronteix, Eugène 235-236
Rosen, Charles 237-243, 252, 396-397

Rossini, Gioachino 30, 34-35, 106, 236, 243-245, 307, 343, 377, 391, 404
Rubinstein, Anton 152, 180, 246-48, 368-369
Arthur Rubinstein 248-251, 269, 397
Rumph, Stephen 2, 51-253, 397

Saint-Saëns, Camille 92, 226, 253-255, 384, 395, 397
Schindler, Anton Felix 8, 211, 255-261, 304, 306-307, 397
Schlosser, Johann Aloys 262-264, 397
Schnabel, Artur 115, 238, 265-274, 332, 397
Schoenberg, Arnold 109, 274-277, 283, 311-312, 361, 364, 372, 375, 392, 399-400
Schrade, Leo 142, 277-279, 285, 398
Schreker, Franz 279-280, 383
Schuller, Gunther 280, 282, 398
Scott, Marion II, 282-283, 398
Sessions, Roger 283-285, 377, 394, 398
Seyfried, Ignaz von 211, 286-288, 304, 307, 398
Shaw, George Bernard 135, 136, 288-289, 291, 293, 346, 374, 378, 399
Shaw, Robert, 292-293
Shostakovich, Dmitri 293-299, 385, 399, 403, 404
Sibelius, Jean 24, 118, 284, 299-301, 380, 382, 388
Smetana, Bedrich 145, 301-303, 373
Solomon, Maynard 49, 51, 91, 252, 303-306, 329, 399-400
Spohr, Louis 135, 158, 211, 307-310, 395, 400
Stanley, Glen 97, 115, 170, 310-311, 400
Stein, Erwin 276, 311-312, 400
Stockhausen, Karl Heinrich 313-314, 378, 387, 405
Strauss, Richard 139, 144, 146, 224,

283, 314-315, 374, 382, 384, 387, 390, 398, 404
Stravinsky, Igor 17, 53, 82, 156, 203, 213, 218, 283, 315-317, 378, 380, 385, 401, 403
Szymanowski, Karol 319-321, 404

Taylor-Coleridge, Samuel 321-322, 397
Tchaikovsky, Peter 85, 138, 222, 322-327, 332, 382, 384, 394, 395, 401
Thayer, Alexander Wheelock 124, 306, 328-329, 401
Thomson, Virgil 268, 269, 272-273, 329-332, 385, 387, 394, 401-402
Tippett, Michael 332-337, 374, 386, 396, 398, 402
Toch, Ernst 337-338, 386
Tovey, Prof. Sir Donald Francis V, 40, 338-341, 378, 401-402

Varèse, Edgard 341-342, 389, 394
Villa-Lobos, Heitor 175, 372

Wagner, Cosima 343-346, 383
Wagner, Richard 13, 23, 28, 63, 64, 71, 92, 94-95, 113, 116, 122, 179, 203-204, 225, 227, 244-245, 275, 276, 292, 296, 331, 343, 345-349, 353, 358, 368, 375, 380, 385, 388, 395, 403
Walter, Bruno II 295, 358-360, 374, 376, 377, 403
Webern, Anton 360-365, 373, 391, 396
Weill, Kurt 40, 365-366, 387
Weingartner, Felix 366-367, 404
Williams, Ralph Vaughan 139, 367, 374, 378, 386, 404
Wolf, Hugo 368-370, 393, 395, 400, 403

ABOUT THE AUTHOR

Terence M. Russell graduated with first class honours in architecture and was a nominee for the coveted Silver Medal of the Royal Institute of British Architects. He is a Fellow of the Royal Incorporation of Architects in Scotland (retired), was formerly Reader in the School of Arts, Culture and Environment at the University of Edinburgh, a Fellow of the British Higher Education Academy, and Senior Assessor to the Scottish Higher Education Funding Council. Alongside his professional work in the field of architecture — embracing practice, teaching and research — he has maintained a lifetime's interest in the music and musicology of Beethoven. He has an equal admiration for the work of Franz Schubert and was for many years an active member of the Schubert Institute, UK. His book writings in the field of architecture include the following:

The Built Environment: A Subject Index, Gregg Publishing (1989):
- Vol. 1: Town planning and urbanism, architecture, gardens and landscape design
- Vol. 2: Environmental technology, constructional engineering, building and materials
- Vol. 3: Decorative art and industrial design, international exhibitions and collections, recreational and performing arts
- Vol. 4: Public health, municipal services, community welfare

Architecture in the Encyclopédie of Diderot and D'Alemebert: The Letterpress Articles and Selected Engravings, Scolar Press (1993)

The Encyclopaedic Dictionary in the Eighteenth Century: Architecture, Arts and Crafts, Scolar Press (1997):
- Vol. 1: John Harris, Lexicon Technicum
- Vol. 2: Ephraim Chambers, Cyclopaedia
- Vol. 3: The Builder's Dictionary
- Vol. 4: Samuel Johnson, A Dictionary of the English Language
- Vol. 5: A Society of Gentlemen, Encyclopaedia Britannica

Gardens and Landscapes in the Encyclopédie of Diderot and D'Alemebert: The Letterpress Articles and Selected Engravings, 2 Vols., Ashgate (1999)

The Napoleonic Survey of Egypt: The Monuments and Customs of Egypt, 2 Vols., Ashgate (2001)

The Discovery of Egypt: Vivant Denon's Travels with Napoleon's Army, History Press (2005)